Typography is what language looks like.

Dedicated to GEORGE SADEK (1928–2007) *and all my teachers.*

ELLEN LUPTON

thinking
with

type

A CRITICAL GUIDE

FOR DESIGNERS,

WRITERS, EDITORS,

& STUDENTS

SECOND, REVISED AND
EXPANDED EDITION

PRINCETON ARCHITECTURAL PRESS · NEW YORK

Published by
Princeton Architectural Press
37 East Seventh Street
New York, New York 10003

Visit our web site at www.papress.com

© 2004, 2010 Princeton Architectural Press

Princeton Architectural Press
Second, revised and expanded edition
Printed and bound in China
15 14 13   9 8 7

Library of Congress Cataloging-in-Publication Data
Lupton, Ellen.
  Thinking with type : a critical guide for designers,
writers, editors, & students / Ellen Lupton. — 2nd
rev. and expanded ed.
    244 p. : ill. (chiefly col.) : 22 cm.
  Includes bibliographical references and index.
  ISBN 978-1-56898-969-3 (alk. paper)
  1. Graphic design (Typography) 2. Type and
type-founding. I. Title.
  Z246.L87 2010
  686.2'2—dc22
                                    2010005389

eISBN 978-1-61689-022-3

BOOK DESIGNER
Ellen Lupton

EDITOR
First edition: Mark Lamster
Second edition: Nicola Bednarek

COVER DESIGNERS
Jennifer Tobias and Ellen Lupton

DIVIDER PAGES
Paintings by Ellen Lupton

PHOTOGRAPHER
Dan Meyers

PRIMARY TYPEFACES
Scala Pro, designed by Martin Majoor
Thesis, designed by Luc(as) de Groot

SPECIAL THANKS TO
Nettie Aljian, Bree Anne Apperley, Sara Bader, Janet Behning,
Becca Casbon, Carina Cha, Tom Cho, Penny (Yuen Pik) Chu,
Carolyn Deuschle, Russell Fernandez, Pete Fitzpatrick,
Wendy Fuller, Jan Haux, Linda Lee, Laurie Manfra, John Myers,
Katharine Myers, Steve Royal, Dan Simon, Andrew Stepanian,
Jennifer Thompson, Paul Wagner, Joe Weston, and Deb Wood
of Princeton Architectural Press
—Kevin C. Lippert, publisher

This project was produced with editorial support from the
Center for Design Thinking, Maryland Institute College of Art.

CONTENTS

HOOD'S SARSAPARILLA Advertisement, lithograph, 1884.
Reproduced at actual size. *A woman's healthy face bursts through a
sheet of text, her bright complexion proving the product's efficacy better
than any written claim. Both text and image were drawn by hand,
reproduced via color lithography.*

INTRODUCTION

Since the first edition of *Thinking with Type* appeared in 2004, this book has been widely adopted in design programs around the world. Whenever a young designer hands me a battered copy of *Thinking with Type* to sign at a lecture or event, I am warmed with joy from serif to stem. Those scuffed covers and dinged corners are evidence that typography is thriving in the hands and minds of the next generation.

I've put on some weight since 2004, and so has this book. For the new edition, I decided to let out the seams and give the content more room to breathe. If you—like most graphic designers—like to sweat the little stuff, you'll find a lot to love, honor, and worry about in the pages that follow. Finicky matters such as kerning, small capitals, non-lining numerals, punctuation, alignment, and baseline grids that were touched on briefly in the first edition are developed here in more detail, along with new topics that were previously omitted, such as how to style a drop capital, what you need

Worried? See page 81

to know about optical sizes, and when to say "typeface" instead of "font" at your next AIGA wine-and-carrot-stick party. This new book has more of everything: more fonts, more exercises, more examples, a more bodacious index, and best of all, more type crimes—more disgraceful "don'ts" to complement the dignified "do's."

I was inspired to write the first edition of this book while searching for a textbook for my own type classes, which I have been teaching at Maryland Institute College of Art (MICA) since 1997. Some books on typography focus on the classical page; others are vast and encyclopedic, overflowing with facts and details. Some rely heavily on illustrations of their authors' own work, providing narrow views of a diverse practice, while others are chatty and dumbed down, presented in a condescending tone.

I sought a book that is serene and intelligible, a volume where design and text gently collaborate to enhance understanding. I sought a work that is small and compact, economical yet well constructed—a handbook designed for the hands. I sought a book that reflects the diversity of typographic life, past and present, exposing my students to history, theory, and ideas. Finally, I sought a book that would be relevant across the media of visual design, from the printed page to the glowing screen.

I found no alternative but to write the book myself.

Thinking with Type is assembled in three sections: LETTER, TEXT, and GRID, building from the basic atom of the letterform to the organization of words into coherent bodies and flexible systems. Each section opens with a narrative essay about the cultural and theoretical issues that fuel typographic design across a range of media. The demonstration pages that follow each essay show not just *how* typography is structured, but *why*, asserting the functional and cultural basis for design habits and conventions. Throughout the book, examples of design practice demonstrate the elasticity of the typographic system, whose rules can (nearly) all be broken.

The first section, LETTER, reveals how early typefaces referred to the body, emulating the work of the hand. The abstractions of neoclassicism bred the strange progeny of nineteenth-century commercial typography. In the twentieth century, avant-garde artists and designers explored the alphabet as a theoretical system. With the rise of digital design tools, typography revived its connections with the body.

The second section, TEXT, considers the massing of letters into larger bodies. Text is a field or texture whose grain, color, density, and silhouette can be endlessly adjusted. Technology has shaped the design of typographic space, from the concrete physicality of metal type to the flexibility—and constraints—offered by digital media. Text has evolved from a closed, stable body to a fluid and open ecology.

The third section, GRID, looks at spatial organization. In the early twentieth century, Dada and Futurist artists attacked the rectilinear constraints of metal type and exposed the mechanical grid of letterpress. Swiss designers in the 1940s and 1950s created design's first total methodology by rationalizing the grid. Their work, which introduced programmatic thinking to a field governed by taste and convention, remains profoundly relevant to the systematic thinking required when designing for multimedia.

This book is about thinking *with* typography—in the end, the emphasis falls on *with*. Typography is a tool for doing things *with*: shaping content, giving language a physical body, enabling the social flow of messages. Typography is an ongoing tradition that connects you *with* other designers, past and future. Type is *with* you everywhere you go—the street, the mall, the web, your apartment. This book aims to speak to, and *with*, all the readers and writers, designers and producers, teachers and students, whose work engages the ordered yet unpredictable life of the visible word.

ACKNOWLEDGMENTS

As a designer, writer, and visual thinker, I am indebted to my teachers at the Cooper Union, where I studied art and design from 1981 to 1985. Back then, the design world was neatly divided between a Swiss-inflected modernism and an idea-based approach rooted in American advertising and illustration. My teachers, including George Sadek, William Bevington, and James Craig, staked out a place between those worlds, allowing the modernist fascination with abstract systems to collide with the strange, the poetic, and the popular.

The title of this book, *Thinking with Type*, is an homage to James Craig's primer *Designing with Type*, the utilitarian classic that was our textbook at the Cooper Union. If that book was a handyman's manual to basic typography, this one is a naturalist's field guide, approaching type as a phenomenon that is more evolutionary than mechanical. What I really learned from my teachers was not rules and facts but how to think: how to use visual and verbal language to develop ideas. For me, discovering typography was like finding the bridge that connects art and language.

To write my own book for the twenty-first century, I decided to educate myself again. In 2003 I enrolled in the Doctorate in Communications Design program at the University of Baltimore and completed my degree in 2008. There I worked with Stuart Moulthrop and Nancy Kaplan, world-class scholars, critics, and designers of networked media and digital interfaces. Their influence is seen throughout this book.

My colleagues at MICA have built a distinctive design culture at the school; special thanks go to Ray Allen, Fred Lazarus, Guna Nadarajan, Brockett Horne, Jennifer Cole Phillips, and all my students.

The editor of *Thinking with Type*'s first edition, Mark Lamster, remains one of my most respected colleagues. The editor of the second edition, Nicola Bednarek, helped me balance and refine the expanded content. I thank Kevin Lippert, publisher at Princeton Architectural Press, for many, many years of support. Numerous designers and scholars helped me along the way, including Peter Bilak, Matteo Bologna, Vivian Folkenflik, Jonathan Hoefler, Eric Karnes, Elke Gasselseder, Hans Lijklema, William Noel, and Jeffrey Zeldman, as well as all the other designers who shared their work.

I learn something every day from my children, Jay and Ruby, and from my parents, my twin sister, and the amazing Miller family. My friends—Jennifer Tobias, Edward Bottone, Claudia Matzko, and Joy Hayes—sustain my life. My husband, Abbott Miller, is the greatest designer I know, and I am proud to include his work in this volume.

{LETTER}

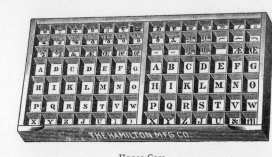

Upper Case.

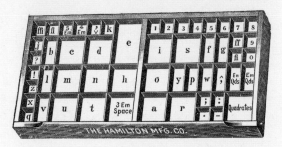

Lower Case.
A PAIR OF CASES.

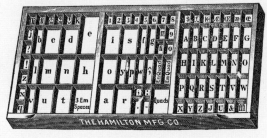

California Job Case.
FIG. 2.—Showing Lay of Cases.

TYPE, SPACES, AND LEADS
Diagram, 1917. Author: Frank S. Henry. *In a letterpress printing shop, gridded cases hold fonts of type and spacing material. Capital letters are stored in a drawer above the minuscule letters. Hence the terms "uppercase" and "lowercase" are derived from the physical space of the print shop.*

LETTER

THIS IS NOT A BOOK ABOUT FONTS. It is a book about how to use them. Typefaces are an essential resource employed by graphic designers, just as glass, stone, steel, and other materials are employed by architects. Graphic designers sometimes create their own typefaces and custom lettering. More commonly, however, they tap the vast library of existing typefaces, choosing and combining them in response to a particular audience or situation. To do this with wit and wisdom requires knowledge of how—and why—letterforms have evolved.

Words originated as gestures of the body. The first typefaces were directly modeled on the forms of calligraphy. Typefaces, however, are not bodily gestures—they are manufactured images designed for infinite repetition. The history of typography reflects a continual tension between the hand and the machine, the organic and the geometric, the human body and the abstract system. These tensions, which marked the birth of printed letters over five hundred year ago, continue to energize typography today.

Movable type, invented by Johannes Gutenberg in Germany in the early fifteenth century, revolutionized writing in the West. Whereas scribes had previously manufactured books and documents by hand, printing with type allowed for mass production: large quantities of letters could be cast from a mold and assembled into "forms." After the pages were proofed, corrected, and printed, the letters were put away in gridded cases for reuse.

Movable type had been employed earlier in China but had proven less useful there. Whereas the Chinese writing system contains tens of thousands of distinct characters, the Latin alphabet translates the sounds of speech into a small set of marks, making it well-suited to mechanization. Gutenberg's famous Bible took the handmade manuscript as its model. Emulating the dense, dark handwriting known as "blackletter," he reproduced its erratic texture by creating variations of each letter as well as numerous ligatures (characters that combine two or more letters into a single form).

JOHANNES GUTENBERG
Printed text, 1456.

This chapter extends and revises "Laws of the Letter," Ellen Lupton and J. Abbott Miller, *Design Writing Research: Writing on Graphic Design* (New York: Kiosk, 1996; London: Phaidon, 1999), 53–61.

NICOLAS JENSON *learned to print in Mainz, the German birthplace of typography, before establishing his own printing press in Venice around 1465. His letters have strong vertical stems, and the transition from thick to thin emulates the path of a broad-nibbed pen.*

ĩlos appellatur mariti
euir dicitur frater mar
ratriæ appellantur qua
mitini fratrum & mat
atrueles matrum fratr
õſobrini ex duabus ed
ta ſunt in antiquis au

the iiii wekis, and how 1
lord, yet the chirche mak
that is to wete, of that he
and of that he cometh to
in thoffyce of the chircl
tynges that ben in this
one partie, & that othe
cause of the comynge of
ben of joye and gladne

GOLDEN TYPE *was created by the English design reformer William Morris in 1890. He sought to recapture the dark and solemn density of Jenson's pages.*

CENTAUR, *designed from 1912 to 1914 by Bruce Rogers, is a revival of Jenson's type that emphasizes its ribbonlike stroke.*

Lorem ipsum dolor si
consectetuer adipiscing el
Integer pharetra, nisl u
luctus ullamcorper, au
tortor egestas ante, vel
pede urna ac neque. N
ac mi eu purus tincidu

Lorem ipsum dolor si
consectetuer adipiscin
Integer pharetra, nisl
luctus ullamcorper, au
tortor *egestas* ante, vel
pharetra pede urna ac
neque. Mauris ac mi e

ADOBE JENSON *was designed in 1995 by Robert Slimbach, who reconceives historical type-faces for digital use. Adobe Jenson is less mannered and decorative than Centaur.*

RUIT *was designed in the 1990s by the Dutch typographer, teacher, and theorist Gerrit Noordzij. This digitally constructed font captures the dynamic, three-dimensional quality of fifteenth-century roman*

vanum laboraverunt
si Dominus custodie
ſtra vigilavit qui cos
num est vobis ante l
rgere postquam sede
i manducatis panem
m dederit dilectis sui
ALMI IVXTA LXX

Lorem ipsum dolor s
consectetuer adipisci
Integer pharetra, nis
ullamcorper, augue t
ante, vel *pharetra* pe
neque. Mauris ac mi
tincidunt faucibus. P
dignissim lectus. Nun

typefaces as well as their gothic (rather than humanist) origins. As Noordzij explains, Jenson "adapted the German letters to Italian fashion (somewhat rounder, somewhat lighter), and thus created roman type."

SCALA *was introduced in 1991 by the Dutch typographer Martin Majoor. Although this thoroughly contemporary typeface has geometric serifs and rational, almost modular forms, it reflects the calligraphic origins of type, as seen in letters such as a.*

HUMANISM AND THE BODY

In fifteenth-century Italy, humanist writers and scholars rejected gothic scripts in favor of the *lettera antica*, a classical mode of handwriting with wider, more open forms. The preference for *lettera antica* was part of the Renaissance (rebirth) of classical art and literature. Nicolas Jenson, a Frenchman who had learned to print in Germany, established an influential printing firm in Venice around 1469. His typefaces merged the gothic traditions he had known in France and Germany with the Italian taste for rounder, lighter forms. They are considered among the first—and finest—roman typefaces.

Many typefaces we use today, including Garamond, Bembo, Palatino, and Jenson, are named for printers who worked in the fifteenth and sixteenth centuries. These typefaces are generally known as "humanist." Contemporary revivals of historical typefaces are designed to conform with modern technologies and current demands for sharpness and uniformity. Each revival responds to—or reacts against—the production methods, printing styles, and artistic habits of its own time. Some revivals are based on metal types, punches (steel prototypes), or drawings that still exist; most rely solely on printed specimens.

Italic letters, also introduced in fifteenth-century Italy, were modeled on a more casual style of handwriting. While the upright humanist scripts appeared in expensively produced books, the cursive form thrived in the cheaper writing shops, where it could be written more rapidly than the carefully formed *lettera antica*. Aldus Manutius, a Venetian printer, publisher, and scholar, used italic typefaces in his internationally distributed series of small, inexpensive printed books. For calligraphers, the italic form was economical because it saved time, while in printing, the cursive form saved space. Aldus Manutius often paired cursive letters with roman capitals; the two styles still were considered fundamentally distinct.

In the sixteenth century, printers began integrating roman and italic forms into type families with matching weights and x-heights (the height of the main body of the lowercase letter). Today, the italic style in most fonts is not simply a slanted version of the roman; it incorporates the curves, angles, and narrower proportions associated with cursive forms.

S ed ne forte tuo careà
Hic timor est ipsis
N on adeo leuiter nost
Vt meus oblito pulu
I llic phylacides iucu
Non potuit cæcis im
S ed cupidus falfis atti
Theffalis antiquam
I llic quicquid ero fer
Traicit & fati litto
I llic formofæ uenian
Quas dedit arguit
Quarum nulla tua fu
Gratior, & tellus h
Quamuis te longæ rei
Cara tamen lachry

FRANCESCO GRIFFO *designed roman and italic types for Aldus Manutius. The roman and italic were conceived as separate typefaces.*

JEAN JANNON *created roman and italic types for the Imprimerie Royale, Paris, 1642, that are coordinated into a larger type family.*

comme i'ay des-ia remarqué, [a] S. Augu-
ftin demande aux Donatiftes en vne fem-
blable occurrence : *Quoy donc ? lors que*
nous lifons, oublions nous comment nous auons
accouftumé de parler ? l'efcriture du grand Dieu

[a] *Aug. lib.33. contra Fauft.c. 7. Quid ergo? cum legimus, obliuifcimur quemadmodum loquifoleamus? An feriptura Dei aliter no-*

On the complex origins of roman type, see Gerrit Noordzij, *Letterletter* (Vancouver: Hartley and Marks, 2000).

GEOFROY TORY *argued that letters should reflect the ideal human body. Regarding the letter A, he wrote: "the cross-stroke covers the man's organ of generation, to signify that Modesty and Chastity are required, before all else, in those who seek acquaintance with well-shaped letters."*

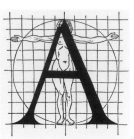

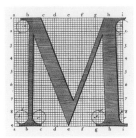

LOUIS SIMONNEAU *designed model letterforms for the printing press of Louis XIV. Instructed by a royal committee, Simonneau designed his letters on a finely meshed grid. A royal typeface (romain du roi) was then created by Philippe Grandjean, based on Simonneau's engravings.*

WILLIAM CASLON *produced typefaces in eighteenth-century England with crisp, upright characters that appear, as Robert Bringhurst has written, "more modelled and less written than Renaissance forms."*

By WILLIAM CASLON, Letter-Founder, in Chiswe

ABCD
ABCDE
ABCDEFG

DOUBLE PICA ROMAN.
Quousque tandem abutere, Catilina, patientia nostra? quamdiu nos etiam furor iste tuus eludet? quem ad finem sese effrenata jac-
ABCDEFGHIJKLMNOP

GREAT PRIMER ROMAN.
Quousque tandem abutere, Catilina, pa-

Double Pica Italick.
Quousque tandem abutere, Catilina, patientia nostra? quam nos etiam furor iste tuus elu- quem ad finem sese effrenata
ABCDEFGHJIKLM.

Great Primer Italick.
Quousque tandem abutere, Catilina,

SPECIMEN

By *JOHN BASKERVILLE of Birmingham.*

I·Am indebted to you for two Letters dated from Corcyra.

if to mean well to the Interest of my Country and to approve that meaning

JOHN BASKERVILLE *was a printer working in England in the 1750s and 1760s. He aimed to surpass Caslon by creating sharply detailed letters with more vivid contrast between thick and thin elements. Whereas Caslon's letters were widely used during his own time, Baskerville's work was denounced by many of his contemporaries as amateur and extremist.*

AUSTERLITI.

RELATAM A GALL

DUCE

GIAMBATTISTA BODONI *created letters at the close of the eighteenth century that exhibit abrupt, unmodulated contrast between thick and thin elements, and razor-thin serifs unsupported by curved brackets. Similar typefaces were designed in the same period by François-Ambroise Didot (1784) in France and Justus Erich Walbaum (1800) in Germany.*

Aabcdef

A B C D

aabbccddee,

A B C D

N O P 2

GEORGE BICKHAM, 1743.
*Samples of "Roman Print"
and "Italian Hand."*

Renaissance artists sought standards of proportion in the idealized human body. The French designer and typographer Geofroy Tory published a series of diagrams in 1529 that linked the anatomy of letters to the anatomy of man. A new approach—distanced from the body—would unfold in the age of scientific and philosophical Enlightenment.

A committee appointed by Louis XIV in France in 1693 set out to construct roman letters against a finely meshed grid. Whereas Tory's diagrams were produced as woodcuts, the gridded depictions of the *romain du roi* (king's alphabet) were engraved, made by incising a copper plate with a tool called a graver. The lead typefaces derived from these large-scale diagrams reflect the linear character of engraving as well as the scientific attitude of the king's committee.

Engraved letters—whose fluid lines are unconstrained by the letterpress's mechanical grid—offered an apt medium for formal lettering. Engraved reproductions of penmanship disseminated the work of the great eighteenth-century writing masters. Books such as George Bickham's *The Universal Penman* (1743) featured roman letters—each engraved as a unique character—as well as lavishly curved scripts.

Eighteenth-century typography was influenced by new styles of handwriting and their engraved reproductions. Printers such as William Caslon in the 1720s and John Baskerville in the 1750s abandoned the rigid nib of humanism for the flexible steel pen and the pointed quill, writing instruments that rendered a fluid, swelling path. Baskerville, himself a master calligrapher, would have admired the thinly sculpted lines that appeared in the engraved writing books. He created typefaces of such sharpness and contrast that contemporaries accused him of "blinding all the Readers in the Nation; for the strokes of your letters, being too thin and narrow, hurt the Eye." To heighten the startling precision of his pages, Baskerville made his own inks and hot-pressed his pages after printing.

At the turn of the nineteenth century, Giambattista Bodoni in Italy and Firmin Didot in France carried Baskerville's severe vocabulary to new extremes. Their typefaces—which have a wholly vertical axis, sharp contrast between thick and thin, and crisp, waferlike serifs—were the gateway to an explosive vision of typography unhinged from calligraphy.

This accusation was reported to Baskerville in a letter from his admirer Benjamin Franklin. For the full letter, see F. E. Pardoe, *John Baskerville of Birmingham: Letter-Founder and Printer* (London: Frederick Muller Limited, 1975), 68.
See also Robert Bringhurst, *The Elements of Typographic Style* (Vancouver: Hartley and Marks, 1992, 1997).

The *romain du roi* was designed not by a typographer but by a government committee consisting of two priests, an accountant, and an engineer. —ROBERT BRINGHURST, 1992

P. VIRGILII MARONIS

BUCOLICA

ECLOGA I. cui nomen TITYRUS.

MELIBOEUS, TITYRUS.

Tityre, tu patulæ recubans sub tegmine fagi
Silvestrem tenui Musam meditaris avena:
Nos patriæ fines, et dulcia linquimus arva;
Nos patriam fugimus: tu, Tityre, lentus in umbra
5 Formosam resonare doces Amaryllida silvas.
   T. O Meliboee, Deus nobis hæc otia fecit:
Namque erit ille mihi semper Deus: illius aram
Sæpe tener nostris ab ovilibus imbuet agnus.
Ille meas errare boves, ut cernis, et ipsum
10 Ludere, quæ vellem, calamo permisit agresti.
   M. Non equidem invideo; miror magis: undique totis
Usque adeo turbatur agris. en ipse capellas
Protenus æger ago: hanc etiam vix, Tityre, duco:
Hic inter densas corylos modo namque gemellos,
15 Spem gregis, ah! silice in nuda connixa reliquit.
Sæpe malum hoc nobis, si mens non læva fuisset,
De coelo tactas memini prædicere quercus:
Sæpe sinistra cava prædixit ab ilice cornix.
Sed tamen, iste Deus qui sit, da, Tityre, nobis.
20   T. Urbem, quam dicunt Romam, Meliboee, putavi
Stultus ego huic nostræ similem, quo sæpe solemus
Pastores ovium teneros depellere foetus.
Sic canibus catulos similes, sic matribus hoedos
                    A   Noram;

VIRGIL (LEFT) Book page, 1757. Printed by John Baskerville. *The typefaces created by Baskerville in the eighteenth century were remarkable—even shocking— in their day for their sharp, upright forms and stark contrast between thick and thin elements. In addition to a roman text face, this page utilizes italic capitals, large-scale capitals (generously letterspaced), small capitals (scaled to coordinate with lowercase text), and non-lining or old-style numerals (designed with ascenders, descenders, and a small body height to work with lowercase characters).*

RACINE (RIGHT) Book page, 1801. Printed by Firmin Didot. *The typefaces cut by the Didot family in France were even more abstract and severe than those of Baskerville, with slablike, unbracketed serifs and a stark contrast from thick to thin. Nineteenth-century printers and typographers called these glittering typefaces "modern."*

Both pages reproduced from William Dana Orcutt, In Quest of the Perfect Book *(New York: Little, Brown and Company, 1926); margins are not accurate.*

LA THÉBAÏDE,

OU

LES FRERES ENNEMIS,

TRAGÉDIE.

ACTE PREMIER.

SCENE I.

JOCASTE, OLYMPE.

JOCASTE.

Ils sont sortis, Olympe? Ah! mortelles douleurs!
Qu'un moment de repos me va coûter de pleurs!
Mes yeux depuis six mois étoient ouverts aux larmes,
Et le sommeil les ferme en de telles alarmes!
Puisse plutôt la mort les fermer pour jamais,
Et m'empêcher de voir le plus noir des forfaits!
Mais en sont-ils aux mains?

440 *Plan for the Improvement of the Art of Paper War.*
whilſt a paſſionate man, engaged in a warm controverſy
would thunder vengeance in

French Canon

It follows of courſe, that writers of great iraſcibility ſhou
be charged higher for a work of the ſame length, than me
authors; on account of the extraordinary ſpace their perfo
mances muſt neceſſarily occupy; for theſe gigantic, wrat
ful types, like ranters on the ſtage, muſt have ſufficie
elbow-room.

For example: Suppoſe a newſpaper quarrel to happen
tween * M and L.   M begins the attack pretty ſmartly in

Long Primer.

L replies in

Pica Roman.

M advances to

Great Primer.

L retorts in

Double Pica.

And ſo the conteſt ſwells to

Raſcal.
Villain

* Leſt ſome ill-diſpoſed perſon ſhould miſapply theſe in
tials, I think proper to declare, that M ſignifies Merchan
and L Lawyer.

Gowa

Cow-
ard,

in five line Pica ; which, indeed, is as far as the art of printing, or a modern quarrel can well go.

A philosophical reason might be given to prove that large
types will more forcibly affect the optic nerve than those of a
smaller size, and are therefore naturally expressive of energy
and vigour. But I leave this discussion for the amusement of
the gentlemen lately elected into our philosophical society.
It is sufficient for me, if my system should be found to be justified by experience and fact, to which I appeal.

I recollect a case in point. Some few years before the war,
the people of a western county, known by the name of Paxton
Boys, assembled, on account of some discontent, in great
numbers, and came down with hostile intentions against the
peace of government, and with a particular view to some leading men in the city. Sir John St. Clair, who assumed military
command for defence of the city, met one of the obnoxious
persons in the street, and told him that he had seen the manifesto of the insurgents, and that his name was particularised
in letters as long as his fingers. The gentleman immediately
packed up his most valuable effects, and sent them with his
family into Jersey for security. Had sir John only said that he
had seen his name in the manifesto, it is probable that he would
not have been so seriously alarmed : but the unusual size of
the letters was to him a plain indication, that the insurgents
were determined to carry their revenge to a proportionable
extremity.

I could confirm my system by innumerable instances in
fact and practice. The title-page of every book is a proof in
point. It announces the subject treated of, in conspicuous
characters ; as if the author stood at the door of his edifice,
                                                    calling

H

5

PLAN FOR THE IMPROVEMENT OF
THE ART OF PAPER WAR *Satirical
essay by Francis Hopkinson,* The
American Museum, *Volume 1 (1787).
Courtesy of the Boston Public
Library. This eighteenth-century essay
is an early example of expressive
typography. The author, poking fun at
the emerging news media, suggests a
"paper war" between a lawyer and a
merchant. As the two men toss attacks
at each other, the type gets progressively
bigger. The terms* Long Primer, Pica
Roman, Great Primer, Double Pica,
and Five Line Pica *were used at the
time to identify type sizes. The* ſ *symbol
is an* s. *Hopkinson was no stranger to
design. He created the stars and stripes
motif of the American flag.*

FAT FACE is the name given to the inflated, hyperbold type style introduced in the early nineteenth century. These faces exaggerated the polarization of letters into thick and thin components seen in the typographic forms of Bodoni and Didot.

EXTRA CONDENSED typefaces are designed to fit in narrow spaces. Nineteenth-century advertisements often combined fonts of varying style and proportion on a single page. These bombastic mixtures were typically aligned, however, in static, centered compositions.

EGYPTIAN, or slab, typefaces transformed the serif from a refined detail to a load-bearing slab. As an independent architectural component, the slab serif asserts its own weight and mass. Introduced in 1806, this style was quickly denounced by purists as "a typographical monstrosity."

GOTHIC is the nineteenth-century term for letters with no serifs. Gothic letters command attention with their massive frontality. Although sans-serif letters were later associated with rationality and neutrality, they lent emotional impact to early advertising.

My person was hideous, my stature gigantic. What did this mean? Who was I? What was I?… Accursed creator! Why did you create a monster so hideous that even you turned away from me in disgust? — MARY SHELLEY, *Frankenstein*, 1831

MONSTER FONTS

Although Bodoni and Didot fueled their designs with the calligraphic practices of their time, they created forms that collided with typographic tradition and unleashed a strange new world, where the structural attributes of the letter—serif and stem, thick and thin strokes, vertical and horizontal stress—would be subject to bizarre experiments. In search of a beauty both rational and sublime, Bodoni and Didot had created a monster: an abstract and dehumanized approach to the design of letters.

With the rise of industrialization and mass consumption in the nineteenth century came the explosion of advertising, a new form of communication demanding new kinds of typography. Type designers created big, bold faces by embellishing and engorging the body parts of classical letters. Fonts of astonishing height, width, and depth appeared—expanded, contracted, shadowed, inlined, fattened, faceted, and floriated. Serifs abandoned their role as finishing details to become independent architectural structures, and the vertical stress of traditional letters canted in new directions.

| ANTIQUE | CLARENDON | LATIN/ANTIQUE TUSCAN | TUSCAN |

Type historian Rob Roy Kelly studied the mechanized design strategies that served to generate a spectacular variety of display letters in the nineteenth century. This diagram shows how the basic square serif form—called Egyptian or slab—was cut, pinched, pulled, and curled to spawn new species of ornament. Serifs were transformed from calligraphic end-strokes into independent geometric elements that could be freely adjusted.

Lead, the material for casting metal type, is too soft to hold its shape at large sizes under the pressure of the printing press. In contrast, type cut from wood can be printed at gigantic scales. The introduction of the combined pantograph and router in 1834 revolutionized wood-type manufacture. The pantograph is a tracing device that, when linked to a router for carving, allows a parent drawing to spawn variants with different proportions, weights, and decorative excrescences.

This mechanized design approach treated the alphabet as a flexible system divorced from calligraphy. The search for archetypal, perfectly proportioned letterforms gave way to a new view of typography as an elastic system of formal features (weight, stress, stem, crossbars, serifs, angles, curves, ascenders, descenders). The relationships among letters in a typeface became more important than the identity of individual characters.

For extensive analysis and examples of decorated types, see Rob Roy Kelly, *American Wood Type: 1828–1900, Notes on the Evolution of Decorated and Large Letters* (New York: Da Capo Press, 1969). See also Ruari McLean, "An Examination of Egyptians," in *Texts on Type: Critical Writings on Typography,* ed. Steven Heller and Philip B. Meggs (New York: Allworth Press, 2001), 70–76.

Lithographic trade card, 1878.
*The rise of advertising in the
nineteenth century stimulated
demand for large-scale letters that
could command attention in
urban space. Here, a man is
shown posting a bill in flagrant
disregard for the law, while a
police officer approaches from
around the corner.*

FULL MOON (RIGHT)
Letterpress poster, 1875. *A dozen
different fonts are used in this
poster for a steamship cruise. A
size and style of typeface has been
chosen for each line to maximize
the scale of the letters in the space
allotted. Although the typefaces are
exotic, the centered layout is as
static and conventional as a
tombstone.*

Printing, having found in the book a refuge in which to lead an autonomous existence, is
pitilessly dragged out into the street by advertisements....Locust swarms of print, which
already eclipse the sun of what is taken for intellect in city dwellers, will grow thicker
with each succeeding year. —WALTER BENJAMIN, 1925

FULL MOON.

ST. MICHAEL'S
TEMPERANCE BAND !

Prof. V. Yeager, Leader, will give a

GRAND
MOONLIGHT
EXCURSION

On the Steamer

BELLE !

To Osbrook and Watch Hill,

On Saturday Evening, July 17th,

Leaving Wharf at $7\frac{1}{2}$ o'clock.   Returning to Westerly at $10\frac{1}{2}$ o'clock.   Kenneth will be at Osbrook.

TICKETS, - FORTY CENTS.

G. B. & J. H. Utter, Steam Printers, Westerly, R. I.

THEO VAN DOESBURG, *founder and chief promoter of the Dutch De Stijl movement, designed this alphabet with perpendicular elements in 1919. Applied here to the letterhead of the Union of Revolutionary Socialists, the hand-drawn characters vary in width, allowing them to fill out the overall rectangle. The De Stijl movement called for the reduction of painting, architecture, objects, and letters to elemental units.*

BOND VAN REVOLUTIONNAIR-SOCIALISTISCHE INTELLECTUEELEN

DE STIJL

VILMOS HUSZÁR *designed this logo for the magazine De Stijl in 1917. Whereas van Doesburg's characters are unbroken, Huszár's letters consist of pixel-like modules.*

abcdefghi jklmnopqr s tuvwxyz a   dd

HERBERT BAYER *created this typeface design, called universal, at the Bauhaus in 1925. Consisting only of lowercase letters, it is built from straight lines and circles.*

FETTE FUTURA

GOETH STOFF

PAUL RENNER *designed Futura in Germany in 1927. Although it is strongly geometric, with perfectly round Os, Futura is a practical, subtly designed typeface that remains widely used today.*

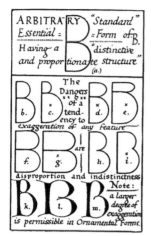

EDWARD JOHNSTON *based this 1906 diagram of "essential" characters on ancient Roman inscriptions. While deriding commercial lettering, Johnston accepted the embellishment of medieval-inspired forms.*

On Futura, see Christopher Burke, *Paul Renner: The Art of Typography* (New York: Princeton Architectural Press, 1998). On the experimental typefaces of the 1920s and 1930s, see Robin Kinross, *Unjustified Texts: Perspectives on Typography* (London: Hyphen Press, 2002), 233–45.

Some designers viewed the distortion of the alphabet as gross and immoral, tied to a destructive and inhumane industrial system. Writing in 1906, Edward Johnston revived the search for an essential, standard alphabet and warned against the "dangers" of exaggeration. Johnston, inspired by the nineteenth-century Arts and Crafts movement, looked back to the Renaissance and Middle Ages for pure, uncorrupted letterforms.

Although reformers like Johnston remained romantically attached to history, they redefined the designer as an intellectual distanced from the commercial mainstream. The modern design reformer was a critic of society, striving to create objects and images that would challenge and revise dominant habits and practices.

The avant-garde artists of the early twentieth century rejected historical forms but adopted the model of the critical outsider. Members of the De Stijl group in the Netherlands reduced the alphabet to perpendicular elements. At the Bauhaus, Herbert Bayer and Josef Albers constructed letters from basic geometric forms—the circle, square, and triangle—which they viewed as elements of a universal language of vision.

Such experiments approached the alphabet as a system of abstract relationships. Like the popular printers of the nineteenth century, avant-garde designers rejected the quest for essential letters grounded in the human hand and body, but they offered austere, theoretical alternatives in place of the solicitous novelty of mainstream advertising.

Assembled like machines from modular components, these experimental designs emulated factory production. Yet most were produced by hand rather than as mechanical typefaces (although many are now available digitally). Futura, completed by Paul Renner in 1927, embodied the obsessions of the avant garde in a multipurpose, commercially available typeface. Although Renner disdained the active movement of calligraphy in favor of forms that are "calming" and abstract, he tempered the geometry of Futura with subtle variations in stroke, curve, and proportion. Renner designed Futura in numerous weights, viewing his type family as a painterly tool for constructing a page in shades of gray.

The calming, abstract forms of those new typefaces that dispense with handwritten movement offer the typographer new shapes of tonal value that are very purely attuned. These types can be used in light, semi-bold, or in saturated black forms. — PAUL RENNER, 1931

new
alphabet

a possibility for the new development	een modelychheid voor de nieuwe onthyltteling	une possibilite pour le developpement nouveau	eine mogdlichteit fur die neue enthylttlung

an introduction for a programmed typography

WIM CROUWEL *published his designs for a "new alphabet,"*
consisting of no diagonals or curves, in 1967. The Foundry (London)
began releasing digital editions of Crouwel's typefaces in 1997.

TYPE AS PROGRAM

Responding in 1967 to the rise of electronic communication, the Dutch designer Wim Crouwel published designs for a "new alphabet" constructed from straight lines. Rejecting centuries of typographic convention, he designed his letters for optimal display on a video screen (CRT), where curves and angles are rendered with horizontal scan lines. In a brochure promoting his new alphabet, subtitled "An Introduction for a Programmed Typography," he proposed a design methodology in which decisions are rule-based and systematic.

WIM CROUWEL presented this "scanned" version of a Garamond a in contrast with his own new alphabet, whose forms accept the gridded structure of the screen. See Wim Crouwel, New Alphabet (Amsterdam: Total Design, 1967).

ZUZANA LICKO created coarse-resolution fonts for desktop screens and printers in 1985. These fonts have since been integrated into Emigre's extensive Lo-Res font family, designed for print and digital media.

See Rudy VanderLans and Zuzana Licko, *Emigre: Graphic Design into the Digital Realm* (New York: Van Nostrand Reinhold, 1993) and *Emigre No. 70: The Look Back Issue, Selections from Emigre Magazine, 1984–2009* (Berkeley: Gingko Press, 2009).

In the mid-1980s, personal computers and low-resolution printers put the tools of typography in the hands of a broader public. In 1985 Zuzana Licko began designing typefaces that exploited the rough grain of early desktop systems. While other digital fonts imposed the coarse grid of screen displays and dot-matrix printers onto traditional typographic forms, Licko embraced the language of digital equipment. She and her husband, Rudy VanderLans, cofounders of Emigre Fonts and *Emigre* magazine, called themselves the "new primitives," pioneers of a technological dawn.

Emperor   Oakland   Emigre

By the early 1990s, with the introduction of high-resolution laser printers and outline font technologies such as PostScript, type designers were less constrained by low-resolution outputs. While various signage systems and digital output devices still rely on bitmap fonts today, it is the fascination with programmed, geometric structures that has enabled bitmap forms to continue evolving as a visual ethos in print and digital media.

Living with computers gives funny ideas. —WIM CROUWEL, 1967

CURATOR : JOSEPH WESNER
Linda Ferguson

Steve Handschu
James Hay
Matthew Holland SCULPTURE
Gary Laatsch
Brian Liljeblad
Dora Natella
Matthew Schellenberg
Richard String

Michell Thomas

Robert Wilhelm

Opening Reception : Friday June 8, 5:30—8:30 pm

SCULPTURE

JUNE 8 – JULY 7, 1990

Detroit   Focus Gallery (313) 962 - 90 2 5
743 Beaubien, Third Floor
DETROIT, MICHIGAN 48226
WEDNESDAY - SATURDAY
Hours: Noon to 6 pm

ALSO IN THE AREA: THE MARKET PRESENTS Peter Gilleran · Gordon Orear   Opening 5 - 7:30 pm. Friday, June 8.

ED FELLA *produced a body of experimental typography that strongly influenced typeface design in the 1990s. His posters for the Detroit Focus Gallery feature damaged and defective forms, drawn by hand or culled from third-generation photocopies or from sheets of transfer lettering. Collection of the Cooper-Hewitt, National Design Museum.*

In the early 1990s, as digital design tools began supporting the seamless reproduction and integration of media, many designers grew dissatisfied with clean, unsullied surfaces, seeking instead to plunge the letter into the harsh and caustic world of physical processes. Letters, which for centuries had sought perfection in ever more exact technologies, became scratched, bent, bruised, and polluted.

Template Gothic: flawed technology

Barry Deck's typeface Template Gothic, designed in 1990, is based on letters drawn with a plastic stencil. The typeface thus refers to a process that is at once mechanical and manual. Deck designed Template Gothic while he was a student of Ed Fella, whose experimental posters inspired a generation of digital typographers. After Template Gothic was released commercially by Emigre Fonts, its use spread worldwide, making it an emblem of digital typography for the 1990s.

Dead History: feeding on the past

P. Scott Makela's typeface Dead History, also designed in 1990, is a pastiche of two existing typefaces: the traditional serif font Centennial and the Pop classic VAG Rounded. By manipulating the vectors of readymade fonts, Makela adopted the sampling strategy employed in contemporary art and music. He also embraced the burden of history and precedent, which play a role in nearly every typographic innovation.

CcDdEeFfGgHhIiJjKk

The Dutch typographers Erik van Blokland and Just van Rossum have combined the roles of designer and programmer, creating typefaces that embrace chance, change, and uncertainty. Their 1990 typeface Beowulf was the first in a series of typefaces with randomized outlines and programmed behaviors.

The industrial methods of producing typography meant that all letters had to be identical....Typography is now produced with sophisticated equipment that doesn't impose such rules. The only limitations are in our expectations. —ERIK VAN BLOKLAND AND JUST VAN ROSSUM, 2000

BACK TO WORK

Although the 1990s are best remembered for images of chaos and decay, serious type designers continued to build general purpose typefaces designed to comfortably accommodate broad bodies of text. Such workhorse type families provide graphic designers with flexible palettes of letterforms.

Mrs Eaves: WORKING *woman* **seeks** *reliable* **mate**

Licko produced historical revivals during the 1990s alongside her experimental display faces. Her 1996 typeface Mrs Eaves, inspired by the eighteenth-century types of Baskerville, became one of the most popular typefaces of its time. In 2009, Mrs Eaves was joined by Mr Eaves, a sans-serif version of the feminine favorite.

Quadraat: *all-purpose* **hardcore** BAROQUE

Fred Smeijers's Quadraat (above) and Martin Majoor's Scala (used for the text of this book) offer crisp interpretations of typographic tradition. These typefaces look back to sixteenth-century printing from a contemporary point of view, as seen in their simply drawn, decisively geometric serifs. Introduced in 1992, the Quadraat family soon expanded to include sans-serif forms in numerous weights and styles.

Gotham: Blue-Collar **Curves**

In 2000 Tobias Frere-Jones introduced Gotham, derived from letters found at the Port Authority Bus Terminal in New York City. With its distinctive yet utilitarian style, Gotham became the signature typeface of Barack Obama's 2008 presidential campaign. By 2009, typography's First Family had over fifty weights and styles.

When choosing a typeface, graphic designers consider the history of typefaces, their current connotations, as well as their formal qualities. The goal is to find an appropriate match between a style of letters and the specific social situation and body of content that define the project at hand. There is no playbook that assigns a fixed meaning or function to every typeface; each designer must confront the library of possibilities in light of a project's unique circumstances.

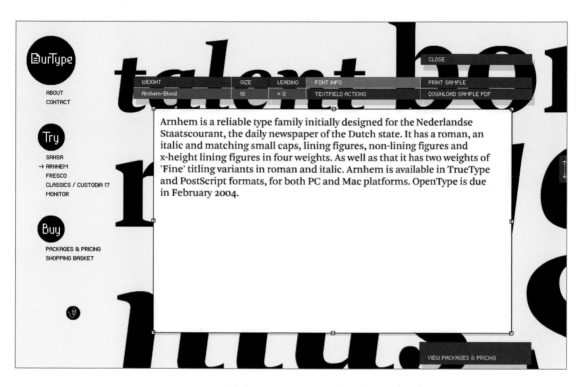

Website, 2004. Design: Fred Smeijers and Rudy Geeraerts. *This Flush-based website for a digital type foundry allows users to test fonts on the fly. The designers launched their own "label" after creating typefaces such as Quadraat for FontShop International. Shown here is Arnhem.*

Can we envision

1. a font that asks more questions than

2. a font that has projective memory that reminds you to

3. a font with a limite

4. a font with an e

5. a font that's

6. a font without temporal inflection, without the imprint

7. an apolitical font, a font that do

8. a font unaffected by the force of gravity and the weight of hum

9. a font without family, withou

10. a Marshall McLuhan font that stubbornly persists in bidding farewe

11. a font that takes advantage of all that promised "processi

12. a font that does something other than sit on its ass in a digita

310

13. a font with the capacity to breed with

14. a recombinant font — every letterform the unruly child of a predictable but rando

15. a font that sounds as good

16. a font that writes its

17. a font that thicker

18. a font that responds and reacts to the meaning it carries ar

19. a font that assumes the intelligence of

20. a font that might sense your level of agitation, fear, or a

21. a font prone to sudden outbursts and

22. a font that exceeds the typograph

23. a font whose parents are Father Time and the Mother of

24. an ambient font, a font withou

25. an everyday font, a font of com

ont that slows the pace of reading for the difficult passages (and skips along through easy bits)

ont that writes between the lines

ont that refuses to utter imperatives or commands

araoke font, a lip-synching font, a font without a voice of its own

ont that listens while it speaks

ont that toggles effortlessly between languages

ont for speaking in tongues

ont that speaks in dialects

metropolitan font for uptown, the ghetto, and suburbia alike

ont that simultaneously translates

ont that sings the plaintive songs of lonely whales

ont that grows

ont that learns

evolutionary font

entropic font

"live" font

promiscuous font, a font that fucks fonts, a font-fucking-font

ont that emerges, unfolds, performs, evolves, and passes away

ont of youth

in fonts, identical but distinct

generative font that renders itself according to behavioral tendencies

ont that is something other than a recording

font that is different every time you "play" it

font with the metabolism of a fly

font with a demographic algorithm that projects itself onto you, the average reader

311

LIFE STYLE Book, 2000. Design: Bruce Mau. Publisher:
Phaidon. Photograph: Dan Meyers. *In this postindustrial
manifesto, graphic designer Bruce Mau imagines a typeface that
comes alive with simulated intelligence.*

CAP HEIGHT · X-HEIGHT · BASELINE · STEM · BOWL · SERIF · DESCENDER

LIGATURE · ASCENDER · FINIAL

TERMINAL · ASCENDER · SPINE

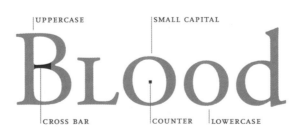

UPPERCASE · SMALL CAPITAL · CROSS BAR · COUNTER · LOWERCASE

ASCENDER HEIGHT
Some elements may extend slightly above the cap height.

CAP HEIGHT
The distance from the baseline to the top of the capital letter determines the letter's point size.

DESCENDER HEIGHT
The length of a letter's descenders contributes to its overall style and attitude.

skin, Body

X-HEIGHT *is the height of the main body of the lowercase letter (or the height of a lowercase x), excluding its ascenders and descenders.*

THE BASELINE *is where all the letters sit. This is the most stable axis along a line of text, and it is a crucial edge for aligning text with images or with other text.*

OVERHANG *The curves at the bottom of letters hang slightly below the baseline. Commas and semicolons also cross the baseline. If a typeface were not positioned this way, it would appear to teeter precariously. Without overhang, rounded letters would look smaller than their flat-footed compatriots.*

Bone

Although kids learn to write using ruled paper that divides letters exactly in half, most typefaces are not designed that way. The x-height usually occupies more than half of the cap height. The larger the x-height is in relation to the cap height, the bigger the letters appear to be. In a field of text, the greatest density occurs between the baseline and the x-height.

Hey, look!
They supersized
my x-height.

Two blocks of text are often aligned along a shared baseline. Here, 14/18 Scala Pro (14-pt type with 18 pts of line spacing) is paired with 7/9 Scala Pro.

*12 points
equal 1 pica*

*6 picas
(72 points)
equal 1 inch*

60-POINT SCALA
A typeface is measured from the top of the capital letter to the bottom of the lowest descender, plus a small buffer space.

In metal type, the point size is the height of the type slug.

HEIGHT Attempts to standardize the measurement of type began in the eighteenth century. The *point system* is the standard used today. One *point* equals 1/72 inch or .35 millimeters. Twelve points equal one *pica*, the unit commonly used to measure column widths. Typography can also be measured in inches, millimeters, or pixels. Most software applications let the designer choose a preferred unit of measure; picas and points are standard defaults.

NERD ALERT:
ABBREVIATING PICAS AND POINTS
8 picas = 8p
8 points = p8, 8 pts
8 picas, 4 points = 8p4
8-point Helvetica with 9 points of line spacing = 8/9 Helvetica

WIDE LOAD

INTERSTATE BLACK
The set width is the body of the letter plus the space beside it.

TIGHT WAD

INTERSTATE BLACK COMPRESSED
The letters in the compressed version of the typeface have a narrower set width.

WIDE LOAD
TIGHT WAD

TYPE CRIME
HORIZONTAL & VERTICAL SCALING
The proportions of the letters have been digitally distorted in order to create wider or narrower letters.

WIDTH A letter also has a horizontal measure, called its *set width*. The set width is the body of the letter plus a sliver of space that protects it from other letters. The width of a letter is intrinsic to the proportions and visual impression of the typeface. Some typefaces have a narrow set width, and some have a wide one.

You can change the set width of a typeface by fiddling with its horizontal or vertical scale. This distorts the line weight of the letters, however, forcing heavy elements to become thin, and thin elements to become thick. Instead of torturing a letterform, choose a typeface that has the proportions you are looking for, such as condensed, compressed, wide, or extended.

32-PT SCALA PRO   32-PT INTERSTATE REGULAR   32-PT BODONI   32-PT MRS EAVES

Do I look fat in this paragraph?

When two typefaces are set in the same point size, one often looks bigger than the other. Differences in x-height, line weight, and set width affect the letters' apparent scale.

Mrs Eaves rejects the twentieth-century appetite for supersized x-heights. This typeface, inspired by the eighteenth-century designs of Baskerville, is named after Sarah Eaves, Baskerville's mistress, housekeeper, and collaborator. The couple lived together for sixteen years before marrying in 1764.

Mr. Big versus *Mrs. & Mr. Little*

32-PT HELVETICA   32-PT MRS EAVES   32-PT MR EAVES

The x-height of a typeface affects its apparent size, its space efficiency, and its overall visual impact. Like hemlines and hair styles, x-heights go in and out of fashion. Bigger type bodies became popular in the mid-twentieth century, making letterforms look larger by maximizing the area within the overall point size.

12/14 HELVETICA

Because of its huge x-height, Helvetica can remain legible at small sizes. Set in 8 pts for a magazine caption, Helvetica can look quite elegant. The same typeface could look bulky and bland, however, standing 12 pts tall on a business card.

8/10 HELVETICA

The default type size in many software applications is 12 pts. Although this generally creates readable type on screen displays, 12-pt text type usually looks big and horsey in print. Sizes between 9 and 11 pts are common for printed text. This caption is 7.5 pts.

Typefaces with small x–heights, such as MRS EAVES, use space less efficiently than those with big lower bodies. However, their delicate proportions have lyrical charm.

12/14 MRS EAVES

Like his lovely wife, **MR EAVES** has a low waist and a small body. His loose letterspacing also makes him work well with his mate.

12/14 MR EAVES

The size of a typeface is a matter of context. A line of text that looks tiny on a television screen may appear appropriately scaled in a page of printed text. Smaller proportions affect legibility as well as space consumption. A diminutive x-height is a luxury that requires sacrifice.

8/10 MRS AND MR EAVES

All the typefaces shown below were inspired by the sixteenth-century printing types of Claude Garamond, yet each one reflects its own era. The lean forms of Garamond 3 appeared during the Great Depression, while the inflated x-height of ITC Garamond became an icon of the flamboyant 1970s.

Grapes of Wrath

30-PT GARAMOND 3   30-PT ITC GARAMOND

GARAMOND IN THE TWENTIETH CENTURY: VARIATIONS ON A THEME

1930s: Franklin D. Roosevelt, SALVADOR DALÍ, Duke

18-PT GARAMOND 3, *designed by Morris Fuller Benton and Thomas Maitland Cleland for ATF, 1936*

Ellington, *Scarface*, chicken and waffles, shoulder pads, radio.

1970s: Richard Nixon, Claes Oldenburg, Van Halen,

18-PT ITC GARAMOND, *designed by Tony Stan, 1976*

The Godfather, bell bottoms, guacamole, sitcoms.

1980s: Margaret Thatcher, BARBARA KRUGER, Madonna,

18-PT ADOBE GARAMOND, *designed by Robert Slimbach, 1989*

Blue Velvet, shoulder pads, pasta salad, desktop publishing.

2000s: Osama Bin Laden, MATTHEW BARNEY, the White

18-PT ADOBE GARAMOND PREMIERE PRO MEDIUM SUBHEAD, *designed by Robert Slimbach, 2005*

Stripes, *The Sopranos*, mom jeans, heirloom tomatoes, Twitter.

A type family with *optical sizes* has different styles for different sizes of output. The graphic designer selects a style based on context. Optical sizes designed for headlines or display tend to have delicate, lyrical forms, while styles created for text and captions are built with heavier strokes.

No Job *Too Small*

48-PT BODONI   8-PT BODONI

TYPE CRIME
*Some typefaces that work well
at large sizes look too fragile
when reduced.*

OPTICAL SIZES

HEADLINES are slim, *high-strung* prima donnas.
27-PT ADOBE GARAMOND PREMIERE PRO DISPLAY

SUBHEADS are *frisky* supporting characters.
27-PT ADOBE GARAMOND PREMIERE PRO SUBHEAD

TEXT is the *everyman* of the printed stage.
27-PT ADOBE GARAMOND PREMIERE PRO REGULAR

CAPTIONS get *heavy* to play small roles.
27-PT ADOBE GARAMOND PREMIERE PRO CAPTION

10 PT

In the era of METAL TYPE, type designers created a different *punch* for each size of type, adjusting its weight, spacing, and other features. Each size required a unique typeface design.

ADOBE GARAMOND PREMIERE PRO DISPLAY

When the type design process became automated in the NINETEENTH CENTURY, many typefounders economized by simply *enlarging or reducing* a base design to generate different sizes.

ADOBE GARAMOND PREMIERE PRO REGULAR

This MECHANIZED APPROACH to type sizes became the norm for photo and digital type production. When a text-sized letterform is enlarged to poster-sized proportions, its thin features become too heavy (and vice versa).

ADOBE GARAMOND PREMIERE PRO CAPTION

8 PT

A DISPLAY or *headline* style looks spindly and weak when set at small sizes. Display styles are intended for use at 24 pts. and larger.

Basic TEXT styles are designed for sizes ranging from 9 to 14 pts. Their features are strong and *meaty* but not too assertive.

CAPTION styles are built with the heaviest stroke weight. They are *designed* for sizes ranging from 6 to 8 pts.

80 PT

Scale is the size of design elements in comparison to other elements in a layout as well as to the physical context of the work. Scale is relative. 12-pt type displayed on a 32-inch monitor can look very small, while 12-pt type printed on a book page can look flabby and overweight. Designers create hierarchy and contrast by playing with the scale of letterforms. Changes in scale help create visual contrast, movement, and depth as well as express hierarchies of importance. Scale is physical. People intuitively judge the size of objects in relation to their own bodies and environments.

THE
WORLD
IS FLAT

TYPE CRIME
Minimal differences in type size make this design look tentative and arbitrary.

THE
WORLD
IS FLAT

SCALE CONTRAST
The strong contrast between type sizes gives this design dynamism, decisiveness, and depth.

THE XIX AMENDMENT Typographic installation at Grand Central Station, New York City, 1995. Designer: Stephen Doyle. Sponsors: The New York State Division of Women, the Metropolitan Transportation Authority, Revlon, and Merrill Lynch. *Large-scale text creates impact in this public installation.*

BLOW-UP: (WARREN NIEDICH) PHOTOGRAPHY, CINEMA AND THE BRAIN

BLOW-UP: PHOTOGRAPHY, CINEMA, AND THE BRAIN
Book cover, 2003. Designers: Paul Carlos and Urshula
Barbour/Pure + Applied. Author: Warren Niedich. *Cropping the
letters increases their sense of scale. The overlapping colors suggest
an extreme detail of a printed or photographic process.*

UNITED NATIONS' OFFICE ON DRUGS AND CRIME (UNODC)
Maps, 2009. Design: Harry Pearce and Jason Ching/
Pentagram. *This series of posters for the United Nations' Office on Drugs and Crime uses typographic scale to compare drug treatment programs, HIV incidence, and other data worldwide. The designers built simple world maps from country abbreviation codes (GBR, USA, RUS, etc.). The posters are aimed specifically at the Russian police, whose country has a poor track record in drug treatment. Note Russia's high incidence of HIV and low availability of addiction rehabilitation programs.*

REVOLVER: ZEITSCHRIFT FÜR
FILM (MAGAZINE FOR FILM)
Magazine, 1998–2003.
Designer: Gerwin Schmidt.
*This magazine is created by and
for film directors. The contrast
between the big type and the small
pages creates drama and surprise.*

SABON

Aa

HUMANIST OR OLD STYLE
The roman typefaces of the fifteenth and sixteenth centuries emulated classical calligraphy. Sabon was designed by Jan Tschichold in 1966, based on the sixteenth-century typefaces of Claude Garamond.

BASKERVILLE

Aa

TRANSITIONAL
These typefaces have sharper serifs and a more vertical axis than humanist letters. When the typefaces of John Baskerville were introduced in the mid-eighteenth century, their sharp forms and high contrast were considered shocking.

BODONI

Aa

MODERN
The typefaces designed by Giambattista Bodoni in the late eighteenth and early nineteenth centuries are radically abstract. Note the thin, straight serifs; vertical axis; and sharp contrast from thick to thin strokes.

A basic system for classifying typefaces was devised in the nineteenth century, when printers sought to identify a heritage for their own craft analogous to that of art history. *Humanist* letterforms are closely connected to calligraphy and the movement of the hand. *Transitional* and *modern* typefaces are more abstract and less organic. These three main groups correspond roughly to the Renaissance, Baroque, and Enlightenment periods in art and literature. Historians and critics of typography have since proposed more finely grained schemes that attempt to better capture the diversity of letterforms. Designers in the twentieth and twenty-first centuries have continued to create new typefaces based on historic characteristics.

CLARENDON

Aa

EGYPTIAN OR SLAB SERIF
Numerous bold and decorative typefaces were introduced in the nineteenth century for use in advertising. Egyptian typefaces have heavy, slablike serifs.

GILL SANS

Aa

HUMANIST SANS SERIF
Sans-serif typefaces became common in the twentieth century. Gill Sans, designed by Eric Gill in 1928, has humanist characteristics. Note the small, lilting counter in the letter a, and the calligraphic variations in line weight.

HELVETICA

Aa

TRANSITIONAL SANS SERIF
Helvetica, designed by Max Miedinger in 1957, is one of the world's most widely used typefaces. Its uniform, upright character makes it similar to transitional serif letters. These fonts are also referred to as "anonymous sans serif."

FUTURA

Aa

GEOMETRIC SANS SERIF
Some sans-serif types are built around geometric forms. In Futura, designed by Paul Renner in 1927, the Os are perfect circles, and the peaks of the A and M are sharp triangles.

CLASSIC TYPEFACES

Sabon
14 PT

This is not a book about fonts. It is a book about how to use them. Typefaces are essential resources for the graphic designer, just as glass, stone, steel, and other materials are employed by the architect.

SABON 9/12

Selecting type with wit and wisdom requires knowledge of how and why letterforms evolved.

7/9

Baskerville
14 PT

This is not a book about fonts. It is a book about how to use them. Typefaces are essential resources for the graphic designer, just as glass, stone, steel, and other materials are employed by the architect.

BASKERVILLE 9/12

Selecting type with wit and wisdom requires knowledge of how and why letterforms evolved.

7/9

Bodoni
14 PT

This is not a book about fonts. It is a book about how to use them. Typefaces are essential resources for the graphic designer, just as glass, stone, steel, and other materials are employed by the architect.

BODONI BOOK 9.5/12

Selecting type with wit and wisdom requires knowledge of how and why letterforms evolved.

7.5/9

Clarendon
14 PT

This is not a book about fonts. It is a book about how to use them. Typefaces are essential resources for the graphic designer, just as glass, stone, steel, and other materials are employed by the architect.

CLARENDON LIGHT 8/12

Selecting type with wit and wisdom requires knowledge of how and why letterforms evolved.

6/9

Gill Sans
14 PT

This is not a book about fonts. It is a book about how to use them. Typefaces are essential resources for the graphic designer, just as glass, stone, steel, and other materials are employed by the architect.

GILL SANS REGULAR 9/12

Selecting type with wit and wisdom requires knowledge of how and why letterforms evolved.

7/9

Helvetica
14 PT

This is not a book about fonts. It is a book about how to use them. Typefaces are essential resources for the graphic designer, just as glass, stone, steel, and other materials are employed by the architect.

HELVETICA REGULAR 8/12

Selecting type with wit and wisdom requires knowledge of how and why letterforms evolved.

6/9

Futura
14 PT

This is not a book about fonts. It is a book about how to use them. Typefaces are essential resources for the graphic designer, just as glass, stone, steel, and other materials are employed by the architect.

FUTURA BOOK 8.5/12

Selecting type with wit and wisdom requires knowledge of how and why letterforms evolved.

6.5/9

In the sixteeenth century, printers began organizing roman and italic typefaces into matched families. The concept was formalized in the early twentieth century.

ANATOMY OF A TYPE FAMILY   ADOBE GARAMOND PRO, *designed by Robert Slimbach, 1988*

The roman form is the core or spine from which a family of typefaces derives.

ADOBE GARAMOND PRO REGULAR

The roman form, also called plain or regular, is the standard, upright version of a typeface. It is typically conceived as the parent of a larger family.

Italic letters, which are based on cursive writing, have forms distinct from roman.

ADOBE GARAMOND PRO ITALIC

The italic form is used to create emphasis. Especially among serif faces, it often employs shapes and strokes distinct from its roman counterpart. Note the differences between the roman and italic a.

SMALL CAPS HAVE A HEIGHT THAT IS SIMILAR TO the lowercase x-height.

ADOBE GARAMOND PRO REGULAR (ALL SMALL CAPS)

Small caps (capitals) are designed to integrate with a line of text, where full-size capitals would stand out awkwardly. Small capitals are slightly taller than the x-height of lowercase letters.

Bold (and semibold) typefaces are used for emphasis within a hierarchy.

ADOBE GARAMOND PRO BOLD AND SEMIBOLD

Bold versions of traditional text fonts were added in the twentieth century to meet the need for emphatic forms. Sans-serif families often include a broad range of weights (thin, bold, black, etc.).

Bold (and semibold) typefaces each need to include an italic version, too.

ADOBE GARAMOND PRO BOLD AND SEMIBOLD ITALIC

The typeface designer tries to make the two bold versions feel similar in comparison to the roman, without making the overall form too heavy. The counters need to stay clear and open at small sizes. Many designers prefer not to use bold and semi-bold versions of traditional typefaces such as Garamond, because these weights are alien to the historic families.

Italics are not *slanted* letters.

TRUE ITALIC

TYPE CRIME: PSEUDO ITALICS *The wide, ungainly forms of these mechanically skewed letters look forced and unnatural.*

Some italics aren't slanted at all. In the type family *Quadraat*, the italic form is upright.

QUADRAAT, *designed by Fred Smeijers, 1992.*

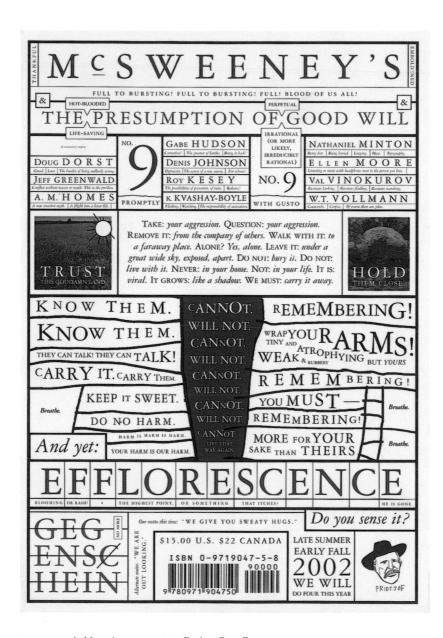

MCSWEENEY'S Magazine cover, 2002. Design: Dave Eggers.
This magazine cover uses the Garamond 3 typeface family in
various sizes. Although the typeface is classical and conservative,
the obsessive, slightly deranged layout is distinctly contemporary.

A traditional roman book face typically has a small family—an intimate group consisting of roman, italic, small caps, and possibly bold and semibold (each with an italic variant) styles. Sans-serif families often come in many more weights and sizes, such as thin, light, black, compressed, and condensed. A *superfamily* consists of dozens of related fonts in multiple weights and/or widths, often with both sans-serif and serif versions. Small capitals and non-lining numerals (once found only in serif fonts) are included in the sans-serif versions of Thesis, Scala Pro, and many other contemporary superfamilies.

ANATOMY OF A SUPERFAMILY

nn nn pp pp

Scala
Scala Italic
SCALA CAPS
Scala Bold

SCALA PRO, *designed by Martin Majoor, includes Scala (1991) and Scala Sans (1993). The serif and sans-serif forms have a common spine. Scala Pro (OpenType format) was released in 2005.*

Scala Sans Light
Scala Sans
Scala Sans Condensed
Scala Sans Cond Bold
Scala Sans Bold
Scala Sans Black
SCALA JEWEL CRYSTAL
SCALA JEWEL DIAMOND
SCALA JEWEL PEARL
SCALA JEWEL SAPHYR

UNIVERS *was designed by the Swiss typographer Adrian Frutiger in 1957. He designed twenty-one versions of Univers, in five weights and five widths. Whereas some type families grow over time, Univers was conceived as a total system from its inception.*

TRILOGY, *a superfamily designed by Jeremy Tankard in 2009, is inspired by three nineteenth-century type styles: sans serif, Egyptian, and fat face. The inclusion of the fat face style, with its wafer-thin serifs and ultrawide verticals, gives this family an unusual twist.*

ANATOMY OF A SUPERFAMILY

This is not a book about fonts. It is a book about how to use them. Typefaces
THE SERIF MEDIUM ROMAN

are essential resources for the graphic designer, just as glass, stone, steel, and
THE SERIF MEDIUM ITALIC

OTHER MATERIALS ARE EMPLOYED BY THE ARCHITECT. SOME DESIGNERS CREATE
THE SERIF MEDIUM SMALL CAPS

their own custom fonts. But most
THE SERIF BLACK ROMAN

graphic designers will tap the vast
THE SERIF EXTRA BOLD ROMAN

store of already existing typefaces,
THE SERIF BOLD ROMAN

choosing and combining each with
THE SERIF SEMI BOLD ROMAN

regard to the audience or situation.
THE SERIF MEDIUM ROMAN

Selecting type with wit and wisdom
THE SERIF SEMI LIGHT

requires knowledge of how and why
THE SERIF LIGHT ROMAN

letterforms have evolved. The history
THE SERIF EXTRA LIGHT ROMAN

of typography reflects a continual tension between the hand and machine, the
THE SANS MEDIUM ROMAN

organic and geometric, the human body and the abstract system. These tensions
THE SANS MEDIUM ITALIC

MARKED THE BIRTH OF PRINTED LETTERS FIVE CENTURIES AGO, AND THEY CONTINUE TO
THE SANS MEDIUM SMALL CAPS

energize typography today. Writing
THE SANS BLACK ROMAN

in the West was revolutionized early
THE SANS EXTRA BOLD ROMAN

in the Renaissance, when Johannes
THE SANS BOLD ROMAN

Gutenberg introduced moveable type
THE SANS SEMI BOLD ROMAN

in Germany. Whereas documents and
THE SANS MEDIUM ROMAN

books had previously been written by
THE SANS SEMI LIGHT ROMAN

hand, printing with type mobilized all
THE SANS LIGHT ROMAN

of the techniques of mass production.
THE SANS EXTRA LIGHT ROMAN

THESIS, *designed by Lu(cas) de Groot, 1994*

A word set in ALL CAPS within running text can look big and bulky, and A LONG PASSAGE SET ENTIRELY IN CAPITALS CAN LOOK UTTERLY INSANE. SMALL CAPITALS are designed to match the x-height of lowercase letters. Designers, enamored with the squarish proportions of true SMALL CAPS, employ them not only within bodies of text but for subheads, bylines, invitations, and more. Rather than MIXING SMALL CAPS WITH CAPITALS, many designers prefer to use ALL SMALL CAPS, creating a clean line with no ascending elements. InDesign and other programs allow users to create FALSE SMALL CAPS at the press of a button; these SCRAWNY LETTERS look out of place.

+ CAPITAL
investment
− CAPITAL
punishment
CAPITAL
crime

CAPITAL
investment
CAPITAL
punishment
CAPITAL
crime

TYPE CRIME
In this stack of lowercase and capital letters, the spaces between lines appear uneven because caps are tall but have no descenders.

ADJUSTED LEADING
The leading has been fine-tuned by selectively shifting the baselines of the small capitals to make the space between lines look even.

PSEUDO SMALL CAPS are shrunken versions of FULL-SIZE CAPS.

TYPE CRIME
PSEUDO SMALL CAPS
Helvetica was never meant to include small caps. These automatically generated characters look puny and starved; they are an abomination against nature.

TRUE SMALL CAPS integrate PEACEFULLY with lowercase letters.

SMALL CAPS, SCALA PRO
Only use small caps when they are officially included with the type family. When working with OpenType fonts (labeled Pro), access small caps in InDesign via the Character Options>OpenType menu. Older formats list small caps as a separate file in the Type>Font menu.

Tasty Vagabonds

The two camps of the burgeoning food-truck phenomenon: stable and nomadic.
BY AILEEN GALLAGHER

TRUCKS THAT ROVE

CUPCAKE STOP
The inevitable cupcakes-only truck rolled out in May. *twitter.com/cupcakestop.*

TREATS TRUCK
Cookies, crispy treats,

NEW YORK MAGAZINE
Design: Chris Dixon, 2009. *This page detail mixes serif types from the Miller family (including true Small Caps) with the sans-serif family Verlag.*

AMUSEMENT MAGAZINE
Design: Alice Litscher, 2009.
*This French culture magazine
employs a startling mix of
tightly leaded Didot capitals in
roman and italic. Running text
is set in Glypha.*

Combining typefaces is like making a salad. Start with a small number of elements representing different colors, tastes, and textures. Strive for contrast rather than harmony, looking for emphatic differences rather than mushy transitions. Give each ingredient a role to play: sweet tomatoes, crunchy cucumbers, and the pungent shock of an occasional anchovy. When mixing typefaces on the same line, designers usually adjust the point size so that the x-heights align. When placing typefaces on separate lines, it often makes sense to create contrast in scale as well as style or weight. Try mixing big, light type with small, dark type for a criss-cross of contrasting flavors and textures.

TYPE CRIME: WHO'S ACCOUNTABLE FOR THIS? *A slightly squeezed variant of the primary font has been used to make the second line fit better (as if we wouldn't notice). Yet another weight appears on the bottom line.*

SINGLE-FAMILY MIXES

Creamy and **Extra Crunchy** | *Differences within a **single family***

UNIVERS 47 LIGHT CONDENSED AND UNIVERS 67 BOLD CONDENSED

Sweet Child of **MINE** | *Differences within a* **SUPERFAMILY**

QUADRAAT REGULAR AND ITALIC; QUADRAAT SANS BOLD

Noodles with **Potato Sauce** | *Bland and blander*

HELVETICA NEUE 56 MEDIUM AND HELVETICA NEUE 75 BOLD

TYPE CRIME
These typefaces are from the same family, but they are too close in weight to mix well.

MULTIPLE-FAMILY MIXES

Jack Sprat and his **voluptuous wife** | *Two-way* **contrast**

THESIS SERIF EXTRA LIGHT AND VAG ROUNDED BOLD

Sweet, SOUR, and **hot** | THREE-*way* **contrast**

BODONI ROMAN, THESIS SERIF EXTRA LIGHT SMALL CAPS, AND FUTURA BOLD

Mr. Potatohead and Mrs. Pearbutt | *Too close for comfort*

ADOBE GARAMOND PRO BOLD AND ADOBE JENSON PRO BOLD

TYPE CRIME
These two type styles are too similar to provide a counterpoint to each other.

The Word

EDITED BY EMMA PEARSE

GLYPHA THIN, *designed by Adrian Frutiger, 1979. The large scale of the letters is counterbalanced by the fine line of the stroke.*

EVENTS

BENOIT DENIZET-LEWIS
The Powerhouse Arena, 37 Main St., nr. Water St., Dumbo (718-666-3049)
The writer from *The New York Times Magazine* reads from *American Voyeur: Dispatches From the Far Reaches of Modern Life*, a collection of his analytical reportage on everything from pro-life summer camps to the clothing company Abercrombie & Fitch; 1/13 at 7.

SOUTHERN WRITERS READING SERIES
Happy Ending Lounge, 302 Broome St., nr. Forsyth St. (212-334-9676)
An open mike for writers from below the Mason-Dixon line, where they'll read and discuss (and drink) all things southern; 1/13 at 8.

SUZE ORMAN
Barnes & Noble, 33 E. 17th St., nr. Broadway (212-253-0810)
The high priestess of financial invincibility presents her latest, *Women and Money: Owning the Power to Control Your Destiny*; 1/14 at 7.

MARY JO BANG
McNally Jackson, 52 Prince St., nr. Mulberry St. (212-274-1160)
Two poets in one room: Susan Wheeler hosts a discussion with the spectacularly named National Book Critics Circle Award winner, whose latest collection is titled *The Bride of E*; 1/14 at 7.

JOYCE CAROL OATES AND ELAINE SHOWALTER
92nd St. Y, 1395 Lexington Ave. (212-415-5500)
What two better authorities to discuss women and writing on the occasion of the publication of Showalter's *A Jury of Her Peers*, a history of American women writers from 1650 to 2000; 1/17 at 11 a.m.

PATTI SMITH
Barnes & Noble, 33 E. 17th St., nr. Broadway (212-253-0810)
The poet queen of punk reads from her book *Just Kids: From Brooklyn to the Chelsea Hotel, a Life of Art and Friendship*, about the fabulous, rocky friendship with Robert Mapplethorpe; 1/19 at 7. *Smith will also appear with the playwright Sam Shepard on January 21 at 8 p.m. at 92nd St. Y, 1395 Lexington Ave. (212-415-5500).*

COUNTESS LUANN DE LESSEPS
Borders, 10 Columbus Circle, nr. Eighth Ave. (212-823-9775)
The Real Housewife of New York, who says that "class is a state of mind," appears in the glamorous flesh to share her intimate knowledge of sophisticated living; 1/21 at 7.

IN THE FLESH
Happy Ending Lounge, 302 Broome St., nr. Forsyth St. (212-334-9676)
Former sex columnist, editor of *Best Sex Writing 2010*, and blogge Rachel Kramer Bussel hosts her monthly series of erotic re this time with the theme of sex and food (and rumo cupcakes all around); 1/21 at 8.

NICK FLYNN
BookCourt, 163 Court St., nr. Pacific
The cult hit memoirist (an Taylor) reads from his lates hitting work about child obsession with torture, of the Iraqi men depic 1/22 at 7.

OZZY OSBOU
Borders, 10 C
The filt
c

MILLER SMALL CAPS, *designed by Matthew Carter with Jonathan Hoefler and Tobias Frere-Jones, 1997–2000. Known as a Scotch Roman typeface, it has crisp serifs and strong contrast between thick and thin.*

EGYPTIAN BOLD CONDENSED, *a Linotype font based on a typeface from 1820. This quirky, chunky face has been used intermittently at* New York Magazine *since the publication was first designed by Milton Glaser in the 1970s. Here, the ultra-black type set at a relatively small size makes an incisive bite in the page.*

VERLAG, *designed by Jonathan Hoefler, 1996. Originally commissioned by Abbott Miller for exclusive use by the Guggenheim Museum, Verlag has become a widely used general-purpose typeface. Its approachable geometric forms are based on Frank Lloyd Wright's lettering for the facade of the Guggenheim.*

THE WORD: NEW YORK MAGAZINE Design: Chris Dixon, 2010. *This content-intensive page detail mixes four different type families from various points in history, ranging from the early advertising face Egyptian Bold Condensed to the functional contemporary sans Verlag. These diverse ingredients are mixed here at different scales to create typographic tension and contrast.*

Lining numerals take up uniform widths of space, enabling the numbers to line up when tabulated in columns. They were introduced around the turn of the twentieth century to meet the needs of modern business. Lining numerals are the same height as capital letters, so they sometimes look big and bulky when appearing in running text.

Non-lining numerals, also called *text* or *old style* numerals, have ascenders and descenders, like lowercase letters. Non-lining numerals returned to favor in the 1990s, valued for their idiosyncratic appearance and their traditional typographic attitude. Like letterforms, old style numerals are proportional; each one has its own set width.

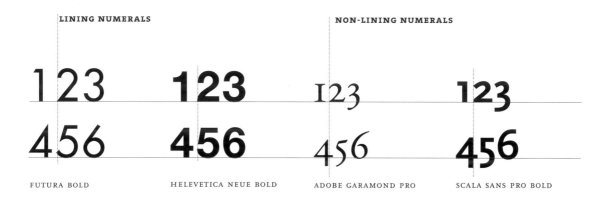

LINING NUMERALS

NON-LINING NUMERALS

FUTURA BOLD

HELEVETICA NEUE BOLD

ADOBE GARAMOND PRO

SCALA SANS PRO BOLD

TEXT SET WITH LINING NUMERALS

What is the cost of *War and Peace*? The cover price of the Modern Library Classics paperback edition is $15.00, discounted 32% by Amazon to $10.50. But what about the human cost in terms of hours squandered reading a super-sized work of literary fiction? If you can read 400 words per minute, double the average, it will take you 1,476 minutes (24.6 hours) to read *War and Peace*. Devoting just four hours per day to the task, you could finish the work in a little over six days. If you earn $7.25 per hour (minimum wage in the U.S.), the cost of reading *War and Peace* will be $184.50 (€130.4716, £11.9391, or ¥17676.299).

ADOBE GARAMOND PRO *includes both lining and non-lining numerals, allowing designers to choose a style in response to the circumstances of the project. The lining numerals appear large, because they have the height of capital letters.*

TEXT SET WITH NON-LINING NUMERALS

What is the cost of *War and Peace*? The cover price of the Modern Library Classics paperback edition is $15.00, discounted 32% by Amazon to $10.50. But what about the human cost in terms of hours squandered reading a super-sized work of literary fiction? If you can read 400 words per minute, double the average, it will take you 1,476 minutes (24.6 hours) to read *War and Peace*. Devoting just four hours per day to the task, you could finish the work in a little over six days. If you earn $7.25 per hour (minimum wage in the U.S.), the cost of reading *War and Peace* will be $184.50 (€130.4716, £11.9391, or ¥17676.299).

Non-lining numerals integrate visually with the text. Different math and currency symbols are designed to match the different numeral styles. Smaller currency symbols look better with non-lining numerals.

99.8	32.3	**DOM** DomCasual	...		26	7451	57.0	-
73.8	16.1	**EGIZ** Egiziano	...		dd	2789	61.6	+
32.7	18.5	**EURO** Eurostile	...		9	1449	99.5	-
69.6	59.4	**FKTR** FetteFraktur	...		dd	3944	87.0	+
66.8	2.8	**FRNK** FrnklinGthc	...		dd	11712	48.8	+
17	7	**FRUT** Frutiger55	...		...	1814	34.5	-
35.8	15	**FUTU** FuturaBook	...		18	11325	20.5	+
52.3	10.1	**GDY** GoudyOldStyl	...		dd	2685	46.5	-
95.3	26.8	**GILL** GillSans	...		dd	10748	72.3	+
96.2	35.4	**GLRD** Galliard	...		26	1566	1.1	-
72.7	9.6	**GMND** Garamond	...		27	2376	62.3	-
102.3	20.7	**GROT** Grotesque9	...		47	6147	8.0	-
87.8	19.1	**HLV** Helvetica	...		dd	3009	63.3	+
79.3	35.6	**HOBO** Hobo	...		dd	5981	25.2	+
97.3	56.9	**HTXT** HoeflerText	.5e	1.3	dd	4548	93.7	+
85.1	11.4	**INTR** Interstate	.32	2.1	dd	10127	19.3	+
72.7	59.1	**JNSN** Janson	...		17	8065	63.2	+
84.8	68.7	**KIS** KisJanson	...		dd	4641	80.9	-
65	7.9	**KSMK** FFKosmik	...		20	510	26.3	+
35.9	8.9	**LTHS** LithosBlack	...		dd	1669	39.8	+
104.7	1.5	**LtrG** LetterGothic	...		dd	8091	20.6	+

HLV Helvetica	...		dd	3009	63.3	+0.35
HOBO Hobo	...		dd	5981	25.2	+0.79
HTXT HoeflerText	.5e	1.3	dd	4548	93.7	+0.99
INTR Interstate	.32	2.1	dd	10127	19.3	+1.86
JNSN Janson	...		17	8065	63.2	+1.11
KIS KisJanson	...		dd	4641	80.9	-0.29
KSMK FFKosmik	...		20	510	26.3	+0.92

123

RETINA, *designed by Tobias Frere-Jones, 2000, was created for the extreme typographic conditions of the Wall Street Journal's financial pages. The numerals are designed to line up into columns. The different weights of Retina have matching set widths, allowing the newspaper to mix weights while maintaining perfectly aligned columns. The notched forms (called ink traps) prevent ink from filling in the letterforms when printed at tiny sizes.*

MONTHLY CALENDAR, 1892
The charming numerals in this calendar don't line up into neat columns, because they have varied set widths. They would not be suitable for setting modern financial data.

{["",·,·""]}

HELVETICA NEUE BOLD

{[""",•,•""]}

BODONI BOLD

COMMONLY ABUSED PUNCTUATION MARKS

5'2" eyes of blue

PRIME OR HATCH MARKS INDICATE INCHES AND FEET

It's a dog's life.

APOSTROPHES SIGNAL CONTRACTION
OR POSSESSION

He said, "That's what she said."

QUOTATION MARKS SET OFF DIALOGUE

A well-designed comma carries the essence of the typeface down to its delicious details. Helvetica's comma is a chunky square mounted to a jaunty curve, while Bodoni's is a voluptuous, thin-stemmed orb. Designers and editors need to learn various typographic conventions in addition to mastering the grammatical rules of punctuation. A pandemic error is the use of straight prime or hatch marks (often called *dumb quotes*) in place of apostrophes and quotation marks (also known as *curly quotes, typographer's quotes,* or *smart quotes*). Double and single quotation marks are represented with four distinct characters, each accessed with a different keystroke combination. Know thy keystrokes! It usually falls to the designer to purge the client's manuscript of spurious punctuation.

"The thoughtless overuse" of quotation marks is a disgrace upon literary style—and on typographic style as well.

TYPE CRIME
Quotation marks carve out chunks of white space from the edge of the text.

See APPENDIX for more punctuation blunders.

"Hanging punctuation" prevents quotations and other marks from taking a bite out of the crisp left edge of a text block.

HANGING QUOTATION MARKS
Make a clean edge by pushing the quotation marks into the margin.

NERD ALERT: To create hanging punctuation in InDesign, insert a word space before the quotation mark. Pressing the option key, use the left arrow key to back the quotation mark into the margin. You can also use the Optical Margin Alignment or Indent to Here tools.

TYPE CRIMES

NEW YORK CITY TOUR
City streets have become a dangerous place. Millions of dollars a year are spent producing commercial signs that are fraught with typographic misdoings. While some of these signs are cheaply made over-the-counter products, others were designed for prominent businesses and institutions. There is no excuse for such gross negligence.

GETTIN' IT RIGHT
Apostrophes and quotation marks are sometimes called curly quotes. Here, you can enjoy them in a meat-free environment.

GETTIN' IT WRONG
The correct use of hatch marks is to indicate inches and feet. Alas, this pizza is the hapless victim of a misplaced keystroke. In InDesign or Illustrator, use the Glyphs palette to find hatch marks when you need them.

Not all typographic elements represent language. For centuries, ornaments have been designed to integrate directly with text. In the letterpress era, printers assembled decorative elements one by one to build larger forms and patterns on the page. Decorative rules served to frame and divide content. In the nineteenth century, printers provided their customers with vast collections of readymade illustrations that could easily be mixed with text. Today, numerous forms of ornament are available as digital fonts, which can be typed on a keyboard, scaled, and output like any typeface. Some contemporary ornaments are modular systems designed to combine into larger patterns and configurations, allowing the graphic designer to invent new arrangements out of given pieces. Themed collections of icons and illustrations are also available as digital fonts.

TYPOGRAPHIC ORNAMENTS Fry and Steele, London, 1794. Collection of Jan Tholenaar, Reinoud Tholenaar, and Saskia Ottenhoff-Tholenaar.

SPEAKUP, *designed by Supisa Wattanasansanee/Cadson Demak, 2008. Distributed by T26.*

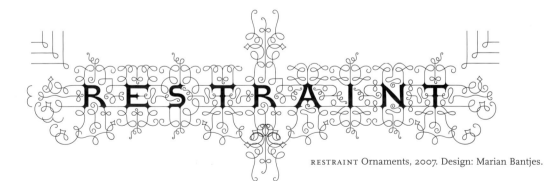

RESTRAINT Ornaments, 2007. Design: Marian Bantjes.

DANCE INK MAGAZINE Design: Abbott Miller, 1996. *The designer repeated a single ornament from the font Whirligigs, designed by Zuzana Licko in 1994, to create an ethereal veil of ink. Whirligigs are modular units that fit together to create an infinite variety of patterns.*

WHIRLIGIGS, *designed by Zuzana Licko, Emigre, 1994.*

GESCHAD. FANTAISIE KAPITALEN

UIT DE

LETTERGIETERIJ VAN JOH. ENSCHEDÉ EN ZONEN TE HAARLEM

Nº 5170. Op 11 Augustijn.

HAARLEM

Nº 5168. Op 11 Augustijn.

ITALIE

Nº 5031. Op 102 Punten.

GRAFT

Nº 5040. Op 10½ Augustijn.

MARS

Dl. V. Bl. 123.

FANTAISIE KAPITALEN Type specimen, 1897. Design: Joh. Enchedé & Zohnen. Collection of Jan Tholenaar, Reinoud Tholenaar, and Saskia Ottenhoff-Tholenaar.

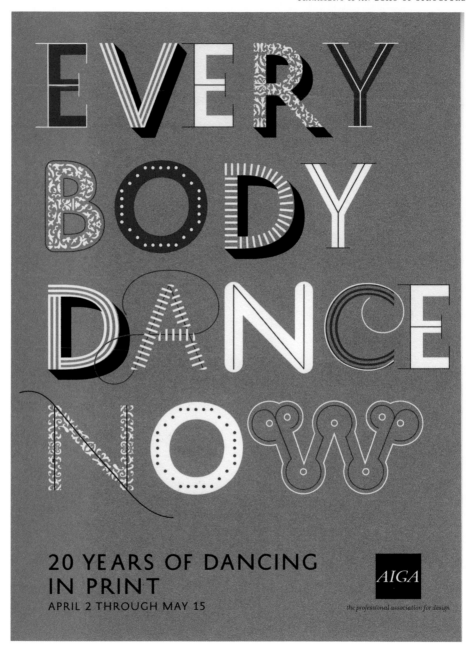

EVERYBODY DANCE NOW Postcard, 2009. Design: Abbott Miller, Kristen Spilman, Jeremy Hoffman/Pentagram. *Peter Bilak's typeface History, designed in 2008, consists of numerous decorative and structural elements that can be layered into distinctive combinations.*

Creating letters by hand allows graphic artists to integrate imagery and text, making design and illustration into fluidly integrated practices. Lettering can emulate existing typefaces or derive from the artist's own drawing or writing style. Designers create lettering by hand and with software, often combining diverse techniques.

KING OF DESIGN

KING OF FASHION

KING OF BEATS

TOKION MAGAZINE: KINGS
Designer: Deanne Cheuk,
2002–2003. *These magazine
headlines combine drawing and
painting with digital techniques.*

THE LOCUST (LEFT) and MELT BANANA (RIGHT) Screenprint
posters, 2002. Designer: Nolen Strals. *Hand lettering is a vibrant
force in graphic design, as seen in these music posters. Lettering is the
basis of many digital typefaces, but nothing is quite as potent as the
real thing.*

A *logotype* uses typography or lettering to depict the name or initials of an organization in a memorable way. Whereas some trademarks consist of an abstract symbol or a pictorial icon, a logotype uses words and letters to create a distinctive visual image. Logotypes can be built with existing typefaces or with custom-drawn letterforms. A logotype is part of an overall visual brand, which the designer conceives as a "language" that lives (and changes) in various circumstances. A complete visual identity can consist of colors, patterns, icons, signage components, and a selection of typefaces. Sometimes a logotype becomes the basis for the design of a complete typeface. Many type designers collaborate with graphic designers to create typefaces that are unique to a given client.

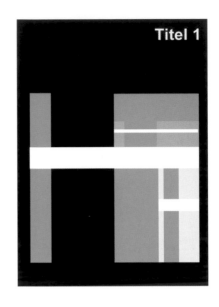

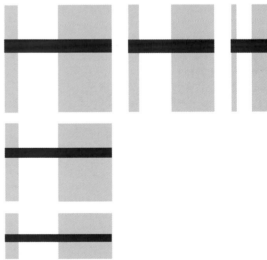

HÜBNER Identity program, 1998. Design: Jochen Stankowski. *This identity for an engineering firm is built around the H, whose proportions change in different contexts.*

STADSSCHOUWBURG UTRECHT

UTRECHT CITY THEATER
Identity, 2009. Design:
Edenspiekermann.
*This ambitious visual identity
program uses custom letterforms
based on the typeface Agenda.
The letters in the custom
typeface are designed to split
apart into elements that can be
mirrored, layered, flipped, and
animated for a variety of
applications, including signage,
posters, printed matter, and
web communications.*

EL BANCO DE UNO Visual branding, 2007. Agency: Saffron.
Identity design: Joshua Distler, Mike Abbink, Gabor Schreier,
Virginia Sardón. Custom typeface design: Mike Abbink, Paul van
der Laan. *This elaborate identity program for a Mexican bank uses
a custom typeface whose blocky forms are inspired by Mayan glyphs.*

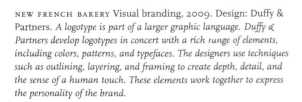

NEW FRENCH BAKERY Visual branding, 2009. Design: Duffy & Partners. *A logotype is part of a larger graphic language. Duffy & Partners develop logotypes in concert with a rich range of elements, including colors, patterns, and typefaces. The designers use techniques such as outlining, layering, and framing to create depth, detail, and the sense of a human touch. These elements work together to express the personality of the brand.*

During the early years of the World Wide Web, designers were forced to work within the narrow range of typefaces commonly installed on the computers of their end users. Since then, several techniques have emerged for embedding fonts within web content or for delivering fonts to end users when they visit a site. In one approach, specially formatted fonts are hosted on a third-party server and then downloaded by users; designers pay a fee for the service. Another approach implements the `@font-face` rule in CSS, which can download any kind of digital font hosted on a server; only typefaces licensed for this use can be accessed legally via `@font-face`.

WEB FONTS 1.0

Verdana was designed by the legendary typographer *Matthew Carter* in 1996 for digital display. Verdana has a large x-height, simple curves, open forms, and loose spacing.

Georgia is a serif screen face built with sturdy strokes, simple curves, open counters, and generous spacing. Designed by Matthew Carter in 1996 for Microsoft, Georgia is widely used on the web.

VERDANA AND GEORGIA, *released in 1996 by Microsoft, were designed specifically for the web. Prior to the rise of font embedding, these were among a handful of typefaces that could be reliably used online.*

FONT EMBEDDING Screen shot, detail, 2009. Typefaces: Greta and Fedra, designed by Peter Bilak/Typotheque. *In 2009, the digital type foundry Typotheque launched a pioneering service that allows designers to display Typotheque fonts on any website in exchange for a one-time license fee. Typotheque's Open Type fonts, which support global languages including Arabic and Hindi, are hosted by Typotheque and accessed using the CSS* `@font-face` *rule.*

BOBULATE Website, 2009. Designed by Jason Santa Maria for Liz Danzico. Typeface: Skolar, designed by David Brezina/Typetogether. *This site design uses Typekit, a third-party service that delivers fonts to end users when they visit a site. Typekit deters piracy by obscuring the origins of the font. Designers or site owners pay a subscription fee to the service.*

Anti-aliasing creates the appearance of smooth curves on screen by changing the brightness of the pixels or sub-pixels along the edges of each letterform. Photoshop and other software packages allow designers to select strong or weak anti-aliasing. When displayed at very small sizes, strongly anti-aliased type can look blurry. It also increases the number of colors in an image file.

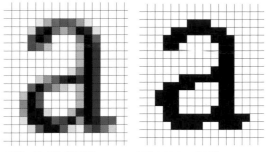

ANTI-ALIASED LETTER   BITMAPPED LETTER

smooth smooth

ANTI-ALIASED TYPE: SMOOTH SETTING *(simulated screen capture)*

none none

ANTI-ALIASING DISABLED: NONE SETTING *(simulated screen capture)*

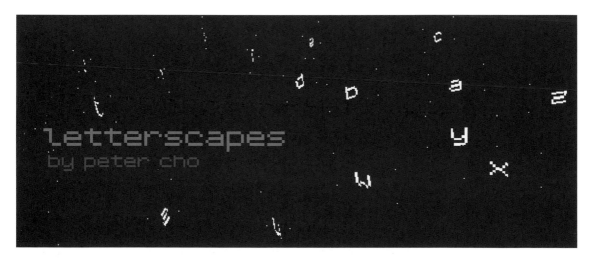

LETTERSCAPES Website, 2002. Design: Peter Cho. *Simple bitmapped letters are animated in three-dimensional space.*

Bitmap typefaces are built out of the *pixels* (picture elements) that structure a screen display or other output device. While a PostScript letter consists of a vector outline, a true bitmap character contains a fixed number of rectilinear units that are displayed either on or off. True bitmap characters are used on devices such as cash registers, signboard displays, and various small-scale screens.

Most contemporary bitmap typefaces are not true bitmaps. They are drawn as outlines on a grid and then output as PostScript, TrueType, or OpenType fonts. Thus they can be easily used with any standard layout software. Many designers like to exploit the visible geometry of pixelated characters.

LoResNine	**LoResNine**
LoResTwelve	**LoResTwelve**
LoResFifteen	**LoResFifteen**
LoResTwentyEight	LoResTwentyEight
Set at size of root resolution (9, 12, 15, and 28 pts)	*All set at 28 pts*

```
BOEKHANDEL NIJHOF & LEE
 STAALSTRAAT 13-A
 1011 JK AMSTERDAM


22/05/03 13:12        01
000000 #0094    BED.1

VERZENDKOST.      42.50
TYPOGRAFIE         6.00
TYPOGRAFIE        16.50
TYPOGRAFIE        19.50
TYPOGRAFIE        33.95
TYPOGRAFIE        55.35
TYPOGRAFIE        32.00
TYPOGRAFIE        59.00
TYPOGRAFIE        40.00
TYPOGRAFIE        50.40
TYPOGRAFIE        47.25
TYPOGRAFIE        80.00
TYPOGRAFIE        37.70
SUBTOTAL         520.15
BTW LAAG          29.44

STUKS               13Q
CREDIT        520.15

  OOK ANTIQUARIAAT
  TEL:020-6203980
  FAX:020-6393294
```

LO-RES NARROW, *designed by Zuzana Licko, Emigre. Released in 2001, the Lo-Res type family is a collection of outline (PostScript) fonts based on bitmap designs created by Licko in 1985. Lo-Res Narrow consists of a series of different sizes, each one constructed with a one-pixel stroke weight. Thus Lo-ResTwentyEight Narrow has dramatically lighter and tighter forms than Lo-ResNine Narrow, which gets blockier as it is enlarged. Designed for display on screen at low resolutions, a bitmap font should be used at its root size or at integer multiples of that size. (Enlarge 9-pixel type to 18, 27, 36, and so on).*

NIJHOF & LEE *Receipt, 2003. This cash register receipt, printed with a bitmap font, is from a design and typography bookstore in Amsterdam.*

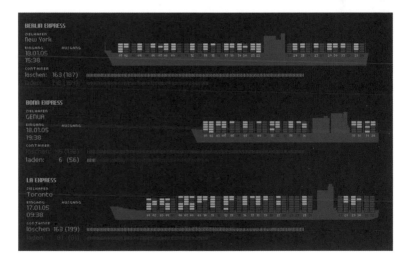

ELEMENTAR, *designed by Gustavo Ferreira in 2009 and distributed by Typotheque. Elementar is a bitmap type family consisting of dozens of weights and styles made by manipulating common parameters such as height, width, and the degree of contrast between horizontal and vertical elements. Elementar is suitable for print, screen, and interfaces. It is inspired by Adrian Frutiger's Univers type family.*

Fontlab and other applications allow designers to create functional fonts that work seamlessly with standard software programs such as InDesign and Photoshop.

The first step in designing a typeface is to define a basic concept. Will the letters be serif or sans serif? Will they be modular or organic? Will you construct them geometrically or base them on handwriting? Will you use them for display or for text? Will you work with historic source material or invent the characters more or less from scratch?

The next step is to create drawings. Some designers start with pencil before working digitally, while others build their letterforms directly with font design software. Begin by drawing a few core letters, such as *o*, *u*, *h*, and *n*, building curves, lines, and shapes that will reappear throughout the font. All the letters in a typeface are distinct from each other, yet they share many attributes, such as x-height, line weight, stress, and a common vocabulary of forms and proportions.

You can control the spacing of the typeface by adding blank areas next to each character as well as creating kerning pairs that determine the distance between particular characters. Producing a complete typeface is an enormous task. However, for people with a knack for drawing letterforms, the process is hugely rewarding.

Castaways

CASTAWAYS Drawing and finished type, 2001. Art and type direction: Andy Cruz. Typeface design: Ken Barber/House Industries. Font engineering: Rich Roat. *House Industries is a digital type foundry that creates original typefaces inspired by popular culture and design history. Designer Ken Barber makes pencil drawings by hand and then digitizes the outlines. Castaways is from a series of typefaces based on commercial signs from Las Vegas. The shapes of the letters recall the handpainted strokes made by traditional sign painters and lettering artists.*

MERCURY BOLD Page proof and screen shot, 2003. Design: Jonathan Hoefler/Hoefler & Frere-Jones. *Mercury is a typeface designed for modern newspapers, whose production demands fast, high-volume printing on cheap paper. The typeface's bullet-proof letterforms feature chunky serifs and sturdy upright strokes. The notes marked on the proof below comment on everything from the width or weight of a letter to the size and shape of a serif. Many such proofs are made during the design process. In a digital typeface, each letterform consists of a series of curves and lines controlled by points. In a large type family, different weights and widths can be made automatically by interpolating between extremes such as light and heavy or narrow and wide. The designer then adjusts each variant to ensure legibility and visual consistency.*

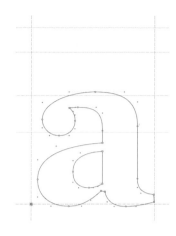

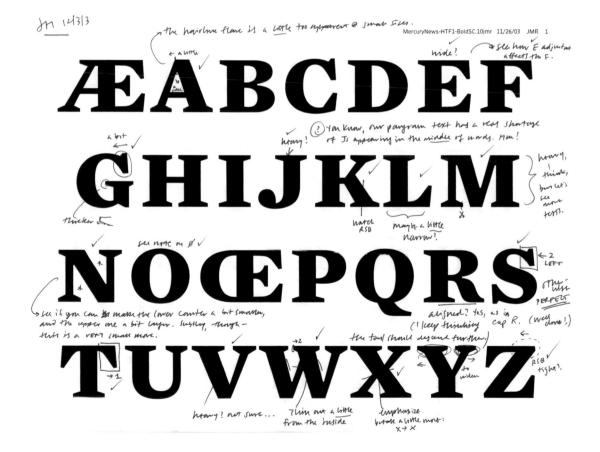

Create a prototype for a bitmap typeface by designing letters on a grid of squares or a grid of dots. Substitute the curves and diagonals of traditional letterforms with gridded and rectilinear elements. Avoid making detailed "staircases," which are just curves and diagonals in disguise. This exercise looks back to the 1910s and 1920s, when avant-garde designers made experimental typefaces out of simple geometric parts. The project also speaks to the structure of digital technologies, from cash register receipts and LED signs to on-screen font display, showing that a typeface is a system of elements.

Wendy Neese

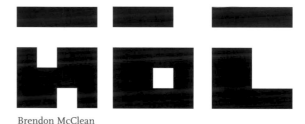

Brendon McClean

Bruce Willen

James Alvarez

Examples of student work from
Maryland Institute College of Art

Joey Potts

READ

Becky Slogeris

PUSH

Bryan Connor

Look

Virginia Sasser

SPAM

Julia Kim

copy

Michelle Ghiotti

Where do fonts come from, and why are there so many different formats? Some come loaded with your computer's operating system, while others are bundled with software packages. A few of these widely distributed typefaces are of the highest quality, such as Adobe Garamond Pro and **Hoefler Text**, while others (including **Comic Sans**, *Apple Chancery*, and Papyrus) are reviled by design snobs everywhere.

If you want to expand your vocabulary beyond this familiar fare, you will need to purchase fonts from digital type foundries. These range from large establishments like Adobe and FontShop, which license thousands of different typefaces, to independent producers that distribute just a few, such as Underware in the Netherlands or Jeremy Tankard Typography in the U.K. You can also learn to make your own fonts as well as find fonts that are distributed for free online.

The different font formats reflect technical innovations and business arrangements developed over time. Older font formats are still generally usable on modern operating systems.

POSTSCRIPT/TYPE 1 was developed for desktop computer systems in the 1980s by Adobe. Type 1 fonts are output using the PostScript programming language, created for generating high-resolution images on paper or film. A Type 1 font consists of two files: a screen font and a printer font. You must install both files in order to fully use these fonts.

TRUETYPE is a later font format, created by Apple and Microsoft for use with their operating systems. TrueType fonts are easier to install than Type 1 fonts because they consist of a single font file rather than two.

OPENTYPE, a format developed by Adobe, works on multiple platforms. Each file supports up to 65,000 characters, allowing multiple styles and character variations to be contained in a single font file. In a TrueType or Type 1 font, small capitals, alternate ligatures, and other special characters must be contained in separate font files (sometimes labelled "Expert"); in an OpenType font they are part of the main font. These expanded character sets can also include accented letters and other special glyphs needed for typesetting a variety of languages. OpenType fonts with expanded character sets are commonly labeled "Pro." OpenType fonts also automatically adjust the position of hyphens, brackets, and parentheses for letters set in all-capitals.

{[(HALF-BAKED?)]}

SCALA, *PostScript/Type 1 font format*

{[(HALF-BAKED?)]}

SCALA PRO, *OpenType font format*

£ § ¥ ¼ ½ ¾ É Ë Ì Å
Ã Â Á Ý ø å ë ð ñ ò þ
ÿ Ą ą ě ę ġ ġ dž z ž ž
ő ġ ġ į į ĭ † ‡ ☜ ☞

SCALA PRO, *OpenType font, designed by Martin Majoor, 2005. Scala Pro has numerous special characters for typesetting diverse European languages. You can access these characters using the Glyphs palette in InDesign.*

SMALL CAPS AND OLD-STYLE NUMERALS, WHERE ARE YOU HIDING?

NERD ALERT: Access small caps and numerals quickly through the Type>OpenType options menu or other OpenType layout tool in your design software. Small caps will not appear as a style variant in the Font menu, because OpenType treats them as part of the main font. With any font, you can view all the special characters through the Type and Tables>Glyphs menu. You will find many unexpected elements, including swashes, ligatures, ornaments, fractions, and more. Double click a glyph to insert it into to your text frame.

SAVE YOURSELF SOME EMBARRASSMENT
AND LEARN TO USE THESE COMMONLY
ABUSED TERMS CORRECTLY.

typeface or font?

A *typeface* is the design of the letterforms; a *font* is the delivery mechanism. In metal type, the design is embodied in the punches from which molds are made. A font consists of the cast metal printing types. In digital systems, the typeface is the visual design, while the font is the software that allows you to install, access, and output the design. A single typeface might be available in several font formats. In part because the design of digital typefaces and the production of fonts are so fluidly linked today, most people use the terms interchangeably. Type nerds insist, however, on using them precisely.

character or glyph?

Type designers distinguish *characters* from *glyphs* in order to comply with Unicode, an international system for identifying all of the world's recognized writing systems. Only a symbol with a unique function is considered a character and is thus assigned a code point in Unicode. A single character, such as a lowercase *a*, can be embodied by several different glyphs (a, *a*, A). Each glyph is a specific expression of a given character.

Roman or roman?

The Roman Empire is a proper noun and thus is capitalized, but we identify roman letterforms, like italic ones, in lowercase. The name of the Latin alphabet is capitalized.

Who is the user of a typeface? In the end, the user is the reader. But before a set of letters can find their way onto the cover of a book or the back of a cereal box, they must pass through the hands of another user: the graphic designer.

Digital fonts are easy to copy, alter, and distribute, but when you purchase a font, you accept an *end user license agreement* (EULA) that limits how you can use it. Intellectual property law in the United States protects the font as a piece of software (a unique set of vector points), but it does not protect the visual design of the typeface. Thus it is a violation of standard EULAs to copy a digital font and share it with other people (your friends, your clients, or your Uncle Bob). It is also illegal to open a font file in FontLab, add new glyphs or alter some of its characters, and save the font under a new name or under its trademarked name. In additon to having economic concerns, typeface designers worry about their work being corrupted as users edit their fonts and then share them with other people.

Most EULAs do allow you to alter the outlines of a font for use in a logo or headline, however, as long as you do not alter the software itself. It is also legal to create new digital versions of printed type specimens. For example, you could print out an alphabet in Helvetica, redraw the letters, digitize them with font design software, and release your own bespoke edition of Helvetica. If nothing else, this laborious exercise would teach you the value of a well-designed typeface. A broadly usable typeface includes numerous weights, styles, and special characters as well as a strong underlying design. Fonts are expensive because they are carefully crafted products.

FREE FONTS

Most of the FREE FONTS found on the Internet have poor spacing and incomplete character sets. Many are *stolen property* distributed without CONSENT. The fonts displayed here, however, are freely given by their creators. A typeface comes to life and finds a voice as people begin to use it.

FONTIN, *designed by Jos Buivenga/Ex Ljbris, 2004*

DESIGNERS have long sought to CONTROL the behavior of users, clients, manufacturers, retailers, and the press. How will a work be interpreted? Will it survive over time in its DESIRED STATE of completion? An architect succeeds when the occupants of his house behave ACCORDING TO PLAN. The rise of online tools has challenged designers' sense of CONTROL in every discipline: the user has become a designer.

AUDIMAT, *designed by Jack Usine/SMeltery.net, 2003*

Some fonts are *distributed freely* in order to preserve UNFAMILIAR traditions. Disseminating a historic revival at no cost to users encourages a broader understanding of history. Reviving typefaces is a DEEP-ROOTED practice. Why should one creator *claim ownership* of another's work? Who controls the past?

ANTYKWA POLTAWSKIEGO, *designed by Adam Półtawski, 1920s–1930s; digitized by Janusz Marian Nowacki, 1996*

SOME FREE FONTS are produced for *underserved linguistic communities* for whom few typefaces are available. Still others are created by people who want to participate in the *open source movement*. The OFL (Open Font License) permits users to alter a typeface and contribute to its ongoing evolution.

GENTIUM *Open Font License, designed by Victor Gaultney, 2001*

TO PARTICIPATE IN a viable, diverse *ecology of content* (journalism, design, art, typography, and more), *everyone has to pay*. BUT PERHAPS everyone shouldn't have to *pay for everything*. If some resources are willingly given away, the result is a RICHER WORLD.

OFL SORTS MILL GOUDY, *revival of Frederic W. Goudy's Goudy Old Style, 1916, designed by Barry Schwartz, 2010; distributed by the League of Moveable Type*

EVERY OBJECT IN THE WORLD CAN PASS FROM A

LEAGUE GOTHIC, *designed by the League of Moveable Type, 2009; revival of Morris Fuller Benton's*

CLOSED, SILENT EXISTENCE TO AN ORAL STATE,

ALTERNATE GOTHIC NO.1., *released by American Type Founders Company (ATF) in 1903.*

OPEN TO APPROPRIATION BY SOCIETY, FOR THERE

DOWNCOME, *designed by Eduardo Recife/ Misprinted Type, 2002*

IS NO LAW, WHETHER NATURAL OR NOT, WHICH

FORBIDS TALKING ABOUT THINGS. A TREE IS A

SHORTCUT, *designed by Eduardo Recife, 2003*

TREE. YES, OF COURSE. BUT A TREE AS EXPRESSED BY

Minou Drouet was a French child poet and composer widely derided by intellectuals in the 1950s.

MINOU DROUET IS NO LONGER QUITE A TREE, IT IS A

DIRTY EGO, *designed by Eduardo Recife, 2001*

TREE WHICH IS DECORATED, ADAPTED TO A CERTAIN

TYPE OF CONSUMPTION, LADEN WITH LITERARY SELF-

MISPROJECT, *designed by Eduardo Recife, 2001*

INDULGENCE, REVOLT, IMAGES, IN SHORT WITH A TYPE

OF SOCIAL USAGE WHICH IS ADDED TO PURE MATTER.

TEXT: *Roland Barthes, "Myth Today," 1957; translated by Annette Lavers.*

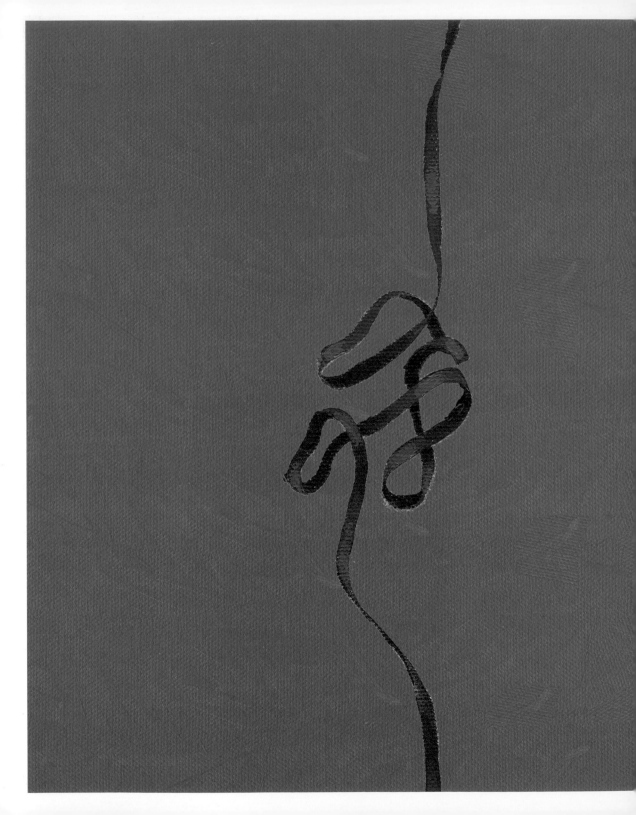

{TEXT}

CYBERSPACE AND CIVIL
SOCIETY Poster, 1996.
Designer: Hayes Henderson.
*Rather than represent
cyberspace as an ethereal grid,
the designer has used blotches
of overlapping text to build an
ominous, looming body.*

TEXT

LETTERS GATHER INTO WORDS, WORDS BUILD INTO SENTENCES. In typography, "text" is defined as an ongoing sequence of words, distinct from shorter headlines or captions. The main block is often called the "body," comprising the principal mass of content. Also known as "running text," it can flow from one page, column, or box to another. Text can be viewed as a thing—a sound and sturdy object—or a fluid poured into the containers of page or screen. Text can be solid or liquid, body or blood.

As body, text has more integrity and wholeness than the elements that surround it, from pictures, captions, and page numbers to banners, buttons, and menus. Designers generally treat a body of text consistently, letting it appear as a coherent substance that is distributed across the spaces of a document. In digital media, long texts are typically broken into chunks that can be accessed by search engines or hypertext links. Contemporary designers and writers produce content for various contexts, from the pages of print to an array of software environments, screen conditions, and digital devices, each posing its own limits and opportunities.

Designers provide ways into—and out of—the flood of words by breaking up text into pieces and offering shortcuts and alternate routes through masses of information. From a simple indent (signaling the entrance to a new idea) to a highlighted link (announcing a jump to another location), typography helps readers navigate the flow of content. The user could be searching for a specific piece of data or struggling to quickly process a volume of content in order to extract elements for immediate use. Although many books define the purpose of typography as enhancing the readability of the written word, one of design's most humane functions is, in actuality, to help readers *avoid* reading.

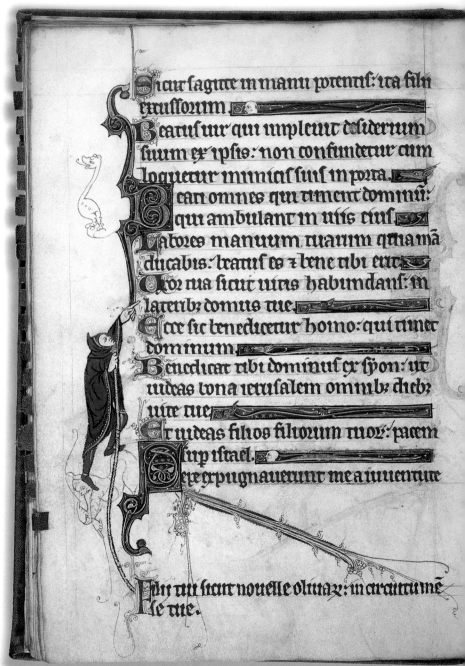

PSALTER-HOURS English
manuscript, thirteenth
century. Walters Ms. W.102,
fol. 33v. Collection of the
Walters Art Museum,
Baltimore. *The monk is
climbing up the side of the page
to replace a piece of faulty text
with the corrected line in the
bottom margin.*

ERRORS AND OWNERSHIP

Typography helped seal the literary notion of "the text" as a complete, original work, a stable body of ideas expressed in an essential form. Before the invention of printing, handwritten documents were riddled with errors. Copies were copied from copies, each with its own glitches and gaps. Scribes devised inventive ways to insert missing lines into manuscripts in order to salvage and repair these laboriously crafted objects.

Marshall McLuhan, *The Gutenberg Galaxy* (Toronto: University of Toronto Press, 1962).

Printing with movable type was the first system of mass production, replacing the hand-copied manuscript. As in other forms of mass production, the cost of manufacturing (setting type, insuring its correctness, and running a press) drops for each unit as the size of the print run increases. Labor and capital are invested in tooling and preparing the technology, rather than in making the individual unit. The printing system allows editors and authors to correct a work as it passes from handwritten manuscript to typographic galley. "Proofs" are test copies made before final production begins. The proofreader's craft ensures the faithfulness of the printed text to the author's handwritten original.

Yet even the text that has passed through the castle gates of print is inconstant. Each edition of a book represents one fossil record of a text, a record that changes every time the work is translated, quoted, revised, interpreted, or taught. Since the rise of digital tools for writing and publishing, manuscript originals have all but vanished. ~~Electronic redlining is replacing the hieroglyphics of the editor.~~ Online texts can be downloaded by users and reformatted, repurposed, and recombined.

On the future of intellectual property, see Lawrence Lessig, *Free Culture: How Big Media Uses Technology and the Law to Lock Down Culture and Control Creativity* (New York: Penguin, 2004).

Print helped establish the figure of the author as the owner of a text, and copyright laws were written in the early eighteenth century to protect the author's rights to this property. The digital age is riven by battles between those who argue, on the one hand, for the fundamental liberty of data and ideas, and those who hope to protect—sometimes indefinitely—the investment made in publishing and authoring content.

A classic typographic page emphasizes the completeness and closure of a work, its authority as a finished product. Alternative design strategies in the twentieth and twenty-first centuries reflect the contested nature of authorship by revealing the openness of texts to the flow of information and the corrosiveness of history.

Typography tended to alter language from a means of perception and exploration to a portable commodity. —MARSHALL MCLUHAN, 1962

On the Way to Lainguage

"How indeed could I aim my argument at some singular destination, at one or another among you whose proper name I might know? And then, is knowing a proper name tantamount to knowing someone?" (*MC*, 2). Derrida demonstrates for his part that the most general structure of the mark participates in a speech destined in advance to addressees (*destinataires*) who are not easily determinable or who, as far as any possible calculation is concerned, in any case command a great reserve of indetermination. This involves a language operating as a system of marks: "Language, however, is only one among those systems of *marks* that claim this curious tendency as their property: they *simultaneously* incline towards increasing the reserves of random indetermination *as well as* the capacity for coding and overcoding or, in other words, for control and self-regulation" (*MC*, 2). We begin to discern how the simultaneity of determining, coding, and even supercoding forms a deep cooperation with the inclination in language toward anticoding, or what Derrida sees as the inflated reserves of random indeterminateness. This double-edged coding, we must remember, regards, as it were, nonschizophrenic language, if such a thing there be. "Such competition between randomness and code disrupts the very systematicity of the system while it also, however, regulates the restless, unstable interplay of the system. Whatever its singularity in this respect, the linguistic system of these traces or marks would merely be, it seems to me, just a particular example of the law of destabilization" (*MC*, 2). It may be useful to note that Derrida understands language in terms primarily of traces and marks, where Lainguage concerns signs in the first place, and in particular the broken rapport of that which is signifying to what ostensibly lies hidden behind it, or the disconnection between signs and signs or signs and referents. Laing is led to assume the latency of a single, unique, localizable but timid presence—rather than trace or residual mark—from where it could be securely determined who speaks, and to whom. This all too brief excursion into "My Chances," which may unwittingly reproduce the effect and trauma of a chance encounter, means to engage a dialogue between the question of address raised by Laing and the ones raised in turn by Derrida. For it now appears that Laing places his bets on the sustained systematicity of the system which Derrida shows always already to fall under a law of destabilization.[89] Moreover, Derrida does not suggest lan-

guage to be sor... seems to want *translation* of s... light of an audi... been saying as... make contact w... stract or terror... touch. In fact I... that I throw, ... come across to... and Laing had... part, that, thro... whose destination... the case with their... muteness was... guage were arr... release-controls structurally ma... ratus. The Other fully retrievable is there to be given... agement begins wit... or alive, traversing *fort* slashing into the... as self or Other telephone to raise the telephone speak... sound waves: "'she'... tem as though it wa... be hallucinated" (*D*... "Anything she wan... one time. Reality di... or fear. Every wish and every dread... tom way. Thus 203). He reads The case history weed garden. Is taneity of omn...

THE TELEPHONE BOOK: TECHNOLOGY, SCHIZOPHRENIA, ELECTRIC SPEECH Book, 1989. Designer: Richard Eckersley. Author: Avital Ronell. Compositor: Michael Jensen. Publisher: University of Nebraska Press. Photograph: Dan Meyers. *This book, a philosophical study of writing as a material technology, uses typography to emphasize the rhetorical argument of the text. This spread, for example, is fractured by typographic "rivers," spaces that connect vertically through the page. Rivers violate the even, unified texture that is a sacred goal within traditional typographic design.*

SPACING

Design is as much an act of spacing as an act of marking. The typographer's art concerns not only the positive grain of letterforms, but the negative gaps between and around them. In letterpress printing, every space is constructed by a physical object, a blank piece of metal or wood with no raised image. The faceless slugs of lead and slivers of copper inserted as spaces between words or letters are as physical as the relief characters around them. Thin strips of lead (called "leading") divide the horizontal lines of type; wider blocks of "furniture" hold the margins of the page.

Although we take the breaks between words for granted, spoken language is perceived as a continuous flow, with no audible gaps. Spacing has become crucial, however, to alphabetic writing, which translates the sounds of speech into multiple characters. Spaces were introduced after the invention of the Greek alphabet to make words intelligible as distinct units. Tryreadingalineoftextwithoutspacingtoseehowimportantithasbecome.

With the invention of typography, spacing and punctuation ossified from gap and gesture to physical artifact. Punctuation marks, which were used differently from one scribe to another in the manuscript era, became part of the standardized, rule-bound apparatus of the printed page. The communications scholar Walter Ong has shown how printing converted the word into a visual object precisely located in space: "Alphabet letterpress printing, in which each letter was cast on a separate piece of metal, or type, marked a psychological breakthrough of the first order....Print situates words in space more relentlessly than writing ever did. Writing moves words from the sound world to the world of visual space, but print locks words into position in this space." Typography made text into a thing, a material object with known dimensions and fixed locations.

Walter Ong, *Orality and Literacy: The Technologizing of the Word* (London and New York: Methuen, 1981). See also Jacques Derrida, *Of Grammatology,* trans. Gayatri Chakravorty Spivak (Baltimore: Johns Hopkins University Press, 1976).

The French philosopher Jacques Derrida, who devised the theory of deconstruction in the 1960s, wrote that although the alphabet represents sound, it cannot function without silent marks and spaces. Typography manipulates the silent dimensions of the alphabet, employing habits and techniques—such as spacing and punctuation—that are seen but not heard. The Latin alphabet, rather than evolve into a transparent code for recording speech, developed its own visual resources, becoming a more powerful technology as it left behind its connections to the spoken word.

That a speech supposedly alive can lend itself to spacing in its own writing is what relates to its own death. —JACQUES DERRIDA, 1976

LINEARITY

In his essay "From Work to Text," the French critic Roland Barthes presented two opposing models of writing: the closed, fixed "work" versus the open, unstable "text." In Barthes's view, the work is a tidy, neatly packaged object, proofread and copyrighted, made perfect and complete by the art of printing. The text, in contrast, is impossible to contain, operating across a dispersed web of standard plots and received ideas. Barthes pictured the text as "woven entirely with citations, references, echoes, cultural languages (what language is not?), antecedent and contemporary, which cut across and through in a vast stereophony....The metaphor of the Text is that of the *network*." Writing in the 1960s and 1970s, Barthes anticipated the Internet as a decentralized web of connections.

Roland Barthes, "From Work to Text," in *Image/Music/Text,* trans. Stephen Heath (New York: Hill and Wang, 1977), 155–64.

Barthes was describing literature, yet his ideas resonate for typography, the visual manifestation of language. The singular body of the traditional text page has long been supported by the navigational features of the book, from page numbers and headings that mark a reader's location to such tools as the index, appendix, abstract, footnote, and table of contents. These devices were able to emerge because the typographic book is a fixed sequence of pages, a body lodged in a grid of known coordinates.

All such devices are attacks on linearity, providing means of entrance and escape from the one-way stream of discourse. Whereas talking flows in a single direction, writing occupies space as well as time. Tapping that spatial dimension—and thus liberating readers from the bonds of linearity—is among typography's most urgent tasks.

Although digital media are commonly celebrated for their potential as nonlinear potential communication, linearity nonetheless thrives in the electronic realm, from the "CNN crawl" that marches along the bottom of the television screen to the ticker-style LED signs that loop through the urban environment. Film titles—the celebrated convergence of typography and cinema—serve to distract the audience from the inescapable tedium of a contractually decreed, top-down disclosure of ownership and authorship. Basic electronic book readers, such as Amazon's Kindle (2007), provide a highly sequential, predominantly linear experience; flipping back or skipping ahead is more cumbersome in some electronic books than in paper ones.

Linearity dominates many commercial software applications. Word processing programs, for example, treat documents as a linear stream.

A text...is a multi-dimensional space in which a variety of writings, none of them original, blend and clash. —ROLAND BARTHES, 1971

On the linearity of word processing, see Nancy Kaplan, "Blake's Problem and Ours: Some Reflections on the Image and the Word," *Readerly/Writerly Texts*, 3.2 (Spring/Summer 1996), 125. On PowerPoint, see Edward R. Tufte, "The Cognitive Style of PowerPoint," (Cheshire, Conn.: Graphics Press, 2003).

(In contrast, page layout programs such as Quark XPress and Adobe InDesign allow users to work spatially, breaking up text into columns and pages that can be anchored and landmarked.) PowerPoint and other presentation software programs are supposed to illuminate the spoken word by guiding the audience through the linear unfolding of an oral address. Typically, however, PowerPoint enforces the one-way flow of speech rather than alleviating it. While a single sheet of paper could provide a map or summary of an oral presentation, a PowerPoint show drags out in time across numerous screens.

Not all digital media favor linear flow over spatial arrangement, however. The database, one of the defining information structures of our time, is a nonlinear form. Providing readers and writers with a simultaneous menu of options, a database is a system of elements that can be arranged in countless sequences. Page layouts are built on the fly from chunks of information, assembled in response to user feedback. The web is pushing authors, editors, and designers to work inventively with new modes of microcontent (page titles, key words, alt tags) that allow data to be searched, indexed, tagged, or otherwise marked for recall.

On the aesthetics of the database, see Lev Manovich, *The Language of New Media* (Cambridge: MIT Press, 2002).

Databases are the structure behind electronic games, magazines, and catalogues, genres that create an information *space* rather than a linear *sequence*. Physical stores and libraries are databases of tangible objects found in the built environment. Media critic Lev Manovich has described language itself as a kind of database, an archive of elements from which people assemble the linear utterances of speech. Many design projects call for the emphasis of space over sequence, system over utterance, simultaneous structure over linear narrative. Contemporary design often combines aspects of architecture, typography, film, wayfinding, branding, and other modes of address. By dramatizing the spatial quality of a project, designers can foster understanding of complex documents or environments.

The history of typography is marked by the increasingly sophisticated use of space. In the digital age, where characters are accessed by keystroke and mouse, not gathered from heavy drawers of manufactured units, space has become more liquid than concrete, and typography has evolved from a stable body of objects to a flexible system of attributes.

Database and narrative are natural enemies. Competing for the same territory of human culture, each claims an exclusive right to make meaning of the world. —LEV MANOVICH, 2002

VISUAL THESAURUS 2.0. Interactive media, 2003. Designers: Plumb Design Inc. *This digital thesaurus presents words within a dynamic web of relationships. The central term is linked to nodes representing that word's different senses. The more connections each of these satellite nodes contain, the bigger and closer it appears on the screen. Clicking on a satellite word brings it to the center.*

IMAGE/MUSIC/TEXT
Concordance and text stats
for Roland Barthes's book
Image/Music/Text. Publisher:
Amazon.com, 2010. *Amazon
presents automated analyses
of a book's text in order to
give readers an idea of what is
inside. The concordance feature
lists the book's one hundred
most commonly used words
in alphabetical order and
sizes them according to their
frequency.*

Concordance (learn more)

These are the 100 most frequently used words in this book.

according action again always analysis another art author between body cannot case certain characters code comes connotation different discourse does elements even example fact first form functions given historical however idea image itself know language least level linguistic longer may meaning message moment music must name narrative nature new nothing now object once order own part perhaps person photograph place point possible precisely reader reading relation say see seen sense sentence sequence set signified signifier signs simply since social society speech still story structural structure subject system term text though thus time two units voice whole without word work writing

Text Stats

These statistics are computed from the text of this book. (learn more)

Readability (learn more)		Compared with other books		
Fog Index:	22.1	98% are easier		2% are harder
Flesch Index:	24.3	93% are easier		7% are harder
Flesch-Kincaid Index:	18.8	98% are easier		2% are harder
Complexity (learn more)				
Complex Words:	19%	70% have fewer		30% have more
Syllables per Word:	1.7	67% have fewer		33% have more
Words per Sentence:	36.1	99% have fewer		1% have more
Number of				
Characters:	396,905	48% have fewer		52% have more
Words:	64,614	49% have fewer		51% have more
Sentences:	1,791	25% have fewer		75% have more

**Succeeding the Author, the scriptor no longer bears within him passions, humours, feelings, impressions, but rather this immense dictionary from which he draws a writing that can know no halt.
—ROLAND BARTHES, 1968**

KATHERINE mcCoy
MICHAEL
mcCoy

ART science
Nothing pulls you into the territory between art and science quite so quickly as design. It is the borderline where contradictions and tensions exist between the quantifiable and the poetic. It is the field between desire and necessity. Designers thrive in those conditions, moving between land and water. A typical critique at Cranbrook can easily move in a matter of minutes between MATHEMATIC poetic a discussion of the object as a validation of being to the precise mechanical proposal for actuating the object. The discussion moves from Heidegger to the "strange material of the week" or from Lyotard to printing technologies without missing a beat. The free flow of ideas, and the leaps from the technical to the mythical, stem from the attempt to maintain a studio plat- DESIRE necessity find his or her own voice as a designer. The studio is a hothouse that enables students the and faculty to encounter their own visions of the world and act on them — a new process that is at times chaotic, conflicting, and occasionally inspiring.

Watching the process of students absorbing new ideas and influences, and the incredible range of in- terpretations of those ideas into design, is MYTHOLOGY technology an annual experience that is always amaz- ing. In recent years, for example, the de- discourse partment has had the experience of watching wood craftsmen metamorphose into high technologists, and graphic designers into software humanists. Yet it all seems consistent. They are bringing a very personal vision to an area that desperately needs it. The messiness of human experi- PURIST pluralist ence is warming up the cold precision of technology to make it livable, and lived in.

Unlike the Bauhaus, Cranbrook never embraced a singular teaching method or philosophy, other than Saarinen's exhortation to each student to find his or her own way, in the company of other artists and designers who were engaged in the same search. The energy at Cranbrook seems to come from the fact of INDIVIDUAL communal the mutual search, although not the mutual conclusion. If design is about life, why shouldn't it have all the complexity, vari- ety, contradiction, and sublimity of life?

Much of the work done at Cranbrook has been dedicated to changing the status quo. It is polemical, calculated to ruffle designers' feathers. And DANGEROUS rigorous

BIRTH OF THE USER

Barthes's model of the text as an open web of references, rather than a closed and perfect work, asserts the importance of the reader over the writer in creating meaning. The reader "plays" the text as a musician plays an instrument. The author does not control its significance: "The text itself plays (like a door, like a machine with 'play') and the reader plays twice over, playing the Text as one plays a game, looking for a practice which reproduces it." Like an interpretation of a musical score, reading is a performance of the written word.

Graphic designers embraced the idea of the readerly text in the 1980s and early 1990s, using layers of text and interlocking grids to explore Barthes's theory of the "death of the author." In place of the classical model of typography as a crystal goblet for content, this alternative view assumes that content itself changes with each act of representation. Typography becomes a mode of interpretation.

Redefining typography as "discourse," designer Katherine McCoy imploded the traditional dichotomy between seeing and reading. Pictures can be read (analyzed, decoded, taken apart), and words can be seen (perceived as icons, forms, patterns). Valuing ambiguity and complexity, her approach challenged readers to produce their own meanings while also trying to elevate the status of designers within the process of authorship.

Another model, which undermined the designer's new claim to power, surfaced at the end of the 1990s, borrowed not from literary criticism but from human-computer interaction (HCI) studies and the fields of interface and usability design. The dominant subject of our age has become neither reader nor writer but *user*, a figure conceived as a bundle of needs and impairments—cognitive, physical, emotional. Like a patient or child, the user is a figure to be protected and cared for but also scrutinized and controlled, submitted to research and testing.

How texts are *used* becomes more important than what they mean. Someone clicked here to get over there. Someone who bought this also bought that. The interactive environment not only provides users with a degree of control and self-direction but also, more quietly and insidiously, it gathers data about its audiences. Barthes's image of the text as a game to be played still holds, as the user responds to signals from the system. We may play the text, but it is also playing us.

CRANBROOK DESIGN:
THE NEW DISCOURSE
Book, 1990. Designers:
Katherine McCoy, P. Scott
Makela, and Mary Lou
Kroh. Publisher: Rizzoli.
Photograph: Dan Meyers.
*Under the direction of
Katherine and Michael
McCoy, the graduate program
in graphic and industrial
design at Cranbrook Academy
of Art was a leading center
for experimental design from
the 1970s through the early
1990s. Katherine McCoy
developed a model of
"typography as discourse," in
which the designer and reader
actively interpret a text.*

Design a human-machine interface in accordance with the abilities and foibles of humankind, and you will help the user not only get the job done, but be a happier, more productive person. —JEF RASKIN, 2000

Graphic designers can use theories of user interaction to revisit some of our basic assumptions about visual communication. Why, for example, are readers on the web less patient than readers of print? It is commonly believed that digital displays are inherently more difficult to read than ink on paper. Yet HCI studies conducted in the late 1980s proved that crisp black text on a white background can be read just as efficiently from a screen as from a printed page.

The impatience of the digital reader arises from culture, not from the essential character of display technologies. Users of websites have different expectations than users of print. They expect to feel "productive," not contemplative. They expect to be in search mode, not processing mode. Users also expect to be disappointed, distracted, and delayed by false leads. The cultural habits of the screen are driving changes in design for print, while at the same time affirming print's role as a place where extended reading can still occur.

Another common assumption is that icons are a more universal mode of communication than text. Icons are central to the GUIs (graphical user interfaces) that routinely connect users with computers. Yet text can often provide a more specific and understandable cue than a picture. Icons don't actually simplify the translation of content into multiple languages, because they require explanation in multiple languages. The endless icons of the digital desktop, often rendered with gratuitous detail and depth, function more to enforce brand identity than to support usability. In the twentieth century, modern designers hailed pictures as a "universal" language, yet in the age of code, text has become a more common denominator than images—searchable, translatable, and capable of being reformatted and restyled for alternative or future media.

Perhaps the most persistent impulse of twentieth-century art and design was to physically integrate form and content. The Dada and Futurist poets, for example, used typography to create texts whose content was inextricable from the concrete layout of specific letterforms on a page. In the twenty-first century, form and content are being pulled back apart. Style sheets, for example, compel designers to think globally and systematically instead of focusing on the fixed construction of a particular surface. This way of

On screen readability, see John D. Gould *et al.*, "Reading from CRT Displays Can Be as Fast as Reading from Paper," *Human Factors*, 29, 5 (1987): 497–517.

On the restless user, see Jakob Nielsen, *Designing Web Usability* (Indianapolis: New Riders, 2000).

On the failure of interface icons, see Jef Raskin, *The Humane Interface: New Directions for Designing Interactive Systems* (Reading, Mass.: Addison-Wesley, 2000).

Web users don't like to read....They want to keep moving and clicking.
—JAKOB NIELSEN, 2000

thinking allows content to be reformatted for different devices or users, and it also prepares for the afterlife of data as electronic storage media begin their own cycles of decay and obsolescence.

In the twentieth century, modern artists and critics asserted that each medium is specific. They defined film, for example, as a constructive language distinct from theater, and they described painting as a physical medium that refers to its own processes. Today, however, the medium is not always the message. Design has become a "transmedia" enterprise, as authors and producers create worlds of characters, places, situations, and interactions that can appear across a variety of products. A game might live in different versions on a video screen, a desktop computer, a game console, and a cell phone, as well as on t-shirts, lunch boxes, and plastic toys.

On transmedia design thinking, see Brenda Laurel, *Utopian Entrepreneur* (Cambridge: MIT Press, 2001).

The beauty and wonder of "white space" is another modernist myth that is subject to revision in the age of the user. Modern designers discovered that open space on a page can have as much physical presence as printed areas. White space is not always a mental kindness, however. Edward Tufte, a fierce advocate of visual density, argues for maximizing the amount of data conveyed on a single page or screen. In order to help readers make connections and comparisons, as well as to find information quickly, a single surface packed with well-organized information is sometimes better than multiple pages with a lot of blank space. In typography as in urban life, density invites intimate exchange among people and ideas.

In our much-fabled era of information overload, a person can still process only one message at a time. This brute fact of cognition is the secret behind magic tricks: sleights of hand occur while the attention of the audience is drawn elsewhere. Given the fierce competition for their attention, users have a chance to shape the information economy by choosing what to look at. Designers can help them make satisfying choices.

Jef Raskin talks about the scarcity of human attention as well as the myth of white space in *The Humane Interface: New Directions for Designing Interactive Systems*, cited on p. 74.

Typography is an interface to the alphabet. User theory tends to favor normative solutions over innovative ones, pushing design into the background. Readers usually ignore the typographic interface, gliding comfortably along literacy's habitual groove. Sometimes, however, the interface should be allowed to fail. By making itself evident, typography can illuminate the construction and identity of a page, screen, place, or product.

If people weren't good at finding tiny things in long lists, the *Wall Street Journal* would have gone out of business years ago. —JEF RASKIN, 2000

Typography, invented in the Renaissance, allowed text to become a fixed and stable form. Like the body of the letter, the body of text was transformed into an industrial commodity that gradually became more open and flexible.

Critics of electronic media have noted that the rise of networked communication did not lead to the much feared destruction of typography (or even to the death of print), but rather to the burgeoning of the alphabetic empire. As Peter Lunenfeld points out, the computer has revived the power and prevalence of writing: "Alphanumeric text has risen from its own ashes, a digital phoenix taking flight on monitors, across networks, and in the realms of virtual space." The computer display is more hospitable to text than the screens of film or television because it offers physical proximity, user control, and a scale appropriate to the body.

The printed book is no longer the chief custodian of the written word. Branding is a powerful variant of literacy that revolves around symbols, icons, and typographic standards, leaving its marks on buildings, packages, album covers, websites, store displays, and countless other surfaces and spaces. With the expansion of the Internet, new (and old) conventions for displaying text quickly congealed, adapting metaphors from print and architecture: window, frame, page, banner, menu. Designers working within this stream of multiple media confront text in myriad forms, giving shape to extended bodies but also to headlines, decks, captions, notes, pull quotes, logotypes, navigation bars, alt tags, and other prosthetic clumps of language that announce, support, and even eclipse the main body of text.

The dissolution of writing is most extreme in the realm of the web, where distracted readers safeguard their time and prize function over form. This debt of restlessness is owed not to the essential nature of computer monitors, but to the new behaviors engendered by the Internet, a place of searching and finding, scanning and mining. The reader, having toppled the author's seat of power during the twentieth century, now ails and lags, replaced by the dominant subject of our own era: the *user*, a figure whose scant attention is our most coveted commodity. Do not squander it.

On electronic writing, see Peter Lunenfeld, *Snap to Grid: A User's Guide to Digital Arts, Media, and Cultures* (Cambridge: MIT Press, 2001); Jay David Bolter, *Writing Space: Computers, Hypertext, and the Remediation of Print* (Mahwah, NJ: Lawrence Erlbaum Associates, 2001), and Stuart Moulthrop, "You Say You Want a Revolution? Hypertext and the Laws of Media," in *The New Media Reader*, ed. Noah Wardrip-Fruin and Nick Monfort (Cambridge: MIT Press, 2003), 691–703.

Hypertext means the end of the death of literature. —STUART MOULTHROP, 1991

DESIGNOBSERVER.COM Website, 2010.
Design: Jessica Helfand, William Drenttel,
Michael Bierut, and Betsy Vardell. *Packing
an enormous volume of content onto its home
page, this design discourse supersite brings
print-quality typography to the screen.*

Kerning is an adjustment of the space between two letters. The characters of the Latin alphabet emerged over time; they were never designed with mechanical or automated spacing in mind. Thus some letter combinations look awkward without special spacing considerations. Gaps occur, for example, around letters whose forms angle outward or frame an open space (*W, Y, V, T*). In metal type, a kerned letter extends past the lead slug that supports it, allowing two letters to fit more closely together. In digital fonts, the space between letter pairs is controlled by a *kerning table* created by the type designer, which specifies spaces between problematic letter combinations.

Working in a page layout program, a designer can choose to use *metric kerning* or *optical kerning* as well as adjusting the space between letters manually where desired. A well-designed typeface requires little or no additional kerning, especially at text sizes.

METRIC KERNING uses the kerning tables that are built into the typeface. When you select metric kerning in your page layout program, you are using the spacing that was intended by the type designer. Metric kerning usually looks good, especially at small sizes. Cheap novelty fonts often have little or no built-in kerning and will need to be optically kerned.

OPTICAL KERNING is executed automatically by the page layout program. Rather than using the pairs addressed in the font's kerning table, optical kerning assesses the shapes of all characters and adjusts the spacing wherever needed. Some graphic designers apply optical kerning to headlines and metric kerning to text. You can make this process efficient and consistent by setting kerning as part of your character styles.

Takes Two

SCALA PRO, WITH KERNING SUPPRESSED
Spacing appears uneven, with gaps around T/a, T/w, and w/o.

Takes Two

SCALA PRO, WITH METRIC KERNING
Spacing appears more even between T/a and T/w.

Takes Two

SCALA PRO, WITH OPTICAL KERNING
Spacing seems more even between T/a, T/w, and w/o.

Warm Type

SCALA PRO ITALIC, WITH KERNING SUPPRESSED
Spacing appears uneven between W/a and T/y.

Warm Type

SCALA PRO ITALIC, WITH METRIC KERNING
Spacing appears more even between W/a and T/y.

Warm Type

SCALA PRO ITALIC, WITH OPTICAL KERNING
Spacing is comparable to metric kerning.

LOVE LETTERS

SCALA PRO ALL CAPITALS, WITH KERNING SUPPRESSED
Spacing is tight between T/T.

LOVE LETTERS

SCALA PRO ALL CAPITALS, WITH METRIC KERNING
Improved spacing between T/T.

LOVE LETTERS

SCALA PRO ALL CAPITALS, WITH OPTICAL KERNING
Improved spacing between T/ T and O/V.

KERNING HEADLINES The subtle differences between metric and optical kerning become more apparent at larger sizes. Most problems occur between capital and lowercase letters. The spacing between *H/a, T/a,* and *T/o* improves with optical kerning. The optical kerning applied here in InDesign has created tighter spacing for large text and looser spacing for small text. Look at both effects before choosing a kerning method.

Ha

METRIC KERNING

Ha

OPTICAL KERNING

METRIC VERSUS OPTICAL KERNING

Books And Harlots Have Their Quarrels In Public.

Books And Harlots Can Be Taken To Bed.

Books and harlots— footnotes in one are as banknotes in the stockings of the other.

—WALTER BENJAMIN, 1925

QUADRAAT SANS, WITH METRIC KERNING

Books And Harlots Have Their Quarrels In Public.

Books And Harlots Can Be Taken To Bed.

Books and harlots— footnotes in one are as banknotes in the stockings of the other.

—WALTER BENJAMIN, 1925

QUADRAAT SANS, WITH OPTICAL KERNING

NERD ALERT: *In addition to using optical kerning, the text above has word spacing reduced to 80 percent. With large type, normal word spacing often looks too wide. Adjust word spacing in the Paragraph>Justification menu in InDesign.*

Adjusting the overall spacing of a group of letters is called *tracking* or *letterspacing*. By expanding the tracking across a word, line, or entire block of text, the designer can create a more airy, open field. In blocks of text, tracking is usually applied in small increments, creating a subtle effect not noticeable to the casual reader. Occasionally, a single word or phrase is tracked for emphasis, especially when CAPS or SMALL CAPS are used within a line. Negative tracking, rarely desirable in text sizes, can be used sparingly to help bring up a short line of text. White type on a black background is considered more legible when it is tracked.

SCALY-BREASTED PARTRIDGE
Arborophila chloropus
12 in (30 cm)
Southeast Asia

CRIMSON-HEADED PARTRIDGE
Haematortyx sanguiniceps
10 in (25 cm)
Borneo

BIRDS OF THE WORLD Book, 2007. Author: Les Beletsky. Publisher: The Johns Hopkins University. Art Director: Charles Nix. Designers: Charles Nix, Whitney Grant, and May Jampathom. *This book, set in Adobe Caslon and Caslon 540, uses tracked small capitals for caption headings.*

TRACKING TEXT TYPE

NORMAL TRACKING
Letters do love one another. However, due to their anatomical differences, some letters have a hard time achieving intimacy. Consider the letter *V*, for example, whose seductive valley makes her limbs stretch out above her base. In contrast, *L* solidly holds his ground yet harbors a certain emptiness above the waist. Capital letters, being square and conservative, prefer to keep a little distance from their neighbors.

POSITIVE TRACKING (+20)
Letters do love one another. However, due to their anatomical differences, some letters have a hard time achieving intimacy. Consider the letter *V*, for example, whose seductive valley makes her limbs stretch out above her base. In contrast, *L* solidly holds his ground yet harbors a certain emptiness above the waist. Capital letters, being square and conservative, prefer to keep a little distance from their neighbors.

NEGATIVE TRACKING (-20)
Letters do love one another. However, due to their anatomical differences, some letters have a hard time achieving intimacy. Consider the letter *V*, for example, whose seductive valley makes her limbs stretch out above her base. In contrast, *L* solidly holds his ground yet harbors a certain emptiness above the waist. Capital letters, being square and conservative, prefer to keep a little distance from their neighbors.

TYPE CRIME
TIGHTLY TRACKED TEXT
Letters are tracked too close for comfort.

Books and harlots—both have their type of man, who both lives off and harasses them. In the case of books, critics. WALTER BENJAMIN, 1925

REVERSED TYPE, NO TRACKING

Books and harlots—both have their type of man, who both lives off and harasses them. In the case of books, critics. WALTER BENJAMIN, 1925

REVERSED TYPE, TRACKED +25

Designers most commonly apply tracking to headlines and logos (where kerning adjustments are also frequently required). As text gets bigger, the space between letters expands, and some designers use tracking to diminish overall spacing in large-scale text. Loose or open tracking is commonly applied to capitals and small capitals, which appear more regal standing slightly apart.

TRACKING HEADLINES AND LOGOTYPES

LOVE LETTERS

CAPITALS: NORMAL TRACKING

LOVE LETTERS

CAPITALS: LOOSE TRACKING (+75)

LOVE LETTERS, LOVE LETTERS

SMALL CAPS: NORMAL VS. LOOSE TRACKING (+75)

love letters, *love letters*

LOWER CASE: NORMAL TRACKING

love letters, *love letters*

LOWER CASE: LOOSE TRACKING (+75)

TYPE CRIME: TRACKING LOWERCASE LETTERS
Loosely spaced lowercase letters—especially italics—look awkward because these characters are designed to sit closely together on a line.

EROS Logotype, 1962. Design: Herb Lubalin. *Ultra-tight letterspacing was a hallmark of progressive commercial graphics in the 1960s and 1970s. Here, the letters cradle each other with an intimacy appropriate to the subject matter.*

CRUET & WHISK and THYMES Logotypes, 2006. Design: Duffy & Partners. *The generously tracked capitals in these logotypes give them an affable, antiquarian flavor while imparting an overall lightness to the designs.*

You can express the meaning of a word or an idea through the spacing, sizing, and placement of letters on the page. Designers often think this way when creating logotypes, posters, or editorial headlines. The compositions shown here express physical processes such as disruption, expansion, and migration through the spacing and arrangement of letters. The round *Os* in Futura make it a fun typeface to use for this project.

Examples of student work from Maryland Institute College of Art

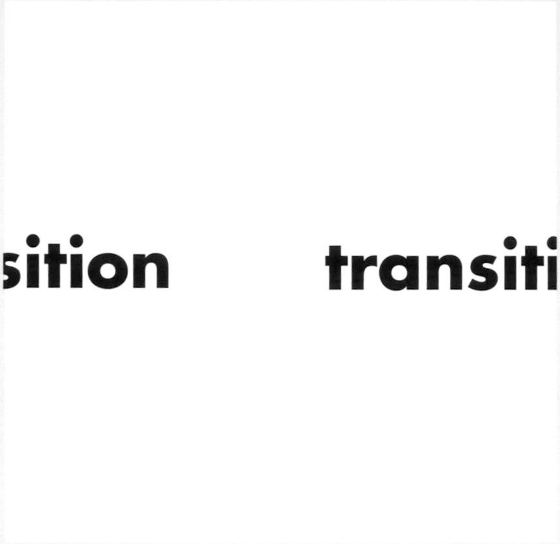

sition   transiti

Johnschen Kudos

disⲅuption

Johnschen Kudos

c o mpression

Johnschen Kudos

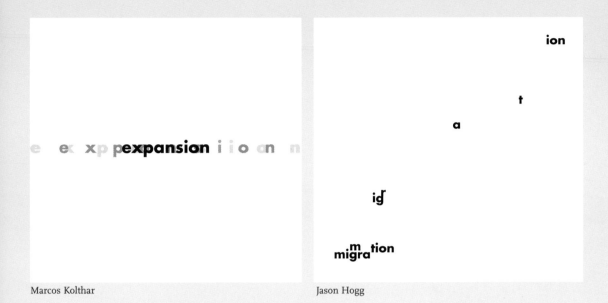

Marcos Kolthar

Jason Hogg

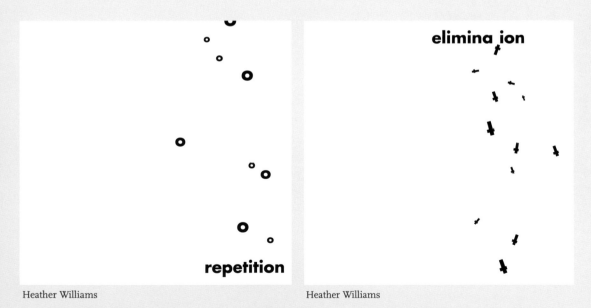

Heather Williams

Heather Williams

The distance from the baseline of one line of type to another is called *line spacing*. It is also called *leading,* in reference to the strips of lead used to separate lines of metal type. The default setting in most layout and imaging software is 120 percent of the type size. Thus 10-pt type is set with 12 pts of line spacing. Designers play with line spacing in order to create distinctive typographic arrangements. Reducing the standard distance creates a denser typographic color, while risking collisions between ascenders and descenders. Expanding the line spacing creates a lighter, more open text block. As leading increases, lines of type become independent graphic elements rather than parts of an overall visual shape and texture.

different
folks
different
strokes

TYPE CRIME
*Here, auto spacing yields
an uneven effect.*

different
folks
different
strokes

*Adjusting line spacing with
the baseline shift tool helps create
an even appearance.*

NERD ALERT: A *baseline shift* is a manual adjustment of the horizontal position of one or more characters. Baseline shifts are often used when mixing different sizes or styles of type. The baseline shift tool can be found in the Type tool bar of standard software applications.

VARIATIONS IN LINE SPACING

The distance from the baseline of one line of type to another is called *line spacing*. It is also called *leading,* in reference to the strips of lead used to separate lines of metal type. The default setting in most layout and imaging software is 120 percent of the type size. Thus 10-pt type is set with 12 pts of line spacing. Designers play with line spacing in order to create distinctive layouts. Reducing the standard distance creates a denser typographic color—while risking collisions between ascenders and descenders.

6/6 SCALA PRO
(6 pt type with 6 pts line spacing, or "set solid")

The distance from the baseline of one line of type to another is called *line spacing*. It is also called *leading,* in reference to the strips of lead used to separate lines of metal type. The default setting in most layout and imaging software is 120 percent of the type size. Thus 10-pt type is set with 12 pts of line spacing. Designers play with line spacing in order to create distinctive layouts. Reducing the standard distance creates a denser typographic color—while risking collisions between ascenders and descenders.

6/7.2 SCALA PRO
(Auto spacing; 6 pt type with 7.2 pts line spacing)

The distance from the baseline of one line of type to another is called *line spacing*. It is also called *leading,* in reference to the strips of lead used to separate lines of metal type. The default setting in most layout and imaging software is 120 percent of the type size. Thus 10-pt type is set with 12 pts of line spacing. Designers play with line spacing in order to create distinctive layouts. Reducing the standard distance creates a denser typographic color—while risking collisions between ascenders and descenders.

6/8 SCALA PRO
(6 pt type with 8 pts line spacing)

The distance from the baseline of one line of type to another is called *line spacing*. It is also called *leading,* in reference to the strips of lead used to separate lines of metal type. The default setting in most layout and imaging software is 120 percent of the type size. Thus 10-pt type is set with 12 pts of line spacing. Designers play with line spacing in order to create distinctive layouts. Reducing the standard distance creates a denser typographic color—while risking collisions between ascenders and descenders.

6/12 SCALA PRO
(6 pt type with 12 pts line spacing)

Ancient maps of the world

An

when the world was flat

Avid

inform us, concerning the void

Dream

where America was waiting

Of

to be discovered,

Trans-

Here Be Dragons. James Baldwin

for-

O to be a dragon. Marianne Moore

mation Adrienne Kennedy, *People Who Led to My Plays*

MARGO JEFFERSON

DANCE INK: AN AVID DREAM
OF TRANSFORMATION
Magazine page, 1992.
Designer: Abbott Miller.
Publisher: Patsy Tarr. *The
extreme line spacing allows two
strands of text to interweave.*

Designers experiment with extreme line spacing to create distinctive typographic textures. Open spacing allows designers to play with the space between the lines, while tight spacing creates intriguing, sometimes uncomfortable, collisions.

interminável do embarque, decido respirar um pouco e procurar o sr. Creso com mais calma, outra hora.

PISO OCIDENTAL – EMBARQUE

A área de embarque é chamada de "aquário": um longo corredor com paredes e portas de vidro que separam o pré-embarque das platafor-mas. O ônibus estaciona nas baias, lá fora, e um funcionário abre as tais portas de vidro, chamando os passageiros. Só então eles passam à região do embarque. Protegem-se, assim, os demais usuários da fuma-ça emitida pelos veículos, em parte absorvida por um enorme tubo exaustor pintado de amarelo.

Em pé, na plataforma 1, enxerga-se o corredor inteiro, até o fim. Em primeiro plano, um relógio de ponteiros e uma larga escada em caracol que leva ao piso superior. No vão embaixo da escada, algumas lanchone-tes e lojas de miudezas encaixam-se com perfeição. De ambos os lados, indicados ao longo do corredor, sucedem-se os números das plataformas 1 a 50, pintados de branco dentro de quadrados verdes, sobrepondo-se ligeiramente uns aos outros como em uma agenda telefônica.

Há poucas crianças vagando pela área. Em compensação, são muitos os seguranças, funcionários de limpeza e vendedores de bebidas caminhando com seus carrinhos. A maioria dos passageiros é compos-

250

ta de adultos que esperam em pé, pois não há lugar para sentar (ape-nas quatro cadeiras de plástico laranja diante de cada plataforma). Consegue-se escutar remotamente o som dos alto-falantes que tocam "Ovelha negra" em versão acústica e diversas músicas instrumentais, para dar a impressão de que o terminal é calmo. "Mas só pra dar a impressão, mesmo", brinca um dos fiscais da Socicam.

Antes da primeira plataforma par, ergue-se uma sala VIP, como a dos aeroportos. É um espaço envidraçado voltado exclusivamente para o bem-estar dos passageiros das empresas Cometa, 1001 e Cata-rinense, em viagens a Santa Catarina, Paraná, Rio de Janeiro e Minas Gerais. A abertura das portas é automática e o usuário é recebido por duas moças de sala azul, salto alto e lencinho amarelo, que con-ferem os bilhetes e aconselham os passageiros a se sentir em casa. Nas paredes, pôsteres de capitais: Curitiba, Florianópolis, São Paulo e Belo Horizonte. No teto, a pintura de um céu azul-escuro com estrelas e o cometa Hailey, símbolo da Viação Cometa. Há longas fileiras que somam ao todo 160 cadeiras estofadas em dois tons: marrom-terra e azul-marinho, sob o piso limpíssimo e brilhante. Há duas TVs sintoni-zadas no canal Globo News, duas máquinas de café e chocolate, uma máquina de refrigerante, quatro aparelhos de ar-condicionado e um galão de água gelada ou natural, "vestido" com um pano branco onde

027

O LIVRO AMERELO DO TERMINAL Book spread, 2008. Designers: Elaine Ramos and Maria Carolina Sampaio. Author: Vanessa Barbara. Publisher: Cosac Naify. *Here, pages of text are set with loose line spacing and printed on thin paper. The vertical placement of the text block varies from spread to spread, allowing text to show through between the lines.*

VISIONARY CITIES: THE
ARCOLOGY OF PAOLO SOLERI
Book, 1970. Design: Paolo
Soleri. *This classic work of
postmodern design uses ultra-
tight line spacing to create
dramatic density on the page.
Produced long before the era of
digital page layout, this book
exploited the possibilities of
phototypesetting and dry
transfer lettering.*

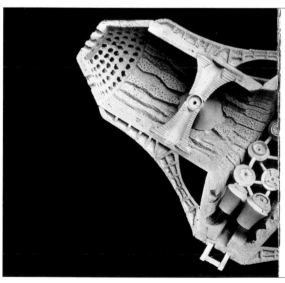

ALIGNMENT

Choosing to align text in justified, centered, or ragged columns is a fundamental typographic act. Each mode of alignment carries unique formal qualities, cultural associations, and aesthetic risks.

Centered text is symmetrical,

like the facade of a classical building.

Centered type often appears on

invitations, title pages, certificates, and tomb stones.

The edges of a centered column

are often dramatically uneven.

Centered lines should be broken to emphasize a key phrase

(such as the name of the bride

or the date of her wedding)

or to allow a new thought to begin on its own line.

Breaking lines in this manner is called

breaking for sense.

Justified text, which has even edges on both the left and right sides of the column, has been the norm since the invention of printing with movable type, which enabled the creation of page after page of straight-edged columns. In metal type setting, the printer justifies each line by hand, using small metal spacers to alter the spaces between words and letters and thus make all the lines the same length. Digital typesetting performs the same labor automatically. Justified type makes efficient use of space. It also creates a clean, compact shape on the page. Ugly gaps can occur, however, when the line length is too short in relation to the size of type used. Hyphenation breaks up long words and helps keep the lines of text tightly packed. Designers often use negative tracking to fit additional characters on a line, or positive tracking to even out a line of type that looks too loose.

CENTERED
Lines of uneven length on a central axis

Centered text is formal and classical. It invites the designer to break a text for sense and create elegant, organic shapes. Centering is often the simplest and most intuitive way to place a typographic element. Used without care, centered text can look staid and mournful, like a tombstone.

JUSTIFIED
Left and right edges are both even

Justified text makes a clean shape on the page. Its efficient use of space makes it the norm for newspapers and books. Ugly gaps can occur, however, as text is forced into lines of even measure. Avoid this by using a line length that is long enough in relation to the size of type. As type gets smaller, more words will fit on each line.

THIS DREARY SHAPE HAS RANDOM LINE BREAKS THAT DON'T RESPOND TO THE RHYTHM OF THE WRITTEN TEXT.

TYPE CRIME
POORLY SHAPED TEXT BLOCK *In most uses, centered text should be broken into phrases with a variety of long and short lines.*

Ugly gaps appear when the designer has made the line length too short, or the author has selected words that are   too   long.

TYPE CRIME
FULL OF HOLES *A column that is too narrow is full of gaps.*

In *flush left/ragged right* text, the left edge is hard and the right edge soft. Word spaces do not fluctuate, so there are never big holes inside the lines of text. This format, which was used primarily for setting poetry before the twentieth century, respects the flow of language rather than submitting to the law of the box. Despite its advantages, however, the flush left format is fraught with danger. Above all, the designer must work hard to control the appearance of the *rag* that forms along the right edge. A good rag looks pleasantly uneven, with no lines that are excessively long or short, and with hyphenation kept to a minimum. A rag is considered "bad" when it looks too even (or too uneven), or when it begins to form regular shapes, like wedges, moons, or diving boards.

Flush right/ragged left is a variant of the more familiar flush left setting. It is common wisdom among typographers that flush right text is hard to read, because it forces the reader's eye to find a new position at the start of each line. This could be true, or it could be an urban legend. That being said, the flush right setting is rarely employed for long bodies of text. Used in smaller blocks, however, flush right text forms effective marginal notes, sidebars, pull quotes, or other passages that comment on a main body or image. A flush or ragged edge can suggest attraction (or repulsion) between chunks of information.

FLUSH LEFT/RAGGED RIGHT
Left edge is hard; right edge is soft

Flush left text respects the organic flow of language and avoids the uneven spacing that plagues justified type. A bad rag can ruin the relaxed, organic appearance of a flush left column. Designers must strive vigilantly to create the illusion of a random, natural edge without resorting to excessive hyphenation.

FLUSH RIGHT/RAGGED LEFT
Right edge is hard; left edge is soft

Flush right text can be a welcome departure from the familiar. Used for captions, side bars, and other marginalia, it can suggest affinities among elements. Because flush right text is unusual, it can annoy cautious readers. Bad rags threaten flush right text just as they afflict flush left, and punctuation can weaken the hard right edge.

A bad rag will fall into weird shapes along the right edge, instead of looking random.

TYPE CRIME
BAD RAG
An ugly wedge shape spoils the ragged edge.

Lots of punctuation (at the ends of lines) will attack, threaten, and generally weaken the flush right edge.

TYPE CRIME
PUNCTUATION EATS THE EDGE *Excessive punctuation weakens the right edge.*

The four modes of alignment (centered, justified, flush left, and flush right) form the basic grammar of typographic composition. Each one has traditional uses that make intuitive sense to readers.

CENTERED

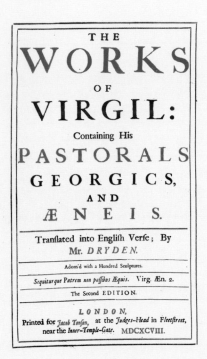

JUSTIFIED

for Coppet. But when the eighty days had passed and the bugaboo was safely on board the *Bellerophon*, she came back to the scenes she loved so well and to what for her was the only heaven: Paris. ¶ She has been called a philosopher and a literary light. But she was only socio-literary. Her written philosophy does not represent the things she felt were true—simply those things she thought it would be nice to say. She cultivated literature, only that she might shine. Love, wealth, health, husband, children—all were sacrificed that she might lead society and win applause. No one ever feared solitude more: she must have those about her who would minister to her vanity and upon whom she could shower her wit. As a type her life is valuable, and in these pages that traverse the entire circle of feminine virtues and foibles she surely must have a place. ¶ In her last illness she was attended daily by those faithful subjects who had all along recognized her sovereignty—in Society she was Queen. She surely now had won her heart's desire, for to that bed from which she was no more to rise, courtiers came and kneeling kissed her hand, and women by the score whom she had befriended paid her the tribute of their tears ❧ She died in Paris at the age of fifty-one.
217

THE WORKS OF VIRGIL Printed for Jacob Tonson, 1698. *Title pages are traditionally set centered. This two-color title page was printed in two passes of the press (note the off-kilter registration of the two colors of ink). Large typefaces were created primarily for use on title pages or in hymn books.*

THE COMPLETE WRITINGS OF ELBERT HUBBARD, VOLUME TWO Printed by the Roycroft Shop, 1908. *This neo-Renaissance book page harkens back to the first century of printing. Not only is the block of text perfectly justified, but paragraph symbols are used in place of indents and line breaks to preserve the solidity of the page.*

FLUSH LEFT

L'ENNEMI

Ma jeunesse ne fut qu'un ténébreux orage,
Traversé çà et là par de brillants soleils;
Le tonnerre et la pluie ont fait un tel ravage,
Qu'il reste en mon jardin bien peu de fruits vermeils.

Voilà que j'ai touché l'automne des idées,
Et qu'il faut employer la pelle et les râteaux
Pour rassembler à neuf les terres inondées,
Où l'eau creuse des trous grands comme des tombeaux.

Et qui sait si les fleurs nouvelles que je rêve
Trouveront dans ce sol lavé comme une grève
Le mystique aliment qui ferait leur vigueur?

— O douleur! ô douleur! Le Temps mange la vie,
Et l'obscur Ennemi qui nous ronge le cœur
Du sang que nous perdons croît et se fortifie!

17

FLUSH RIGHT

132   Technique

things that could not have been done at all had he stuck to his original idea.

No shields   Trade-markery is a country cousin of heraldry; it can claim that kin, but native good taste will keep it from trying to ape its noble relative. I mean that trade-marks in the form of shields are a joke—as comical as those mid-Victorian trade devices surrounded by the Garter. Things like that, in first instances (they are now meaningless survivals), were efforts on the part of Trade to sit in the same pew with Race. Under the modern dispensation, with kings at a discount, the feudal touch may be dispensed with. One makes this comment about shields as trade-marks because a cosmic law operates to convince every expectant proprietor of a new trade-mark that he wants his device in the shape of a shield.

Flexible   A good trade-mark is the thing that lives inside a boundary line—not the boundary line itself. It should be possible for the device to step outside its circle, or triangle, or what not, and still be the same—an unmistakable emblem. In other words, marks that depend for their individuality upon triangular frames, circles, squares, etc., are weak brethren; they are of a low order of trade-mark vitality.

Typographic flavor   For the greater number of advertising uses a trade-mark design needs to be given a typographic flavor. It will stand in close relation to type in the usual advertisement and its stance will be more comfortable if it is brought into sympathy with type. This means that the proprietor will have to relax the rigor of his rule and allow his design (originally rendered in soft lithographic grays and stipples) to be redrawn in positive line, with considerable paper showing. It is not necessary to ape the style of a woodcut in this effort after typographic flavor; but it is necessary to echo, to a certain extent, the crisp black lines and

CHARLES BAUDELAIRE/LES FLEURS DU MAL Printed by Bill Lansing, 1945. *Traditionally, poetry is set flush left, because the line breaks are an essential element of the literary form. Poetry is not ususally set centered, except in greeting cards.*

LAYOUT IN ADVERTISING Designed and written by W. A. Dwiggins, 1928. *In this classic guide to commercial art practices, Dwiggins has placed callouts or subject cues in the margins. On the left-hand (verso) page shown here, the cues are set flush right, drawing them closer to the content they identify.*

Designers sometimes use the archetypal modes of alignment in ways that emphasize their visual qualities. Combining different types of alignment can yield dynamic and surprising layouts.

"Grandma! Grandma! Look at me! I did it!" Oval yelled from the water, her youth taut as a syllogism.

"I saw you darling!" Mother waved. Then she sat back and smiled, nature on her side after all.

"Well sure," Square began—
He heard the suck of Circle's chest cavity, speech lobes echoing the startle of her brain's emotive region to vibrate vocal chords so that the up-rush of breath through her body would come out as,

"What?!"

She pushed her sunglasses up onto her head to reveal that her eyes had widened to the size of an animal's before it pounces. And in response, an electro-chemical jolt contracted his muscles to quickly voice "But it's more complicated than that" (accelerando) as he tried to recover.

Tried and failed, he saw, realizing that Mother would take his words as confirmation of Circle's phobia of conceiving. Circle's eyes remained trained on him. "Sometimes more kids just aren't in the cards," he tried.

"What he means," Circle said, emotion beginning to raise veins, "is that we've decided to limit our family."

"Limit your?—"

"It's not like when you and dad were raising a family. Kids cost a lot. The public schools are worthless so you can't even think about sending them there. And anyway, who's going to watch a baby while I'm at work? Square doesn't have time. He can't even figure out the ending to his dumb…"

Dumb?

"…story, watching Oval after school like he does and I don't have time to be around them. Not like you were with us."

a common story

"Well, things have certainly changed," Mother sighed in that exhausted victim tone she adopted whenever she was about to play her "tired blood" card. "In my day, children just came or they didn't. We were just the organ they did it through."

of a common man

"Geez, that's what you want me to go back to?" Circle laughed, her smile an incipient "fear grin" primates often exhibited just before tension broke into fight or flight. "A crap shoot?" This last was meant for him. He decided to let pass the crack about his "dumb" story.

Homo being common to all men

"I only meant—"

and women (obviously)

"Mother, I can't not know what I know!" Her exasperated tone left a pregnant silence at the table. "Excuse me," she said, "I need a refill on my ice." She stood up and there was the shock of her body: a flat athletic torso, muscular shoulders and arms in a cheetah-print swimsuit (a legacy of African, i.e. savage sexuality) that made him want her. "Anybody else want anything?"

-45

FLUSH LEFT AND FLUSH RIGHT: VAS: AN OPERA IN FLATLAND Book spread, 2002. Designer: Stephen Farrell. Author: Steve Tomasula. *In this typographic novel, texts and images align left and right against a series of thin rules. Hanging punctuation and boldface letters emphasize the flush edges.*

FLUSH LEFT AND FLUSH RIGHT: INFORMAL Book, 2002. Designer: Januzzi Smith. Author: Cecil Balmond. Photograph: Dan Meyers. *This book is a manifesto for an informal approach to structural engineering and architecture. The text columns juxtapose flush right against flush left alignments, creating a tiny but insistent seam or fissure inside the text and irregular rags along the outer edges.*

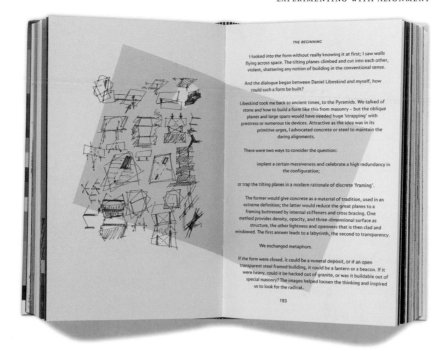

JUSTIFIED: HELLA JONGERIUS Book, 2003. Designers: COMA. Photograph: Dan Meyers. *Transparent paper emphasizes the justified text block. Images hang from a consistent horizontal point, creating a throughline that is visible along the edge of the book.*

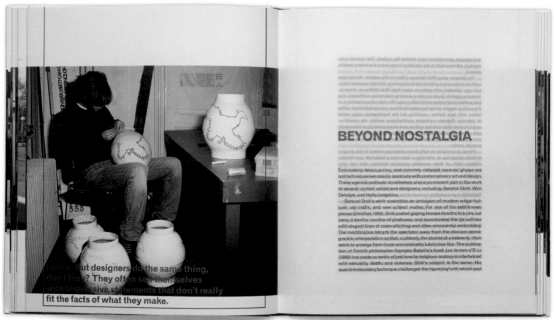

Use modes of alignment (flush left, flush right, justified, and centered) to actively interpret a passage of text. The passage here, from Walter Ong's book *Orality and Literacy: The Technologizing of the Word*, explains how the invention of printing with movable type imposed a new spatial order on the written word, in contrast with the more organic pages of the manuscript era. The solutions shown here comment on the conflicts between hard and soft, industrial and natural, planning and chance, that underlie all typographic composition.

Examples of student work from
Maryland Institute College of Art

PRINT SITUATES WORDS IN SPACE MORE RELENTLESSLY THAN WRITING EVER DID. writing moves words from the sound world BUT PRINT LOCKS WORDS INTO to a world of visual space, POSITION IN THIS SPACE. CONTROL OF POSITION IS EVERYTHING IN PRINT. PRINTED TEXTS LOOK MACHINE-MADE, AS THEY ARE. in handwriting, control of space tends to be ornamental, TYPOGRAPHIC CONTROL TYPICALLY IMPRESSES MOST BY ITS TIDINESS ornate, as in calligraphy. AND INVISIBILITY: THE LINES PERFECTLY REGULAR, ALL JUSTIFIED ON THE RIGHT SIDE, EVERYTHING COMING OUT EVEN VISUALLY, AND WITHOUT THE AID OF GUIDELINES OR RULED BORDERS THAT OFTEN OCCUR IN MANUSCRIPTS. THIS IS AN INSISTENT WORLD OF COLD, NON-HUMAN, FACTS.

Randomly spaced words break free from a rigidly justified column.
Lu Zhang

PRINT
situates words in space more relentlessly
than writing ever did. Control of position
is everything in print. Printed texts look
machine-made, as they are. Typographic
control typically impresses most by its
WRITING tidiness and invisibility: the lines perfectly
moves words from the sound world
regular, all justified on the right side,
to a world of visual space,
everything coming out even visually, and
but print locks words
without the aid of guidelines or ruled
into position in this space.
borders that often occur in manuscripts.
In handwriting, control of space
This is an insistent world of cold,
tends to be ornamental, ornate,
non-human, facts.
as in calligraphy.

Passages of flush left and flush right text hinge from a central axis.
Johnschen Kudos

Print situates words
in space more
relentlessly than
writing ever did.
Writing moves words from the sound world to a world of visual space,
but print locks
words into position
in this space.
Control of position
is everything in
print. Printed texts
look machine-made,
as they are.
In handwriting, control of space tends to be ornamental, ornate.
Typographic control
typically impresses
most by its tidiness
and invisibility: the
lines perfectly regular,
all justified on the
right side, everything
coming out even
visually, and without
the aid of guidelines
or ruled borders that
often occur in
manuscripts.

This is an insistent
world of cold,
non-human, facts.

Long, centered lines are bridges between narrow, ragged columns.
Benjamin Lutz

relentlessly than writing ever did. Writing moves words from the sound world to a world of visual space, but print locks words into position in this space. Control of position is everything in print. Printed texts look machine-made, as they are. In handwriting, control of space tends to be ornamental, ornate, as in calligraphy. Typographic control typically impresses most by its tidiness and invisibility: the lines perfectly regular, all justified on the right side, everything coming out even visually, and without the aid of guidelines or ruled borders that often occur in manuscripts. This is an insistent world of cold, non-human, facts.

Print situates words in space more

The beginning of the paragraph is moved to the end.
Daniel Arbello

Print situates words in space more relentlessly than writing ever did. Writing moves words from the sound world to a world of visual space, but print locks words into position in this space.

Control of position is everything in print.

Printed texts look machine-made, as they are. In handwriting, control of space tends to be ornamental, ornate, as in calligraphy. Typographic control typically impresses most by its tidiness and invisibility: the lines perfectly regular, all justified on the right side, everything coming out even visually, and without the aid of guidelines or ruled borders that often occur in manuscripts. THIS IS AN INSISTENT WORLD OF COLD, NON-HUMAN, FACTS.

A single line slides out of a justified block.
Kapila Chase

Print situates words in space more relentlessly than writing ever did.

Writing moves words from the sound world to a world of

V I S U A L   S P A C E

but print locks words into position in this space. Control of position is everything in print. Printed texts look machine-made, as they are.

In handwriting, control of space tends to be ornamental, ornate, as in calligraphy.

Typographic control typically impresses most by its tidiness and invisibility: the lines perfectly regular, all justified on the right side, everything coming out even visually, and without the aid of guidelines or ruled borders that often occur in manuscripts.

This is an insistent world of cold, non-human, facts.

Elements break away from a justified column.
Efrat Levush

Print situates words in space more relentlessly than writing ever did. Writing moves words from the

sound world to a world of visual space, but print locks words into position in this space.

Control of position is everything in print. Printed texts look

machine-made, as they are. In handwriting, control of space tends to be

ornamental, ornate, as in calligraphy. Typographic control typically impresses most

by its tidiness and invisibility: the lines perfectly regular, all justified on the right side,

everything coming out even visually, and without the aid of guidelines or ruled borders that often occur

in manuscripts. This is an insistent world of cold, non-human, facts.

Text is forced into a grid of ragged squares.
Kim Bender

Roman letters are designed to sit side by side, not on top of one another. Stacks of lowercase letters are especially awkward because the ascenders and descenders make the vertical spacing appear uneven, and the varied width of the characters makes the stacks look precarious. (The letter *I* is a perennial problem.) Capital letters form more stable stacks than lowercase letters. Centering the column helps to even out the differences in width. Many Asian writing systems, including Chinese, are traditionally written vertically; the square shape of the characters supports this orientation. The simplest way to make a line of Latin text vertical is to rotate the text from horizontal to vertical. This preserves the natural affinity among letters sitting on a line while creating a vertical axis.

BOOK SPINES *Stacked letters sometimes appear on the spines of books, but vertical baselines are more common. Starting from the top and reading down is the dominant direction in the United States.*

v e r t i g o

v e r t i g o

V E R T I G O

V E R T I G O

TYPE CRIME
STACKED LOWERCASE

SMALL CAPS, STACKED

VERTIGO A FILM BY ALFRED HITCHCOCK

VERTIGO A FILM BY ALFRED HITCHCOCK

VERTIGO A FILM BY ALFRED HITCHCOCK

top to bottom   *bottom to top*   *both directions*

VERTICAL BASELINES *There is no fixed rule determining whether type should run from top to bottom or from bottom to top. It is more common, however, especially in the United States, to run text on the spines of books from top to bottom. (You can also run text up and down simultaneously.)*

MEXICAN STREET SIGNS
Photographs by Andrea Marks. *Stacked letters often appear on commercial street signs, which often employ thin, vertical slices of space. The letters in these signs were drawn by hand. Wide characters and squared-off Os stack better than narrow letters with traditional rounded forms. In some instances, the letters have been specially aligned to create vertical relationships, as in the "Optica" sign at right, painted on a sliver of flat molding inside a door frame.*

SIMPATICO Poster for
the Public Theater, 1994.
Designer: Paula Scher/
Pentagram. *Type set on
a vertical baseline creates
movement across the poster.
The theater's logo, which also
employs a vertical baseline,
can be easily placed on street
banners.*

PARALLELEN IM
SCHNITTPUNKT
(CROSSING PARALLELS)
Poster, 1997. Designer:
Gerwin Schmidt. Publisher:
Art-Club Karlsruhe. *The axes
of type and landscape intersect
to create posters that are simple,
powerful, and direct. The text
is mirrored in German and
French.*

N THE BEGINNING of a text, the reader needs an invitation to come inside. Enlarged capitals, also called *versals*, commonly mark the entrance to a chapter in a book or an article in a magazine. Many medieval manuscripts are illuminated with elaborately painted rubrics. This tradition continued with the rise of the printing press. At first, initials were hand-painted onto printed pages, making mass-produced books resemble manuscripts, which were more valuable than printed books. Initials soon became part of typography. A printer could set them together with the main text in wood blocks or cast lead characters, or add them with a separate process such as engraving. Today, enlarged caps are easily styled as part of a publication's typographic system.

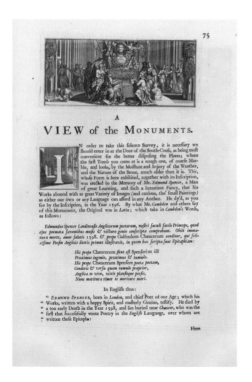

A VIEW OF THE MONUMENTS Book page, eighteenth century. *This page was printed in two passes: letterpress type with engraved illustrations.*

NEW YORK TIMES BOOK REVIEW Newspaper page, 2009. Art director: Nicholas Blechman. Illustrator: Ellen Lupton. *The dropped capital is a separate illustration placed in the layout.*

IN THIS PARAGRAPH, the enlarged capital sits on the same baseline as the text that follows. This simple solution is easy to implement on both page and screen. Setting the first few words of the text block in SMALL CAPITALS helps smooth the transition between the initial and the text.

AN ENLARGED LETTER cut into the text block is called a *dropped capital* or *drop cap*. This example was produced using the Drop Caps feature in InDesign. The software automatically creates a space around one or more characters and drops them the requested number of lines. The designer can adjust the size and tracking of the capital to match it to the surrounding text. Similar solutions can be implemented on the web in CSS. The space around the capital is rectangular, which can be visually awkward, as seen here with the sloping silhouette of the letter *A*.

WAS IT THE BEST OF TIMES, the worst of times, or just Times New Roman? The dropped capital used here (The Serif Bold) was positioned as a separate element. A text wrap was applied to an invisible box sitting behind the capital, so that the text appears to flow around the intruding right prow of the *W*. Likewise, the left prow extends out into the margin, making the character feel firmly anchored in the text block. Hand-crafted solutions like this one cannot be applied systematically.

GRAB YOUR READER BY THE CAHUNAS AND NEVER EVER LET GO DESIGNERS SOMETIMES ADAPT the drop cap convention for other purposes. An illustration or icon can appear in place of a letterform. Purely typographic alternatives are also possible, such as inserting a title or subtitle into space carved from the primary text block. Such devices mobilize a familar page structure for diverse and sometimes unexpected uses.

Paragraphs do not occur in nature. Whereas sentences are grammatical units intrinsic to the spoken language, paragraphs are a literary convention designed to divide masses of content into appetizing portions.

Indents have been common since the seventeenth century. Adding space between paragraphs (*paragraph spacing*) is another standard device. On the web, a paragraph is a semantic unit (the <p> tag in html) that is typically displayed on screen with space inserted after it.

A typical indent is an *em space*, or a *quad*, a fixed unit of space roughly the width of the letter's cap height. An em is thus proportional to the size of the type; if you change the point size or column width, the indents will remain appropriately scaled. Alternatively, you can use the tab key to create an indent of any depth. A designer might use this technique in order to align the indents with a vertical grid line or other page element. Avoid indenting the very first line of a body of text. An indent signals a break or separation; there is no need to make a break when the text has just begun.

Despite the ubiquity of indents and paragraph spacing, designers have developed numerous alternatives that allow them to shape content in distinctive ways.

NERD ALERT: Use the Space After Paragraph feature in your page layout program to insert a precise increment of space between paragraphs. Skipping a full line often creates too open an effect and wastes a lot of space. Get in the habit of inserting a full paragraph return (Enter key) only at the end of paragraphs; insert a line break when you don't want to add additional space (Shift + Enter).

The table is covered with a table cloth which itself is protected by a plastic table cloth. Drapes and double drapes are at the windows. We have carpets, slipcovers, coasters, wainscoting, lampshades. Each trinket sits on a doily, each flower in its pot, and each pot in its saucer.

Everything is protected and surrounded. Even in the garden, each cluster is encircled with wire netting, each path is outlined by bricks, mosaics, or flagstones.

This could be analyzed as an anxious sequestration, as an obsessional symbolism: the obsession of the cottage owner and small capitalist not only to possess, but to underline what he possesses two or three times. There, as other places, the unconscious speaks in the redundancy of signs, in their connotations and overworking.

— *Jean Baudrillard, 1969*

INDENT AND LINE BREAK

The table is covered with a table cloth which itself is protected by a plastic table cloth. Drapes and double drapes are at the windows. We have carpets, slipcovers, coasters, wainscoting, lampshades. Each trinket sits on a doily, each flower in its pot, and each pot in its saucer.

Everything is protected and surrounded. Even in the garden, each cluster is encircled with wire netting, each path is outlined by bricks, mosaics, or flagstones.

This could be analyzed as an anxious sequestration, as an obsessional symbolism: the obsession of the cottage owner and small capitalist not only to possess, but to underline what he possesses two or three times. There, as other places, the unconscious speaks in the redundancy of signs, in their connotations and overworking.

— *Jean Baudrillard, 1969*

LINE BREAK AND 1/2 LINE SPACE (PARAGRAPH SPACING)

The table is covered with a table cloth which itself is protected by a plastic table cloth. Drapes and double drapes are at the windows. We have carpets, slipcovers, coasters, wainscoting, lampshades. Each trinket sits on a doily, each flower in its pot, and each pot in its saucer.

Everything is protected and surrounded. Even in the garden, each cluster is encircled with wire netting, each path is outlined by bricks, mosaics, or flagstones.

This could be analyzed as an anxious sequestration, as an obsessional symbolism: the obsession of the cottage owner and small capitalist not only to possess, but to underline what he possesses two or three times. There, as other places, the unconscious speaks in the redundancy of signs, in their connotations and overworking.

— *Jean Baudrillard, 1969*

OUTDENT (HANGING INDENTATION) AND LINE BREAK

The table is covered with a table cloth which itself is protected by a plastic table cloth. Drapes and double drapes are at the windows. We have carpets, slipcovers, coasters, wainscoting, lampshades. Each trinket sits on a doily, each flower in its pot, and each pot in its saucer. Everything is protected and surrounded. Even in the garden, each cluster is encircled with wire netting, each path is outlined by bricks, mosaics, or flagstones. This could be analyzed as an anxious sequestration, as an obsessional symbolism: the obsession of the cottage owner and small capitalist not only to possess, but to underline what he possesses two or three times. There, as other places, the unconscious speaks in the redundancy of signs, in their connotations and overworking.

— *Jean Baudrillard, 1969*

EXTRA SPACE INSIDE LINE, WITHOUT LINE BREAK

The table is covered with a table cloth which itself is protected by a plastic table cloth. Drapes and double drapes are at the windows. We have carpets, slipcovers, coasters, wainscoting, lampshades. Each trinket sits on a doily, each flower in its pot, and each pot in its saucer. ■ Everything is protected and surrounded. Even in the garden, each cluster is encircled with wire netting, each path is outlined by bricks, mosaics, or flagstones. ■ This could be analyzed as an anxious sequestration, as an obsessional symbolism: the obsession of the cottage owner and small capitalist not only to possess, but to underline what he possesses two or three times. There, as other places, the unconscious speaks in the redundancy of signs, in their connotations and overworking.

— *Jean Baudrillard, 1969*

SYMBOL, WITHOUT INDENT OR LINE BREAK

The table is covered with a table cloth which itself is protected by a plastic table cloth. Drapes and double drapes are at the windows. We have carpets, slipcovers, coasters, wainscoting, lampshades. Each trinket sits on a doily, each flower in its pot, and each pot in its saucer.

Everything is protected and surrounded. Even in the garden, each cluster is encircled with wire netting, each path is outlined by bricks, mosaics, or flagstones.

This could be analyzed as an anxious sequestration, as an obsessional symbolism: the obsession of the cottage owner and small capitalist not only to possess, but to underline what he possesses two or three times. There, as other places, the unconscious speaks in the redundancy of signs, in their connotations and overworking.

— *Jean Baudrillard, 1969*

TYPE CRIME: TOO MANY SIGNALS *Using paragraph spacing and indents together squanders space and gives the text block a flabby, indefinite shape.*

Different kinds of content invite different approaches to marking paragraphs. In early printed books, paragraphs were indicated with a symbol, such as ||, with no additional space or line break. In the seventeenth century, it became standard to indent the first line of a paragraph and break the line at the end. Commercial printing tends to embrace fragmentation over wholeness, allowing readers to sample bits and pieces of text. Modern literary forms such as the interview invite designers to construct inventive typographic systems.

Dominus Salomoni secundò apparens, iubet sua seruare praecepta, addita comminatione nisi seruata fuerint. Salomon plures aedificat ciuitates, gentes sibi facit tributarias, & classe in Ophir missa plurimum auri recipit.

CAP.   IX.

¹ ACTVM est autem cùm perfecisset Salomon ædificium domus Domini , & ædificium regis , & omne quod optauerat & volue-rat facere, ² apparuit ei Dominus secundò || sicut apparuerat ei in Gabaon. ³ Dixítque Dominus ad eum , Exaudiui orationem tuam & deprecationem tuam, quam de-precatus es coram me: sanctificaui domū hanc quam ædificasti , vt ponerem nomen meum ibi in sempi-ternum , & erunt oculi mei & cor meum ibi cunctis diebus, ⁴ Tu quoque si ambulaueris coram me, si-cut ambulauit * pater tuus , in simplicitate cordis & in æquitate:& feceris omnia quæ præcepi tibi, & le-gitima mea & iudicia mea seruaueris,⁵ ponam thro-num regni tui super Israel in sempiternum,||sicut lo-cutus sum Dauid patri tuo, dicens , Non auferetur vir de genere tuo de solio Israel. ⁶ Si autem auer-sione auersi fueritis vos & filij vestri,non sequentes me , nec custodientes mandata mea, & ceremonias meas quas proposui vobis, sed abieritis & colueritis deos alienos , & adoraueritis eos : ⁷ auferam Israel de superficie terræ quam dedi eis, & templum quod sanctificaui nomini meo proijciam à cōspectu meo, erítque Israel in prouerbium , & in fabulam cunctis populis. ⁸ Et domus hæc erit in exemplum : omnis qui transierit per eam, stupebit & sibilabit, & dicet, ||Quare fecit Dominus sic terræ huic & domui huic? ⁹ Et respondebunt , Quia dereliquerunt Dominum Deum suum , qui eduxit patres eorum de terra-Æ-gypti , & secuti sunt deos alienos , & adorauerunt eos,& colnerunt eos : idcirco induxit Dominus su-per eos omne malum hoc. ¹⁰ || Expletis autem an-nis viginti postquàm ædificauerat Salomon duas domos , id est , domum Domini & domum regis. ¹¹ (Hiram rege Tyri præbente Salomoni ligna ce-drina & abiegna , & aurum iuxta omne quod opus habuerat:)tunc dedit * Salomon Hiram viginti op-pida in terra-Galilææ. ¹² Et egressus est Hiram de Tyro,vt videret oppida quæ dederat ei Salomon, & non placuerunt ei , ¹³ & ait , Hæcine sunt ciuitates quas dedisti mihi , frater ? Et appellauit eas Ter-ram-chabul , vsque in diem hanc. ¹⁴ Misit quoque Hiram

A

2.Par.7. c. 11.
Sup.3.4.5.

* Dauid 2.

2.Re.7.b.12 c.16.
1.Pa.22. b. 10.

B

De.29.d. 24.
Iere.22.b.5.

2.Par.8.a.1

*rex L

C

ALL BUILT-IN FIXTURES are furnished with nickel hardware and 1½-inch casing, to be used as a casing or as a ground for the finished casing.

Stock carried in pine (unfinished).

All ironing boards carried in stock are 12 inches wide—any width made to order.

"PEERLESS" equipment is very simple to install, will require no special arrangements of your plans and will make your house or apart-ment a real home, a good investment and add a distinction you could not acquire otherwise.

Hoosier Cabinets furnished in oak or flat white finish. Also with aluminum or porceliron table slides.

dominate its board?

I'd be interested to know what Maxwell Anderson and David Ross think about the possibility of changing the membership of museum boards so that they more fully represent the communities they claim to serve. Can we imagine a Whitney Museum board that is not a rich man's club?

Irving Sandler

There are diverse museum audiences. A significant constituency consists of artists. They need what they see to make art. In talking to artists, at least of my generation, everyone has told me of the importance of the Museum of Modern Art's permanent collection in the development of their art. I would hope that museums could serve all of their diverse audiences, but the health of art and its future depends on how they meet the needs of artists.

Maurice Berger

Dan, you wrote: "Because of this feeling of being excluded, I believe that one of the most important commitments any museum professional can make is to try to reach out and connect to the public through continuous lectures, gallery tours, workshops, and the difficult but necessary writing of readable wall and brochure texts."

This is a very important point, yet I suspect that you may be the exception rather than the rule. All too often, I have found (as a consultant to a number of museums) resistance on the part of many curators to examining and improving their pedagogical skills. Indeed, education departments are often marginal to or left out of the curatorial process. On Thursday, I will open a two-day session on museum education, public address, and pedagogy.

Irving, you wrote: "A significant constituency consists of artists. They need what they see to make art. . . . I would hope that museums could serve all of their diverse audiences, but the health of art and its future depends on how they meet the needs of artists."

A very important observation—the museum as a space of education, inspiration, and motivation for other artists.

Maxwell L. Anderson

Alan asked about the possibility of opening up major museum boards. It took me quite some time to persuade the Whitney Museum board that it would be logical to have a seat for an artist. I was lucky enough to have three artists on the board of Toronto's Art Gallery of Ontario, a much larger museum spanning from the Renaissance to the present with a budget comparable to the Whitney's.

The concern expressed by the Whitney's board was that having an artist could create conflicts of interest. I noted that it might well be a conflict of interest to have trustees who actively collected in the general areas that the museum does, but that I trust members to recuse themselves when discussions warrant it.

Eventually, I was given the green light by the Nominating Committee to invite Chuck Close, who graciously accepted over a bottle of Glenlivet in his studio, and proved to be a superb trustee. Chuck has helped keep the conversation alive and focused on the museum's mission. His term was up this June.

My nominee to succeed him would have provided a return engagement to mine a museum, in this case the Whitney, but that was not to be. Chuck's term has been extended, and he will be terrific as long as he cares to stay on. My preference was to alternate, at the end of each three-year term, between a more senior artist and a midcareer artist.

As far as other positions on boards, the prevailing desire of most nominating committees is to have trustees with the means necessary to fuel a campaign and support the annual fiscal burden of the operating budget. One can understand the impulse. On the other hand, across the nation there is still an unfilled need for greater ethnic diversity and better representation of various segments of an artistic spectrum—in the Whitney's case, for example, for more collectors of contemporary art.

For the makeup of a board to change, there has to be an overarching will to do it. That is not the impulse around the United States today. When times are tight, whatever will there might be is put to the side in a quest to find people with proven capacity to give.

Mary Kelly

Over the years, I have noticed how the same work, shown in different contexts, draws vastly different audiences, in terms of numbers and responses, and perhaps this is why I placed emphasis on the issue of reception in my earlier remarks. Of course, in making a work, there is a subjective investment that presupposes an audience, or put another way, the desire of the other. I think artists are always speaking, consciously or unconsciously, to very specific people—friends, lovers, patrons, collectors, and sometimes to certain communities—professional, political, social, generational, or geographic, but this is never the same audience constructed by the exhibition.

Considered as a "statement," you could say an exhibition is formulated by a curator/author who is given the

124   125

MUSEUMS OF TOMORROW: A VIRTUAL DISCUSSION Book spread, 2004. Designed by Franc Nunoo-Quarcoo and Karen Howard. *Outdents (instead of indents) mark paragraph breaks in this multi-authored text.*

DESIGN BEYOND DESIGN Book spread, 2004. Designed and edited by Jan van Toorn. *Lines and blocks of text slide into the margin to mark changes of voice in an ongoing conversation.*

discussion

hasn't been any talking about artistic practice and political practice. So how can artists and graphic designers intervene? At the same time, it is not for the others that one intervenes, it is with the others and for oneself. That is very important; we should not be paternalistic missionaries. I think that politics itself is an art, politics is the art of managing conflicts, the art of relations of force, and therefore necessarily involves the people who possess the power of expression. For let me remind you that expression and the orderly transfer of ideas play a very, very important role in conflicts.

Member of the audience

I would like to ask Jörg Petruschat how he sees the relation between social conflict and artistic practice, especially in relation to design.

Jörg Petruschat

I can hear..., but today it's the seventh of november and... at school I had to learn russian. I'll try it.

I came here for three reasons. I see that revolution in technology served to cement the social status quo. Many designers hope to change the world when they go to technologies and I think that is a big illusion. And my duty is not to say to you what you have to do in future, but my duty is to think about what I see in the present. And I think it's an illusion to run behind the technology changes in the hope of changing the social status quo. In my opinion we should not make the mistake of thinking that we are the greatest because we are the latest. We have to look into the history and the problems of history because the situation, as I showed, from the fifteenth down to the nineteenth century has many similarities with the situation today. That's the first.

The second is that technology is a political structure, it transmits a kind of power, of economic power, and this is a new form that we cannot touch in our everyday life. This technology functions behind a façade. So the political is also structural in this case. When designers think there are possibilities to change the world in contact with these technological systems they think like Walter Gropius, that the computer's only an instrument. I think that is false. The computer is not only an instrument but a big structure with many standards, and standards affect everyday life. That's the third reason.

Member of the audience

I enjoyed Susan's talk very much. But I have some doubts. Are you really saying you: I want to go back to the original meaning of the word aesthetics, to go back to perception, and I want to see how perception is displaced in our culture?

Susan Buck-Morss

I do think that there is this opacity of representation, in other words, the way art is not just communication, the way that there's something

friday 7 november

else going on there. Either it's the medium itself, or it's something else that is extremely important. That's the most political we can do better to concentrate on that, than to think about exactly what message is getting across in the sense of a representational message, a direct message. But when you speak about aesthetics and an aesthetics problematic, I think it's what the avant-garde can only hope to do now. I think the avant-garde legitimated its leadership in the past by thinking it knew where history was going. I think this notion of history in progress is very dangerous. You can't be elitist if you know where we're going and you know what's holding us. I really agree with Benjamin that one has to stay radical but give up absolutely the notion of progress or automatic progress.

What does that leave for an avant-garde? That is my question and I was trying to argue as one part of political art. but not all of political art. And in this avant-garde possibility I was thinking about interruption in a temporal sense, or displacement. Maybe it is a very important political intervention to even use their own bodies as this kind of space where not very pleasant things happen. I do think that it's still possible, and for me rather fruitful, to think of a tradition of avant-garde art and how that could be reformulated, not in the way that would say what political art should be about, but something that gives some description and direction.

Lorraine Wild

My question... do you think that in the context of what you're talking about, that it keeps being useful to talk about art, even at all as the definition of what is actually avant-garde or necessary at the moment? I was thinking about that when you opened up with the installation by Ramírez in Tijuana's public plaza, that in fact is a building that demonstrates a code. You could actually not call that art at all, you could call that an informational exhibition, but that somehow this nomenclature that we attach to the activity immediately sets it out into a different round, makes it more difficult to talk about; and that encrusted with the whole idea of cultural hierarchy that in fact works against the very thing.

Susan Buck-Morss

Well, I mean it's interesting, what you say. What the difference is between the word design and the word art. Art is the code word in late western bourgeois society for disinterested interest, for non-instrumental practice. And so I am trying to occupy that or to use it. In fact you're talking about public space of communication; you're not actually talking about anything that obeys the conventional definitions of art. Somehow, we get stuck with this almost retrogressive notion of art, but then actually that very same definition has been used to prevent or tends to create a wall when it comes to this sort of activi-

90   91

The placement and styling of captions affect the reader's experience as well as the visual economy and impact of page layouts. Some readers are primarily attracted to pictures and captions, while others prefer to follow a dominant written narrative, consulting illustrations in support of the text. From a reader's perspective, close proximity of captions and images is a welcome convenience. Placing captions adjacent to pictures is not always an efficient use of space, however. Designers should approach such problems editorially. If captions are essential to understanding the visual content, keep them close to the pictures. If their function is merely documentary, adjacency is more easily sacrificed.

EL BANCO DE UNO | Signage proposal | Agency: Saffron | Design: Joshua Distler, Mike Abbink, Gabor Schreier, Virginia Sardón

EL BANCO DE UNO
Signage proposal
Agency: Saffron
Design: Joshua Distler,
Mike Abbink, Gabor
Schreier, Virginia Sardón

EL BANCO DE UNO
Signage proposal
Agency: Saffron
Design: Joshua Distler,
Mike Abbink, Gabor
Schreier, Virginia Sardón

EL BANCO DE UNO
Signage proposal
Agency: Saffron
Design: Joshua Distler,
Mike Abbink, Gabor
Schreier, Virginia Sardón

1 Newspaper, 2009. Design: Nick Mrozowski. © www.ionline.pt. *Captions tell a story in this layout from the Portuguese newspaper* i.

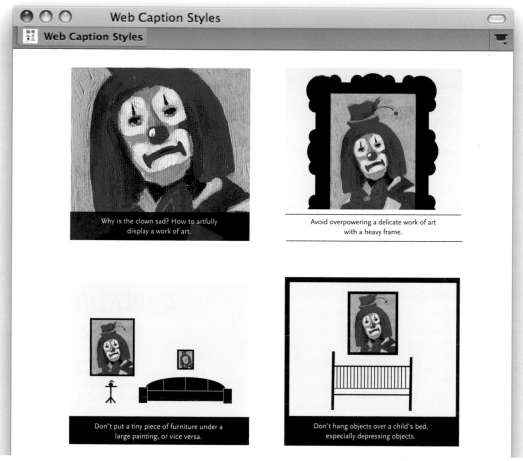

Why is the clown sad? How to artfully display a work of art.

Avoid overpowering a delicate work of art with a heavy frame.

Don't put a tiny piece of furniture under a large painting, or vice versa.

Don't hang objects over a child's bed, especially depressing objects.

CAPTIONS FOR THE WEB *Online content management systems coordinate pictures and captions in a database. Designers use rules, frames, overlays, and color blocks to visually connect images and captions, creating coherent units. Shown here are four different ways to style captions for the web.*

INTERACTIVE WEB CAPTIONS Guardian.co.uk, 2009. Design director: Mark Porter. *A secondary caption reveals itself when users rolls over this image on the Guardian's home page.*

COMMUNICATING HIERARCHY Complex content requires a deeply layered hierarchy. In magazines and websites, a typographic format is often implemented by multiple users, including authors, editors, designers, and web producers. If a hierarchy is clearly organized, users are more likely to apply it consistently. Designers create *style guides* to explain the princples of a hierarchy to the system's users and demonstrate how the system should be implemented.

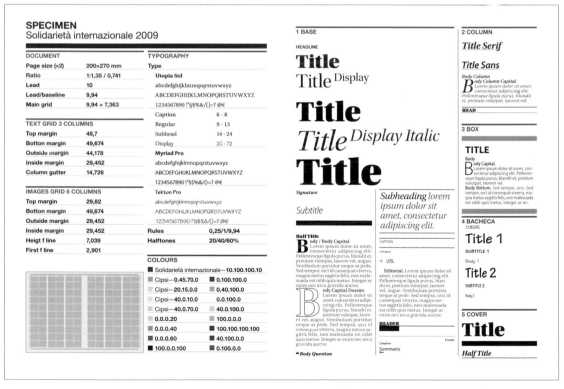

SOLIDARIETÀ INTERNAZIONALE Magazine redesign, 2009. Design: Sezione Aurea. *Publications often commission design firms to create new formats that can be implemented by staff designers and editors. This redesign uses the typefaces Myriad and Utopia, designed by Robert Slimbach. A comprehensive style guide serves to communicate the new format to the magazine's staff.*

STRUCTURAL HIERARCHY Designers and editors should organize content structurally rather than stylistically, especially in digital documents. When creating style sheets in a page layout program, label the elements with terms such as "title," "subtitle," and "caption" rather than "bold," "tiny," or "apple green Arial." In CSS, elements such as em (emphasis), strong, and p (paragraph) are structural, whereas i (italic), b (bold), and br (break) are visual. As a body of content is translated into different media, the styles should continue to refer to the parts of the document rather than to specific visual attributes.

Structural hierarchies help make websites accessible to search engines and users. HTML5 employs the following sectioning elements: <section>, <article>, <aside>, and <nav>. A section can be a parent of another section. When marked off inside another section, the child section is subordinate to its parent. Designers are encouraged to apply headings (<h1>, <h2>, <h3>, and so on) within sections in a manner that reflects the structure of the document.

For more on web standards, see Jeffrey Zeldman with Ethan Marcotte, *Designing with Web Standards*, third edition (Berkeley, CA: New Riders, 2009).

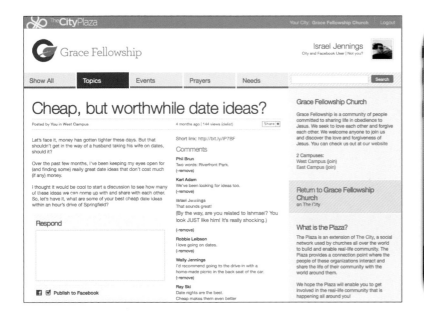

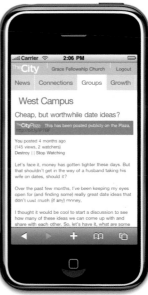

THE CITY Website, 2010. Designer: Graham Stinson. *The City is a social networking site that helps churches and non-profits engage in community activities. Auto-detection determines whether the reader is using a desktop or mobile phone and then re-routes layout characteristics in order to create a custom view. Each layout references a different CSS file; the main HTML for each page remains the same.*

HIERARCHY AND ACCESSIBILITY The web was invented in order to provide universal access to information, regardless of a person's physical abilities or access to specialized hardware or software. Many users lack the browsers or software plug-ins required for displaying certain kinds of files, while visually impaired users have difficulty with small type and non-verbal content. Creating structural hierarchies allows designers to plan alternate layouts suited to the software, hardware, and physical needs of diverse audiences.

Sometimes good typography is heard, not seen. Visually impaired users employ automated screen readers that linearize websites into a continuous text that can be read aloud by a machine. Techniques for achieving successful linearization include avoiding layout tables; consistently using alt tags, image captions, and image descriptions; and placing page anchors in front of repeated navigation elements that enable users to go directly to the main content. Various software programs allow designers to test the linearization of their pages.

CLAPHAMINSTITUTE.ORG Website, 2003. Designer: Colin Day/Exclamation Communications. Publisher: The Clapham Institute. *This site was designed to be accessible to sighted and non-sighted users. Below is a linearized version of the home page. A visually impaired reader would hear this text, including the alt tags for each image. The "skip to content" anchor allows users to avoid listening to a list of navigation elements.*

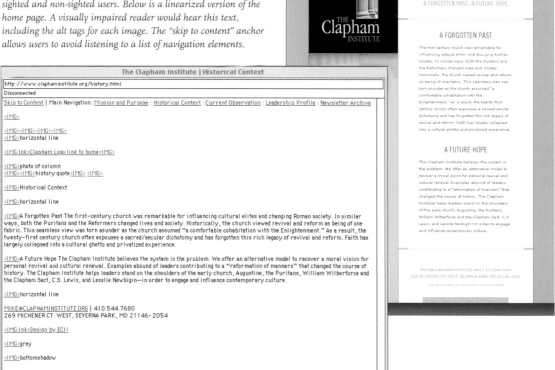

LIGHTHOUSE.ORG Website, 2010. Design: Dan Mall and Kevin Sharon/Happy Cog. Front-end code: Jenn Lukas. Information architecture: Kevin Hoffman. Accessibility research and testing: Angela Colter and Jennifer Sutton. *The visual layout of this website (LEFT) is optimized for sighted users, while the source order of the code (BELOW) is optimized for the visually impaired, allowing users to linearize the text with an automated screen reader. For example, in the visual display, the navigation menu appears immediately below the logo. In the source code, however, the organization name is followed directly by the tagline, preventing the top of the page from clogging up with navigation elements. Such differences between the visual display and the source order are kept to a minimum because not everyone who uses a screen reader is blind, and some people with disabilities who navigate via source order can see the visual layout with their eyes. If the visual layout differs too much from the source code, these users would be confused. The relationship between the visual layout and the source order is also optimized for search engines.*

```html
<body class="home">
<div id="content-wrap">

<div id="header">

    <p class="language"><a href="#">En Espa&ntilde;ol?</a></p>

    <p class="move"><a href="#content">Skip to main content</a></p>

    <h1>
            <img src="/i/logo.gif" alt="" class="hide" />
            <a href="/" title="home">Lighthouse International</a>
    </h1>

    <div class="home-intro">

            <p class="mission"><strong>Dedicated to fighting vision loss through prevention, treatme

            <div class="home-feature">
                    <img src="/i/content/dorrie-smith.png" alt="Dorrie Smith, blog author and Lighth

                    <h2><a href="/services-assistance/help-with-computers-technology/dorries-sight/i

                    <p>Dorrie Smith has found a way to read the Times every morning despite significa
            </div>
            <div id="home-empty-repeat"></div>
    </div>

    <form action="/results/" method="post" id="search">
            <fieldset>
                    <legend><label for="searchtext" class="move-js">Search Lighthouse.org</label></l

                    <p>
                            <input type="text" id="searchtext" name="searchtext" class="filled" valu
                            <input type="image" src="/i/widgets/search.gif" alt="Search" />
                    </p>
            </fieldset>
    </form>

    <div id="secondary">
            <ul>
                    <li class="first"><a href="/services-assistance/">Services &amp; Assistance</a><
                    <li><a href="/low-vision-and-blindness/">About Low Vision &amp; Blindness</a></l
                    <li><a href="/vision-health/">Vision Health</a></li>
                    <li><a href="/research/">Research</a></li>
                    <li><a href="/news-events/">News &amp; Events</a></li>
                    <li><a href="/donate-volunteer/">Donate &amp; Volunteer</a></li>
                    <li class="form-wrap">
                            <form action="/listings/" method="post" id="find-help">
                                    <p>
                                            <label for="searcharea">Find Help In Your Area</label>
                                            <input type="text" id="searcharea" name="searcharea" val
                                            <input type="image" src="/i/widgets/find-help.gif" alt="
                                    </p>
                            </form>
```

abgebildet:

Karl Kraus zählt Wilhelm II. zu „den Schwerverbrechern auf dem Thron" mit der „Beteuerung, daß sie es nicht gewollt haben, woran sie, da sie es taten, doch schuldig sind" [F 595,2].

1920; F 531,52f.

→ gemeinsames **Vorgehen**

→ etwas zum **Vortrag** bringen

→ in die **Falle** gehen

→ ich habe alles reiflich **erwogen**

→ im **Lauf** des Abends

→ ein **Laut** auf den Lippen

→ zum **Schluß**

→ zu **Mantua** in Banden Der treue Hofer war

→ **Gesellschaft** mit beschränkter Haftung / G. m. b. H.

→ **vorlieb** nehmen

seit der Thronbesteigung !) — —

— — So erlebte ich, daß er einen do Major, den Adjutanten des Kronprinzen, Ohr zog, ihm einen tüchtigen Sch gab und sagte: — —

— — empfing er in Tempelhof im minister und den Chef des Militärkabinettes alten Esel glaubt, daß ihr alles besser

*) Deutsche Verlagsanstalt, Stuttgart,

Und daß das »gemeinsame Vorgehen« für war, »sobald Kraus die Satire auf Kaiser Wil werde«, beweist eine Vertrautheit der I Programm, die ich selbst am Nachmittag no ihnen in die Falle gegangen! Aber wenn ei Innsbruck auf Demonstrationen ausgehen, Abends eine Ahnung von dem Vorhandens will ich dem Wilhelm glauben, daß er es nic Josef, daß er alles reiflich erwogen hat. Die einer vagen Kenntnis meiner Gesinnung, ab die ihre auszuleben, in den Saal geführter Abends ein Dutzend weit besserer Anlässe zwei Diebsgenerale — hatten vorübergehen der Laut auf den Lippen erstarb, und erst über die eigene Unregsamkeit ihnen Bew ihre Anwesenheit legitimierten, indem

WÖRTERBUCH DER REDENSARTEN/KARL KRAUS, DIE FACKEL
Book, 1999. Designer: Anne Burdick. Publisher:
Österreichische Akademie der Wissenschaften. *This book
presents essays from the journal* Die Fackel, *published by the
Viennese writer Karl Kraus from 1899 to 1936. The journal's text
appears in the center of each page. This text is sometimes
represented with an image of the original publication and
sometimes filtered through the modern typography of the new
edition. In the beige-colored margins, different styles and sizes of
type indicate different modes of editorial commentary.*

RADAR Magazine, 2008. Designed by Luke Hayman/Pentagram and Kate Elazegui/Radar. *Mass-market magazine covers often combine a big photograph, a big headline, and a big logo with a swarm of teasers about articles to be found inside. Radar's covers present feature stories front and center while enticing readers with numerous compact headlines. In contrast, the magazine's table of contents provides a more leisurely overview. Here, the typographic hierarchy emphasizes the articles' titles and uses the page numbers as easy-to-find anchors.*

THE BELIEVER Magazine, front and back covers, 2009. Design: Dave Eggers. Illustrations: Charles Burns. *The busy but readable covers of this literary magazine use slab serif text in multiple sizes and weights to advertise the content found inside. The line illustrations integrate comfortably with the text. A full table of contents appears on the back cover, providing readers with an easy-to-use interface. Influenced by nineteenth-century almanacs, the design of The Believer uses borders and frames to draw attention to the content and create a memorable visual identity.*

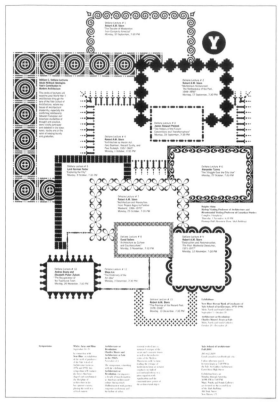

Michael Bierut, Kerrie Powell, Sunnie Guglielmo

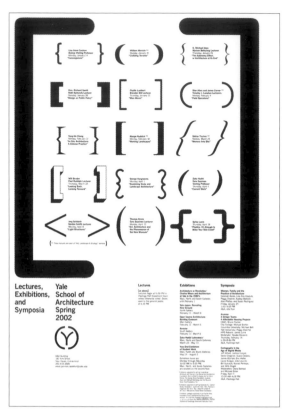

Michael Bierut, Justin Weyers

Michael Bierut

YALE SCHOOL OF ARCHITECTURE Posters, 2003–2006.
Designers: Michael Bierut and team/Pentagram. *Produced
over a series of years for a single client, these posters apply diverse
typographic treatments and hierarchies to similar bodies of content.
The black-and-white palette creates consistency over time.*

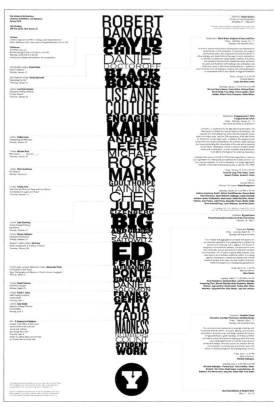

Michael Bierut, Genevieve Panuska

Michael Bierut, Jacqueline Kim

Michael Bierut, Andrew Mapes

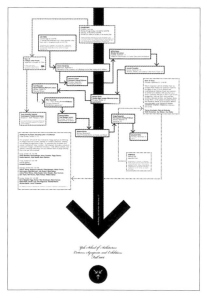

Michael Bierut, Michelle Leong, Sasha Fernando

In the real world of graphic design, managing large quantities of text is a routine challenge. Designers use the principles of hierarchy, alignment, and page layout to make content easy to scan and enjoyable to read. You can try this exercise with any long list of entries: calendar events, dictionary definitions, pithy quotes, classified ads, or a page from a college course catalog. Numbering the elements in the list gives you a graphic element to manipulate. Design a poster that presents the content in a visually interesting way. Work with style sheets to test different type treatments quickly and consistently.

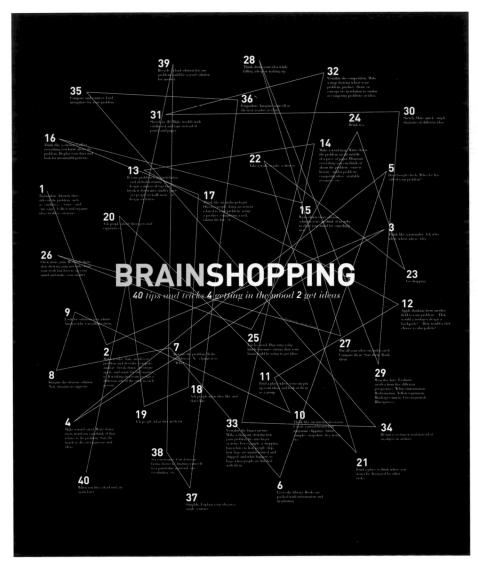

Sabrina Kogan

*Examples of student work from
Maryland Institute College of Art.*

Becky Slogeris

Andy Mangold

HISTORIA NATURALIS
Book, 1472. Printed by
Nicolas Jenson, Venice
Collection of the Walters Art
Museum, Baltimore. *This book
features an elegant, unbroken
text block set in one of the
earliest roman typefaces. The
page has no line breaks or
indents.*

Plauti fabulæ funt indicio. Sãguine canino contra toxica nihil præftantius putatur. Vomitiones quoɋ hoc animal mõftraffe uidetur. Et alios ufus ex eo mire laudatos referemus fuis locis. Nunc ad ftatutũ ordinem pergemus. Aduerfus ferpentiũ ictus efficacia habentur fimum pecudis recens in uino decoctum illitumɋ. Mures diffecti et impofiti quoɋ natura non eft fpernenda præcipue in afcenfu fyderum ut diximus: cum lumine lunæ fibrarum numero crefcente atɋ decrefcente. Tradũt magi iocinere muris dato porcis in fico fequi dantem id animal. In homine quoɋ fimiliter ualere. fed refolui cyatho olei poto. Muftelarũ duo genera. Alterũ filueftre. Diftãt magnitudine. Græci uocant ictides. Harũ fel cõtra afpidas dicitur efficax:cætero uenenũ. Hæc autẽ quæ in domibus noftris obertat:et catulos fuos (ut auctor eft Cicero) quotidie trãfferr:mutatɋ fedem ferpẽtes profequitur. Ex ea inueterata fale denarii põdus in cyathis tribus datur percuffis:aut uentriculus coriandro fartus inueteratufɋ et in uino potus. Et catulus muftelæ etiã efficacius. Quædam pudenda dictu tãta auctorum affeueratione commendantur:ut præterire fas non fit. Siquidem illa concordia rerum aut repugnantia medicinæ gignuntur. Veluti cimicum animalis fetidiffimi:in dictu quoɋ:faftidiẽdi natura contra ferpentium morfus et præcipue afpidum ualere dicitur. Item contra uenena omnia. Argumento ɋ dicũt gallinas quo die id ederint nõ fterfici ab afpide. Carnes quoɋ earũ percuffis plurimũ prodeffe. Ex iis quæ tradunt humaniffimum illitu morfibus cum fanguine teftudinis. Item fuffitu eorũ abigere fanguifugas adhærentes:hauftatɋ ab animalibus reftinguere in potu datos. Quãɋ et oculos quidam iis inungunt tritis cum fale et lacte mulierum. Aurefɋ cum melle et rofaceo ammixtis. Eos qui agreftes fint:et in malua nafcantur crematos cinere p̄ mixto rofaceo infundunt auribus. Cætera quæ de iis tradunt:uomicæ et quartanarũ remedia:alioriũɋ morborũ quãɋ ouo aut cæra aut faba inclufos cenfeant deuorãdos falfa nec referenda arbitror. Lethargi tamen medicinæ cum argumento adhibenti quoniam uincatur afpidum fomnifica uis feptenos ĩ cyatho aquæ dantes puerilibus annis quaternos. Et ftranguriæ fiftulæɋ impofuere:adeo nihil illa rerum omnium parens fine ingentibus caufis genuit. Quin et adalligatos leuo brachio binos lana fubrepta paftonbus refiftere nocturnis febnbus prodiderunt:diurnis in rofeo panno. Rurfus iis aduerfatur fcolopendra fuffituɋ necat. Afpides percuffos torpore & fom- no necant:omnium ferpentium minime fanabiles. Sed et uenenum earum fi fãguis attingit:aut recens uulnus ftatim iterimit. Inueteratũ ulcus tardius. De cætero potu quantalibet copia:non nocet. Non enim eft rabifica uis:itaɋ occifa morfu earum animalia cibis innoxia funt. Contarei in proferendo ex iis remedia:nifi. M. Varronẽ fcirem.lxxxiii.uitæ anno prodidiffe afpidũ ictus efficaciffime curari haufta a puffis ipforum urina. Bafilifci:quem etiam ferpentes ipfi fugiunt alios olfactu necantem: qui hominem uel fi afpiciat tantum dicitur interimere:fanguinem magi miris laudibus celebrant coeuntem picis modo et colore dilutum cinnabari clariorem fieri. Tribuunt et fucceffus petitionum a poteftatibus:& a diis etiam precum:morborum remedia beneficiorum munere. Quidã id Saturni fanguinem appellant. Draco nõ habet uenena. Caput eius limini ianuarum fubditum propitiatis oratione diis fortunatam domum facere promittitur. Oculis eius fueteratis et cum melle tritis functos non paueſcere ad nocturnas imagines etiam pauidos cordis. Pingue in pelle dorcadũ neruis ceruinis adalligatum in lacerto conferre iudiciorum uictoriam. Primũ fpõdy- lum aditus poteftatum mulcere. Dentes eius illigatos pellibus caprearum ceruinis neruis:mites præftare dominos:poteftatefɋ exorabiles. Sed fuper omnia eft cõpofi- tio:qua inuictos faciunt magorum mendacia. Cauda draconis et capite uillis leonis e fronte et medulla eiufdem equi uictoris fpuma canis unguibus adalligatis ceruino corio:neruifɋ cerui alternatis et dorcadis. Quæ arguiffe non minus refertɋ contra ferpentes remedia demonftraffe:quoniam hæc morborum beneficia funt. Draconũ

GRID

A GRID BREAKS SPACE OR TIME INTO REGULAR UNITS. A grid can be simple or complex, specific or generic, tightly defined or loosely interpreted. Typographic grids are all about control. They establish a system for arranging content within the space of a page, screen, or the built environment. Designed in response to the internal pressures of content (text, image, data) and the outer edge or frame (page, screen, window), an effective grid is not a rigid formula but a flexible and resilient structure, a skeleton that moves in concert with the muscular mass of information.

Grids belong to the technological framework of typography, from the concrete modularity of letterpress to the rulers, guides, and coordinate systems employed in graphics applications. Although software generates illusions of smooth curves and continuous tones, every digital image or mark is constructed—ultimately—from a grid of neatly bounded blocks. The ubiquitous language of the GUI (graphical user interface) creates a gridded space in which windows overlay windows in a haphazard way.

In addition to their place in the background of design production, grids have become explicit theoretical tools. Avant-garde designers in the 1910s and 1920s exposed the mechanical grid of letterpress, bringing it to the polemical surface of the page. In Switzerland after World War II, graphic designers built a total design methodology around the typographic grid, hoping to construct with it a new and rational social order.

The grid has evolved across centuries of typographic development. For graphic designers, grids are carefully honed intellectual devices, infused with ideology and ambition, and they are the inescapable mesh that filters, at some level of resolution, nearly every system of writing and reproduction.

LATIN BIBLE Book page, 1497. Printed by Anton Koberger. *A two-column grid engulfs a second set of columns. Each page is a dense mass incised with narrow gutters and open spaces where illuminated capitals would have been added by hand. The layout changes from page to page.*

GRID AS FRAME

Alphabetic writing, like most writing systems, is organized into columns and rows of characters. Whereas handwriting flows into connected lines, the mechanics of metal type impose a stricter order. Each letter occupies its own block, and the letters congregate in orderly rectangles. Stored in gridded cases, the characters become an archive of elements, a matrix of existing forms from which each page is composed.

Until the twentieth century, grids served as frames for fields of text. The margins of a classical book page create a pristine barrier around a flush, solid block of text. A page dominated by a solitary field of type remains today's most common book format, although that perfect rectangle is now broken with indents and line breaks, and the margins are peppered with page numbers and running heads (text indicating the book or chapter title).

In addition to the classical norm of the single-column page, various alternative layouts existed during the first centuries of printing, from the two-column grid of Gutenberg's Bible to more elaborate layouts derived from the medieval scribal tradition, where passages of scripture are surrounded by scholarly commentary. Polyglot (multilingual) books display a text in several languages simultaneously, demanding complex divisions of the surface.

Such formats permit multiple streams of text to coexist while defending the sovereignty of the page-as-frame. The philosopher Jacques Derrida has described the frame in Western art as a form that seems to be separate from the work, yet is necessary for marking its difference from everyday life. A frame or pedestal elevates the work, removing it from the realm of the ordinary. The work thus depends on the frame for its status and visibility.

Typography is, by and large, an art of framing, a form designed to melt away as it yields itself to content. Designers focus much of their energy on margins, edges, and empty spaces, elements that oscillate between present and absent, visible and invisible. With print's ascent, margins became the user interface of the book, providing space for page numbers, running heads, commentary, notes, and ornaments.

The frame... disappears, buries itself, effaces itself, melts away at the moment it deploys its greatest energy. The frame is in no way a background... but neither is its thickness as margin a figure. Or at least it is a figure that comes away of its own accord. —JACQUES DERRIDA, 1987

CAPVT PRIMVM.

N principio creauit Deus cœlum & terrá. Terra autem erat inanis & vacua: & tenebræ erant super facie abyssi: & spiritus Dei ferebatur super aquas. Dixitq; Deus, Fiat lux. & facta est lux. Et vidit Deus lucem quòd esset bona: & diuisit lucem à tenebris. Appellauitq; lucem diem;& tenebras nocte. Factumq; est vespere & mane dies vnus. Dixit quoque Deus, Fiat firmamentu in medio aquarum; & diuidat aquas ab aquis. Et fecit Deus firmamentum, diuisitq; aquas quæ erant sub firmamento, ab his quæ erant super firmamentu. Et factum est ita. Vocauitq; Deus firmamentu,cælum: & factum est vespere, & mane dies secundus.

Dixit verò Deus, Congregentur aquæ quæ sub cœlo sunt, in locum vnum: & appareat arida.Et factum est ita. Et vocauit Deus aridá, terram: congregationesq; aquarum appellauit maria. Et vidit Deus quòd esset bonum. Et ait, Germinet terra herbá virentem & facientem semen; & lignum pomiferu faciens fructu iuxta genus suum, cuius semen in semetipso sit super terram.Et factu est ita. Et protulit terra herbam virente, & faciente semen iuxta genus suu;lignumq; faciens fructu, & habens vnum quodq; sementem secundu speciem suam. Et vidit Deus quòd esset bonum. Et factum est vespere & mane dies tertius. Dixit aute Deus, Fiant luminaria in firmamento cæli; & diuidant diem ac nocte; & sint in signa & tepora & dies & annos; Vt luceát in firmaméto cæli, & illuminent terrá.Et factum est ita. Fecitq; Deus duo luminaria magna: luminare maius, vt præesset diei; & luminare minus, vt præsset nocti: & stellas. Et posuit eas Deus in firmaméto cæli, vt lucerét super terrá: Et præessent diei ac nocti;& diuiderent lucem ac tenebras. Et vidit Deus quòd esset bonu. Et factum est vespere, & mane dies quartus. Dixit etiam Deus,Producantaquæ reptile animæ viuentis, & volatile super terram sub firmamento cæli.

תרגום אונקלוס

בקדמין

BIBLIA POLYGLOTTA Book spread, 1568. Printed by Christopher Plantin, Antwerp. *Plantin's polyglot Bible is zoned for five different translations (Hebrew, Greek, Aramaic, Syriac, and Latin). Each zone is proportioned to accommodate the typographic texture of a particular script. The page is a dense rectangle cut into parts. The pieces— though highly individualized— fit together into a unified whole. Reproduced from* William Dana Orcutt, In Quest of the Perfect Book *(New York: Little, Brown and Co., 1926).*

248 SUPPLEMENT DE L'ANT. EXPLIQ. Liv. VI.

CHAPITRE SECOND.

I. La colonne de Pompée. II. On ne convient pas sur ses mesures. III. Colonne d'Alexandre Severe.

I. LA fameuse colonne de Pompée est auprès d'Alexandrie : on ne sait pour quelle raison elle porte le nom de Pompée ; je croirois volontiers que c'est par quelque erreur populaire. Plusieurs voiageurs en ont parlé, tous conviennent qu'elle est d'une grandeur énorme. Deux des plus modernes en ont donné le dessein & les mesures ; mais ils different considerablement entre eux sur la hauteur du piedestal, de la colonne & du chapiteau : cependant tous deux disent qu'ils l'ont mesurée.

,, Pour ce qui est de la colonne, dit l'un, (c'est Corneille Brun p. 241.)
,, elle est sur un piedestal quarré, haut de sept ou huit pieds & large de qua-
,, torze à chacune de ses faces. Ce piedestal est posé sur une base quarrée,
,, haute d'environ un demi pied, & large de vingt, faite de plusieurs pierres
,, maçonnées ensemble. Le corps de la colonne même n'est que d'une seule
,, pierre, que quelques-uns croient être de granit ; d'autres disent que c'est
,, une espece de pâte ou de ciment, qui avec le tems a pris la forme de pierre.
,, Pour moi je crois que c'est une vraie pierre de taille, du moins autant que
,, j'ai pu le reconnoître par l'épreuve que j'en ai faite. Et si cela est vrai, com-
,, me personne presque n'en doute, il y a sujet de s'étonner comment on a
,, pu dresser une pierre de cette grandeur : car après l'avoir mesurée, j'ai trou-
,, vé qu'elle a quatre-vingt-dix pieds de haut, & que sa grosseur est telle, que
,, six hommes peuvent à peine l'embrasser ; ce qui revient, selon la mesure
,, que j'en ai prise, à trente-huit pieds. Au haut il y a un beau chapiteau pro-
,, portionné à la grosseur de la colonne, mais fait d'une piece separée.
L'autre, qui est M. Paul Lucas, en parle en cette maniere : ,, Un de mes
,, premiers soins fut d'aller examiner la colonne de Pompée, qui est près d'A-
,, lexandrie du côté du couchant, & je crois qu'il seroit difficile de rien ajou-

CAPUT SECUNDUM.

I. Columna Pompeii. II. De ejus mensuris non convenit inter eos qui istæc loca adierunt. III. Columna Alexandri Severi.

I. CEleberrima illa Pompeii columna prope Alexandriam erigitur. Cur Pompeii columna vocetur, ignoratur. Libenter crederem hujusmodi denominationem ex populari errore manavisse. Ex peregrinantibus omnes enormis magnitudinis esse narrant. Duo recentiores & figuram & mensuras dederunt, at inter illos non convenit de stylobatæ, columnæ & capitelli magnitudine. Attamen ambo dicunt se mensuras excepisse.

,, Quantum ad columnam, inquit Cornelius
,, Brunius p. 241. ea imposita est quadrato styloba-
,, tæ cujus altitudo est septem octove pedum, la-
,, tera vero singulis in faciebus sunt quatuordecim
,, pedum. Stylobates autem ille quadratæ basi im-

,, ponitur, altitudine dimidii pedis, ex lapidibus
,, plurimis structa basis est, longitudinis circum-
,, quaque viginti pedes habens. Columna ex uno
,, lapide est, plurimi putant ex marmore granico
,, esse, alii vero quasi cæmentum & compactam
,, materiam esse, quæ procedente tempore, formam
,, lapidis sumserit. Puto ego esse lapidem quantum
,, saltem experiri licuit. Quod si ita sit ; id autem
,, nemo hodie in dubium vocat ; plane mirum
,, quo pacto tantum lapidem erigere potuerint.
,, Nam cum mensuram duxissem, nonaginta pedes
,, altitudinis habere comperi, tantaque ejus est spis-
,, situdo, ut sex viri simul vix illam amplecti pos-
,, sint, id quod ad mensuram a me sumtam redu-
,, citur, circuitus enim ejus est triginta & octo
,, pedum. In culmine capitellum est ex uno lapide
,, secundum columnæ proportionem.
Alius, nempe Paulus Lucas, columnam sic des-
cribit. ,, Ubi primum potui columnam Pompeii
,, adii, quæ prope Alexandriam est versus oc-
,, cidentem. Difficile autem esset ejus mensuras

SUPPLEMENT AU LIVRE DE L'ANTIQUITÈ (LEFT) Book page, Paris, 1724. *The two-column grid devised for this bilingual book provides a large, single-column block for the French text, with two columns below for the Latin. The quotation marks serve as a frame along the left edge of the quoted passage.*

THE ILLUSTRATED LONDON NEWS (RIGHT) Newspaper page, 1861. *Early newspaper advertisements were designed by the paper's printer, not supplied by the client or an advertising agency. This dense field of entries occupies a four-column grid, with ruled lines to create order.*

THE IMPERIAL FAMILY BIBLE (NEXT SPREAD) Book, 1854. *In this unusual book structure, the notes appear in the center of the page rather than along the bottom or the edges. The margin has moved from outside to inside.*

mount Perazim,[1] he shall be wroth as *in* 'the valley of Gibeon, that he may do his work, 'his strange work; and bring to pass his act, his strange act.

22 Now therefore 'be ye not mockers, 'lest your bands be made strong: for I have heard from the LORD GOD of hosts, "a consumption, even determined upon the whole earth.

23 ¶ Give 'ye ear, and hear my voice; hearken, and hear my speech.

24 Doth the ploughman plough all day to sow? doth he open and "break the clods of his ground?

25 When he hath made plain the face thereof, doth he not cast abroad the fitches,[2] and scatter the cummin, and cast in[3] the principal wheat, and the appointed barley, and the rye,[4] in their place?[5]

26 For[6] 'his God doth instruct him to discretion, *and* doth teach him.

27 For the fitches are not 'thrashed[7] with a thrashing-instrument, neither is a cart-wheel turned about upon the cummin; but 'the fitches are beaten out with a staff, and the cummin with a rod.

28 'Bread-*corn* is bruised;[8] because he will not ever be thrashing it, nor break *it with* 'the wheel of his cart, nor bruise it *with* his horsemen.

29 This also 'cometh forth from the LORD of hosts, *which* is wonderful in counsel, *and* excellent in working.

CHAPTER XXIX.

God's heavy judgments upon Jerusalem, 1–6. The unsatiableness of her enemies, 7, 8. The senselessness, 9–12, and deep hypocrisy of the Jews, 13–17. A promise of sanctification to the godly, 18–24.

WOE[9] to Ariel, to Ariel, the[10] city *where* David dwelt! 'add ye year to year; let them kill[11] sacrifices.

2 Yet 'I will distress Ariel, and there shall be heaviness and sorrow: and' it shall be unto me as Ariel.[12]

3 And I will 'camp against thee round about, and will lay siege against thee with a mount, and I will raise forts against thee.

4 And 'thou shalt be brought down, *and* shalt speak out of the ground, and thy speech shall be low out of the dust, and thy voice shall be, as
(748)

of one that hath a familiar spirit, of the ground, and thy speech sh whisper[1] out of the dust.[2]

5 Moreover, 'the multitude of strangers shall be like small dust, a the multitude of the terrible ones *s* be 'as chaff that passeth away; it shall be 'at an instant suddenly

6 Thou shalt be 'visited of LORD of hosts with thunder, and w earthquake, and great noise, w storm and tempest, and the flame devouring fire.

7 And 'the multitude of all nations that fight against Ariel, ev all that fight against her and l munition, and 'that distress her, sh be "as a dream of a night-vision.

8 It shall even be[3] "as when an h gry *man* dreameth, and, behold, eateth; but he awaketh, and his so is empty: or as when a thirsty *man* dreameth, and, behold, he drinket but he awaketh, and, 'behold, *he* faint, and his soul hath appetite: shall the multitude of all the natio be that fight against mount Zion.

9 ¶ Stay yourselves, 'and wonde cry[4] ye out, and cry: 'they a drunken,[5] but not with wine; the stagger, but not with strong drink

10 For 'the LORD hath poured o upon you the spirit of deep sleep, a 'hath closed your eyes: the prophe and your rulers,[6] 'the seers, hath covered.

11 And the vision of all[7] is becom unto you as the words of a 'boo 'that is sealed, which *men* deliver one that is learned, saying, Read I pray thee: and he saith, 'I canno for it *is* sealed.

12 And the book[9] is delivered him that is not learned, saying, Rea this, I pray thee: and he saith, "I a not learned.

13 ¶ Wherefore the LORD[10] said, 'Fo asmuch as this people draw near *m* with their mouth, and with their lip do honour me, but have removed the heart far from me, and 'their fear[11] ward me is taught by the precept o men:

14 Therefore, behold, 'I will pre ceed[9] to do a marvellous work amon

The people threatened for   ISAIAH, XXX.   *their confidence in Egypt.*

this people, *even* a marvellous work and a wonder; "for the wisdom of their wise *men* shall perish, and the understanding of their prudent *men* shall be hid.

15 Woe unto them that *b*seek deep to hide their counsel from the LORD, and*c* their works are in the dark, and they say, *d*Who seeth us? and who knoweth us?

16 Surely*1* *c*your turning of things upside down shall be esteemed *f*as the potter's clay: for shall the work say of him that made it, He made me not? *g*or shall the thing framed say of him that framed it, He had no understanding?

17 *¶ Is* it not *h*yet a very little while and *i*Lebanon* shall be turned into a fruitful field, and *k*the fruitful field shall be esteemed as a forest?

18 And in that day shall *l*the deaf hear the words of the book, and the eyes of the blind shall see out of obscurity, and out of darkness.

19 The *m*meek also shall increase*3* *their* joy in the LORD, and *n*the poor among men shall *o*rejoice in the Holy One of Israel.

20 For *p*the terrible one is brought to nought, and *q*the scorner is consumed, *and* all that watch*4* for iniquity are cut off:

21 That *r*make a man* an offender for a word, *s*and lay a snare for him that reproveth in the gate, *u*and turn aside the just for a thing of nought.

22 Therefore thus saith the LORD, who*5* redeemed Abraham, concerning the house of Jacob,*6* *w*Jacob shall not now be ashamed, neither shall his face now wax pale.

23 But when he seeth his children, the*x* work of mine hands, in the midst of him, they shall *y*sanctify my name, and sanctify the Holy One of Jacob, and shall *z*fear the God of Israel.

24 They *a*also that erred in spirit shall come*b* to understanding, and they that murmured shall learn doctrine.

CHAPTER XXX.

The prophet threateneth the people for their confidence in Egypt, 1—7, and contempt of God's word, 8—17. God's mercies toward his church, 18—26. God's wrath, and the people's joy in the destruction of Assyria, 27—33.

WOE to *a*the rebellious children, saith the LORD, *b*that take coun-

sel, but not of me; and that *c1*cover with a covering, but not of my Spirit, that they may *d*add sin to sin:

2 That *e*walk to go down into Egypt, *f*and have not asked at my mouth; to strengthen themselves in the strength of Pharaoh, and to trust in *g*the shadow of Egypt!

3 Therefore shall *h*the strength of Pharaoh be your shame, and the trust in the shadow of Egypt *i*your confusion.

4 For *k*his princes were at *l*Zoan, and his ambassadors came to *m*Hanes.

5 They were all *n*ashamed of a people *that* could not profit them, nor be an help nor profit, but a shame, and also a reproach.

6 The *o*burden of the *p*beasts of the south:*2* *q*into the land of trouble and anguish, from whence *come* the young and old lion, *r*the viper and fiery flying serpent, they will carry their *r*riches upon the shoulders of young asses, and their treasures upon the bunches of camels, to a people *that* shall not profit *them*.

7 For *t*the Egyptians shall help in vain, and to no purpose: therefore have I cried concerning*3* this, *u*Their strength*4* *is* to sit still.

8 ¶ Now go, *v*write it before them in a table,*5* and note it in a book, that it may be for the*6* time to come for ever and ever;

9 That *w*this *is* a rebellious people, *x*lying children, children *that* *y*will not hear the law of the LORD:

10 Which *z*say to the seers, See not; and to the prophets, Prophesy not unto us right things, *a*speak unto us smooth things, prophesy *7*deceits:

11 Get *b*you out of the way, turn aside out of the path, *c*cause the Holy One of Israel to cease from before us.

12 Wherefore thus saith the Holy One of Israel,*8* *d*Because ye despise this word, *e*and trust in *9*oppression and perverseness, and stay thereon:

13 Therefore this iniquity shall be to you *f*as a breach ready to fall, swelling out*10* in a high wall, whose breaking *g*cometh suddenly at an instant.

14 And *h*he shall break it as the

(749)

LES MOTS EN
LIBERTÉ FUTURISTES:
LETTRE D'UNE JOLIE FEMME
À UN MONSIEUR PASSÉISTE
Poem, 1912. Author: F. T.
Marinetti. *In this Futurist
poem, Marinetti attacked the
conventions of poetry and the
restrictions imposed by the
mechanical grid of letterpress.
The rectilinear pressures of
the grid are nonetheless evident
in the composed work.*

MERZ-MATINÉEN Poster,
1923. Designer: El Lissitzky.
*The Russian Constructivist
artist and designer traveled
extensively in Europe in the
1920s, where he collaborated
with other members of the
international avantgarde,
including the Dadaist Kurt
Schwitters. This precisely
assembled poster for a Dada
event is organized and activated
by the rectilinear grid of
letterpress.*

FORTOLIET Postcard, 1925.
Designer: Piet Zwart.
Collection of Elaine
Lustig Cohen. *The Dutch
graphic designer Piet Zwart was
influenced by the De Stijl
movement as well as
Constructivism. In the visual
identity he created for Fortoliet,
a flooring company, Zwart
built monumental letters out of
typographic rules.*

DIVIDING SPACE

In the nineteenth century, the multi-columned, multimedia pages of news-papers and magazines challenged the supremacy of the book and its insular edge, making way for new typologies of the grid. By questioning the protective function of the frame, modern artists and designers unleashed the grid as a flexible, critical, and systematic tool. Avant-garde artists and poets attacked the barriers between art and everyday life, creating new objects and practices that merged with urban experience.

Leading the assault against print's traditional syntax was F. T. Marinetti, who established the Futurist movement in 1909. Marinetti devised poems that combined different styles and sizes of type and allowed lines of text to span multiple rows. Marinetti's ingenius manipulations of the printing process work against—but inside—the constraints of letterpress, exposing the technological grid even while trying to overturn it. Dada artists and poets performed similar typographic experiments, using letterpress printing as well as collage, montage, and various forms of photomechanical reproduction.

Constructivism, which originated in the Soviet Union at the end of the 1910s, built on Futurist and Dada typography, bringing a more rational approach to the attack on typographic tradition. El Lissitzky employed the elements of the print shop to emphasize the mechanics of letterpress, using printer's rules to make the technological matrix actively and physically present. Constructivism used rules to divide space, throwing its symmetry into a new kind of balance. The page was no longer a fixed, hierarchical window through which content might be viewed, but an expanse that could be mapped and articulated, a space extending beyond the edge.

For Dutch artists and designers, the grid was a gateway to the infinite. The paintings of Piet Mondrian, their abstract surfaces crossed by vertical and horizontal lines, suggest the expansion of the grid beyond the limits of the canvas. Theo van Doesburg, Piet Zwart, and other members of the Dutch De Stijl group applied this idea to design and typography. Converting the curves and angles of the alphabet into perpendicular systems, they forced the letter through the mesh of the grid. Like the Constructivists, they used vertical and horizontal bars to structure the surface of the page.

Typography is mostly an act of dividing a limited surface. —WILLI BAUMEISTER, 1923

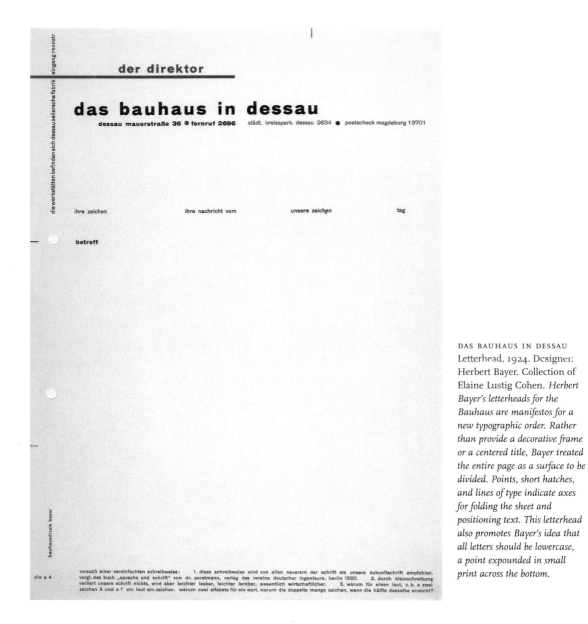

DAS BAUHAUS IN DESSAU
Letterhead, 1924. Designer:
Herbert Bayer. Collection of
Elaine Lustig Cohen. *Herbert
Bayer's letterheads for the
Bauhaus are manifestos for a
new typographic order. Rather
than provide a decorative frame
or a centered title, Bayer treated
the entire page as a surface to be
divided. Points, short hatches,
and lines of type indicate axes
for folding the sheet and
positioning text. This letterhead
also promotes Bayer's idea that
all letters should be lowercase,
a point expounded in small
print across the bottom.*

**The new typography not only contests the classical "framework"
but also the whole principle of symmetry. —PAUL RENNER, 1931**

Jan Tschichold's book *The New Typography*, published in Germany in 1928, took ideas from Futurism, Constructivism, and De Stijl and conveyed them as practical advice for commercial printers and designers. Functionally zoned letterheads using standard paper sizes were central to Tschichold's practical application of modernism. Whereas Futurism and Dada had aggressively attacked convention, Tschichold advocated design as a means of discipline and order, and he began to theorize the grid as a modular system based on standard measures.

By describing the expansion of space in all directions, the modern grid slipped past the classical frame of the page. Similarly, modern architecture had displaced the centered facades of classical building with broken planes, modular elements, and continuous ribbons of windows. The protective frame became a continuous field.

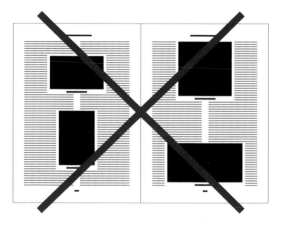

THE NEW TYPOGRAPHY
Diagram, 1928
(redrawn). Designer and
author: Jan Tschichold

Tschichold's diagram of good and bad magazine design advocates staggering images in relation to content instead of forcing text to wrap around blocks moored at the center of the page. Explaining this experiment, Tschichold wrote that his redesigned pages would be even more effective if the photographic halftones (called "blocks") were produced in fixed rather than arbitrary sizes.

I have intentionally shown blocks of different and "accidental" widths, since this is what usually has to be contended with (although in the future, with standard block-sizes, it will happen less often).
—JAN TSCHICHOLD, 1928

ZAHN-NOPPER Store identity, 1961–63. Designer: Anton Stankowski. *This identity system demonstrates a programmatic approach to design, using a limited set of elements to construct diverse yet genetically linked solutions. The system is governed by flexible rules for construction rather than a fixed logotype.*

GRID AS PROGRAM

Classics of Swiss design theory include Josef Müller-Brockmann, *Grid Systems in Graphic Design* (Switzerland: Ram Publications, 1996; first published in 1961) and *The Graphic Artist and His Design Problems* (Switzerland: Arthur Niggli Ltd., 1961); and Karl Gerstner, *Designing Programmes* (Switzerland: Arthur Niggli, 1964). See also Emil Ruder, *Typography* (New York: Hastings House, 1981; first published in 1967).

During the post–World War II period, graphic designers in Switzerland honed ideas from the New Typography into a total design methodology. It was at this time that the term *grid* (*Raster*) became commonly applied to page layout. Max Bill, Karl Gerstner, Josef Müller-Brockmann, Emil Ruder, and others were practitioners and theorists of a new rationalism that aimed to catalyze an honest and democratic society. Rejecting the artistic clichés of self expression and raw intuition, they aspired to what Ruder called "a cool and fascinating beauty."

Gerstner's book *Designing Programmes* (1964) is a manifesto for systems-oriented design. Gerstner defined a design "programme" as a set of rules for constructing a range of visual solutions. Connecting his methodology with the new field of computer programming, Gerstner presented examples of computer-generated patterns that were made by mathematically describing visual elements and combining them according to simple rules.

Expanding on the pioneering ideas of Bayer, Tschichold, Renner, and other designers of the avant garde, the Swiss rationalists rejected the centuries-old model of the page-as-frame in favor of a continuous architectural space. Whereas a traditional book would have placed captions, commentary, and folios within a protective margin, the rationalist grid cut the page into multiple columns, each bearing equal weight within the whole, suggesting an indefinite progression outward. Pictures were cropped to fit the modules of the grid, yielding shapes of unusual proportion. Constructing ever more elaborate grids, the Swiss designers used the confines of a repeated structure to generate variation and surprise. Such grids could be activated in numerous ways within a single publication, always referring back to the root structure.

This approach, which quickly became known as "Swiss design," found adherents (and detractors) around the world. Many American designers dismissed Swiss rationalism as irrelevant to a society driven by pop culture and hungry for rapidly transforming styles. Programmatic thinking is now being revived, however, as designers today confront large-scale information projects. The need is greater than ever for flexible "programs" designed to accommodate dynamic bodies of content.

**The typographic grid is a proportional regulator for composition, tables, pictures, etc….
The difficulty is: to find the balance, the maximum of conformity to a rule with the maximum
of freedom. Or: the maximum of constants with the greatest possible variability."
—KARL GERSTNER, 1961**

14. Eingangshalle

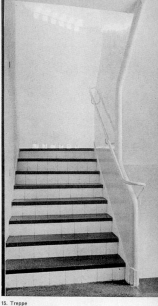

15. Treppe

2 Mehrfamilienhäuser im Doldertal Zürich

Räumliche Organisation
Situation: Die beiden Mehrfamilienhäuser liegen im Villenviertel, auf halber Höhe des westwärts abfallenden „Zürichberg" [4]. Längs dem Grundstück verläuft auf der Nordwestseite eine öffentliche Parkanlage mit einem dichten Baumbestand. Die Zufahrtsstrasse genannt „Doldertal" hat ein Gefälle von 10% und ist nicht durchgehend. Die Schrägstellung der Blöcke zur Baulinie ergibt eine verbesserte Südlage für die Wohnräume, eine Abdrehung der Schlafräume von der Strasse und eine lockere Gesamtanlage, ohne gegenüberliegende Schmalseiten. [5]   (Siehe auch baugesetzliche Sonderheiten.)
Raumprogramm: Es ist versucht worden, die Vorzüge des Einfamilienhauses soweit als möglich auf die Etagenwohnung zu übertragen (freies, schallsicheres Wohnen, Einbeziehung der Landschaft, grosse Wohnterrassen, weitgehende innere Ausstattung). Im Untergeschoss: Gedeckter Vorplatz mit zwei Garagen, Eingangshalle mit Treppenaufgang, Abstellräume, Vorratskeller, Waschküche und Trockenraum, die beiden letztern nur im untern Haus. Unter der Eingangshalle mit besonderem Eingang [9] (7) liegen Heizung und Kohlenraum. Im Parterre: eine Vierzimmerwohnung mit Mädchenzimmer und ein Einzimmer-Appartment mit direktem Eingang vom Garten. Im Obergeschoss: eine 5/6-Zimmerwohnung mit Mädchenzimmer. Zu dieser

Wohnung gehört noch ein auf Höhe Dachgeschoss liegendes Sonnenbad [12] (16), durch eine Eisentreppe von der Terrasse erreichbar. In beiden Wohnungen liegen Treppe und Küche ausserhalb der eigentlichen Wohnfläche (Schallisolation); dennoch hat die Küche eine betriebstechnisch zentrale Lage (Verbindung mit der Terrasse, je eine Durchreiche nach Essplatz und Treppenhaus). Im Dachgeschoss ein grosses und ein kleines Atelier, Abstellräume im Treppenbau.

Technische Durchbildung
(vgl. Technische Details)
Konstruktionsprinzip: Eisenskelett, Eisenbeton-Zwischendecken, Fassadenausmauerung mit gebrannten Hohlsteinen, hintermauert mit Gipsdielen. Die Fassaden sind konstruktiv von den Zwischendecken getrennt. Das zurückgesetzte Dachgeschoss besteht aus Holz mit einer äussern Eternitverkleidung. Zur Fertigstellung des Äussern sind ausschließlich Materialien mit unterhaltsloser Oberfläche verwendet worden: Edelputz (weisser Zement, Natursteinpartikeln, ohne Farbbeigabe); Eternit für Rolladenkasten, Brüstungen, Sonnen-Storen-Vordach und Dachgeschoßaufbau; lackiertes Holz für Rolladen und Garagentore; Kupfer für sämtliche Spenglerarbeiten; feuerverzinktes Eisen für Fensterbleche, Geländer. Gestrichen sind lediglich die Fenster und gewisse Metallteile aus architektonischen Gründen.
Fensterflächen: Horizontal-Schiebefenster in Föhrenholz in den Woh-

nungen. Grösse des Normalfensters 310 × 120 cm, zusammengeba[...] mit dem Rolladenkasten; fester Teil einwärts klappbar zum Reinige[...] Die Südfenster des Wohnraumes sind mit der Brüstung zusamme[...] gebaut (vgl. [21], [22], [23]). Die Küchenfenster sind doppelt, a[...] übrigen Fenster am Bau sind einfach verglast. Die Ateliers ha[...] durchgehende 45 cm hohe Oberlichter unter der Decke mit Lüftung[...] klappen, sowie gewisse fest verglaste Fenster mit normaler Brüstu[...] Verglasung: Wohnungsfenster Spiegelglas 6/7 mm, Atelier-Ob[...] lichter Rohglas, Treppenhausfenster Drahtglas. Sonnenschutz: [...] die Wohnzimmerfenster vor die Fassade gehängte Sonnenstor[...] [21] (44), für die Schlafzimmer Roll-Jalousien. Heizung: Jedes Ha[...] hat seine eigene Warmwasserheizung für Kleinkaliberkoks, [...] gleichzeitig für die Warmwasserbereitung benützt wird. Pro Ha[...] ein Warmwasserboiler mit 1000 Liter Inhalt.
Wohnungsausstattung: Die beiden Häuser sind für anspruchsvo[...] Mieter, jedoch ohne Luxus ausgestattet. Die Zimmer sind de[...] entsprechend geräumig dimensioniert (Wohnraum 35,00 m², Terras[...] 20,00 m²). Die Skelettkonstruktion erlaubt jederzeit eine den Wü[...] schen der Mieter entsprechende Variabilität des Grundrisses.
Wohnraum befindet sich mit offener Kamin und ein breites Fenst[...] brett für Blumen. Eingebaute Schränke im Korridor, in den Zimme[...] kleiner Abstellraum. Fussböden: In den Wohnungen Holzmos[...] (Esche im Wohnraum, Eiche in den übrigen Räumen und im Korrido[...]

2 Mehrfamilienhäuser im Doldertal Zürich   52

16. Teilansicht von Südwest mit Eingang und Garagen

n den Küchen sind Steinzeugplatten, versuchsweise Linoleum; in den Bädern Terrazzo, schwarz, mit weissen Marmorkörnern. Die Treppentritte und Podeste bestehen ebenfalls aus Terrazzo (Tritte fertige Platten, Podeste im Bau gegossen und geschliffen). Die Stirnseiten der Tritte und die Sockel sind mit weissen, hartglasierten Platten belegt [14]. Die Böden der Ateliers sind mit hellgrauem Linoleum belegt. Wandbehandlung: Gipsverputz in sämtlichen Räumen, Kalkabrieb in Küchen, Bädern und Aborten. Die Wände der Zimmer sind mit Leimfarbe gestrichen, mit Ausnahme derjenigen in den Wohnräumen und Gängen (tapeziert mit Grundpapier und Leimfarbanstrich, oder Ölfarbanstrich auf Stoffbespannung). In den Ateliers Verkleidung der Wände in Holzkonstruktion mit Sperrplatten (gewachste finnische Birke).

Im Treppenhaus: Aussenwand stoffbespannt, mit Ölfarbe gestrichen, mittlere Brüstungswand gespachtelt und Hochglanz mit Ripolin gestrichen; der Handlauf in Eisen, im Feuer weiss emailliert. Fenstersimsen: Diese bestehen in allen Räumen der Wohnungen aus perforierten, 3 cm starken Schieferplatten. Ausstattung der Bäder und Küchen: Grösse des Bades in den Wohnungen 6 m² mit Badwanne, Bidet und zwei Lavabos, W.C. Der Spiegel über dem Lavabos ist gegen die festverglaste Fensterfläche gehängt (Licht auf das Gesicht). Die Küchen sind vollständig ausgestattet, je eine Durchreiche ins Treppenhaus und in den Wohn-Essraum, zweiteiliger Aufwaschtisch in Chrom-

nickel - Stahlblech, Kühlschrank, Arbeitsflächen in Ahornholz. Elektrische Beleuchtung: Diese ist in allen Wohn- und Schlafräumen, Gängen, Küchen, Ateliers eine indirekte.

Ökonomische Angaben
Die beiden Häuser sind Privatbesitz von Herrn Dr. S Giedion, Zentralsekretär der Internationalen Kongresse für Neues Bauen. Die Baukosten inkl. Architektenhonorar betragen: 43,5 Maurerstunden pro m³ umbauten Raumes bei total 1985 m³ pro Haus, offene Halle im Parterre zur Hälfte gerechnet. Die durchschnittlichen Baukosten für normale Wohnbauten in Zürich, ohne besonderen Ausbau, betragen 38 bis 40 Maurerstunden pro m³ umbauten Raumes. (1 Mstd.= Fr. 1.72 1935/36)

Ästhetischer Aufbau
Die Schrägstellung der Blöcke ergibt einerseits eine lockere Gesamtanlage und erhöht anderseits deren plastische Selbständigkeit. Der zweigeschossige Charakter der Häuser (Baubestimmung der betreffenden Zone) wird durch das Loslösen des Baukörpers vom Terrain und durch das Zurücksetzen des Dachgeschosses gewahrt. Dieser Eindruck wird verstärkt durch die vom Hauptbau abweichende Konstruktion des Dachgeschosses (Holz und Eternit). In der Südfassade ist durch Weglassen der gemauerten Brüstungen ein äusseres Zusam-

menfassen von Wohnraum und Wohnterrasse erreicht. In der räumlichen Gliederung treten vielfach schräg verlaufende Wände auf, wodurch eine gewisse Auflockerung der Rechtwinkligkeit erreicht wird. Die Eingangshalle ganz in Glas hat eine freie Form und lässt den Durchblick in den rückwärtsliegenden Park frei. Der Garten reicht über die weitergeführten Gartenplatten (Granit) bis zum Treppenaufgang. In den Wohnräumen und Ateliers reichen die Fenster bis zur Decke, in den Schlafräumen ist ein Sturz von 40 cm. In der Dimensionierung von Bauteilen und Ausstattungsdetails ist eine dem betreffenden Material entsprechende Sparsamkeit sowie eine organische und gepflegte Formgebung beobachtet worden. Materialbehandlung und Farbgebung: Aussen wirken die Baustoffe in ihrer natürlichen Struktur und Farbe: Edelputz (weisser Zement mit roten, schwarzen und glimmernden Steinsplittern), Eternit, lackiertes Holz, Eisenteile feuerverzinkt, mit Aluminiumfarbe gestrichen. Farbe an folgenden Stellen: Fensterrahmen dunkelgrau, Geländerrohre, Abdeckbleche weissgrau, die sichtbaren Kellermauern und Säulen sind normal verputzt und hellgrau gestrichen. Im Innern: Die Wände im Treppenhaus, in den Gängen und Nebenräumen sind weissgrau, ebenso das gesamte Holzwerk, in den Gängen und Nebenräumen sind weissgrau, ebenso das Schlafräume sind hell getönt (beige, rosa, hellblau, grau). Besondere farbige Akzente kommen weder aussen noch innen vor; es ist damit der wechselnden Bewohnung des Miethauses Rechnung getragen worden.

53   2 Mehrfamilienhäuser im Doldertal Zürich

DIE NEUE ARCHITEKTUR/
THE NEW ARCHITECTURE
Book, 1940. Designer: Max Bill.
Author: Max Roth. Photograph:
Dan Meyers.

Designed by Max Bill in 1940, this book is considered the first use of a systematic modular grid. Each image is sized to fit the column structure—as Jan Tschichold had predicted in 1928—filling one, two, or three zones. Acknowledging the originality of its layout, the author credits Bill as "the creator of the typographical structure of the book."

Der New-York-Times-Prospekt zeigt die Lösung einer komplexen Aufgabe; zeigt, wie eine Idee, ein Text und die typographische Darstellung über mehrere Phasen hinweg integriert werden. Darüber hinaus kann sich die Aufgabe stellen, Prospekte wie diesen wiederum mit andern Werbemitteln und Drucksachen zu integrieren. Denn heute brauchen Firmen mehr und·mehr nicht bloss hier einen Prospekt, da ein Plakat, dort Inserate usw. Heute braucht eine Firma etwas anderes: Eine Physiognomie, ein optisches Gesicht.

Die Beispiele dieser Seiten geben die Physiognom der boîte à musique, eines Grammophongeschäfts in Basel, wieder. Die boîte à musique hat ein Signe und einen firmeneigenen Stil – und doch wieder nic wenn man unter dem einen ein starres, nachträglic überall dazugesetztes Zeichen und unter dem ande ein bloss ästhetisches Prinzip versteht. Vielmehr: Die einmal definitiv festgelegten, aber jeweils den verschiedenen Funktionen und Proportionen ange passten Elemente selber bilden das Signum und de Stil in einem.

Abbildung 13 zeigt die Struktur. Fixiert sind die Ele mente Schrift und Rahmen; ferner die Verbindung von beiden und das Prinzip der Variabilität: der Ra men kann, ausgehend von der Ecke unten rechts, nach oben sowie nach links beliebig um ganze Ein heiten vergrössert werden. Einen in sich proportio hervorragenden Fall gibt es nicht. Es gibt nur wert gleiche Varianten; und hervorragend ist die Varia dann, wenn sie der jeweiligen Aufgabe am besten gemessen ist.

Abbildung 14 zeigt die Neujahrskarte mit gleichzei verschieden proportionierten Varianten; 15 den Br bogen, wo das Signum dem (gegebenen) Din A4 Format angepasst ist; 16 und 17 Inserate, wieder e sprechend dem zur Verfügung stehenden Insertio raum bemessen; 18 ein Geschenkbon.

13

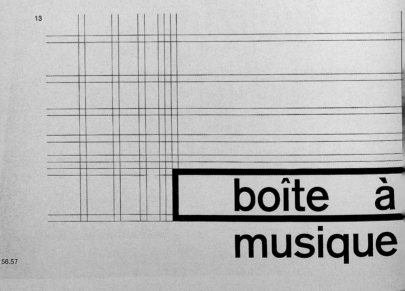

56.57

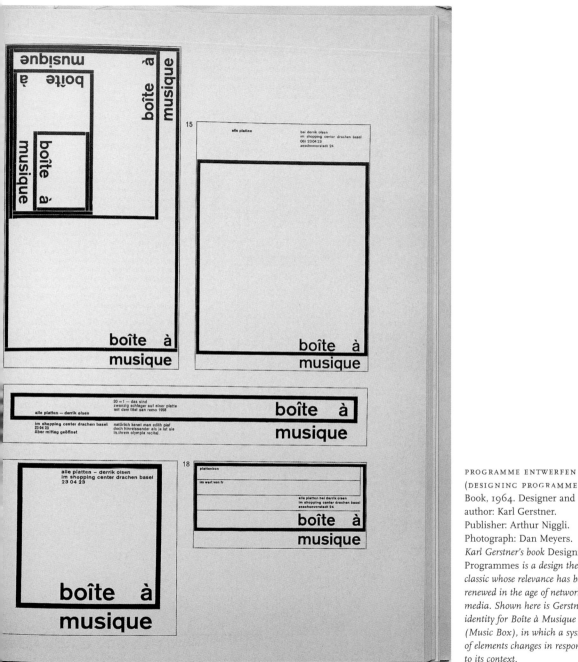

PROGRAMME ENTWERFEN
(DESIGNING PROGRAMMES)
Book, 1964. Designer and
author: Karl Gerstner.
Publisher: Arthur Niggli.
Photograph: Dan Meyers.
Karl Gerstner's book Designing
Programmes *is a design theory
classic whose relevance has been
renewed in the age of networked
media. Shown here is Gerstner's
identity for Boîte à Musique
(Music Box), in which a system
of elements changes in response
to its context.*

GRID AS TABLE

Tables and graphs are a variant of the typographic grid. A table consists of vertical columns and horizontal rows, each cell occupied by data. A graph is a line mapped along the *x* and *y* axes of a grid, each dimension representing a variable (such as time and stock value, shown below). As explained by Edward Tufte, the leading critic and theorist of information design, tables and graphs allow relationships among numbers to be perceived and rapidly compared by the eye. In tables and graphs, the grid is a cognitive tool.

Tables are a central aspect of web design. The table feature was incorporated into HTML code in 1995 so that web authors could present tabular data. Graphic designers, eager to give shape to the web's wide and flacid text bodies, quickly devised unauthorized uses for the HTML table, transforming this tool for representing data into nothing more, nor less, than a typographic grid. Designers have used the table feature to control the placement of images and captions and to build margins, gutters, and multicolumn screens. Designers also use tables to combine multiple styles of alignment—such as flush left and flush right—within a document, and to construct elegantly numbered and bulleted lists.

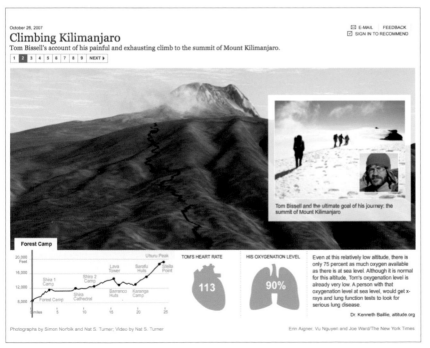

CLMBING KILIMANJARO (BELOW) Interactive information graphic, 2007. Graphics director: Steve Duenes/NYTimes.com. Courtesy of the New York Times. *This interactive three-dimensional travelogue traces Tom Bissell's harrowing climb to the top of Mount Kilimanjaro. The fever graph plots the distance Bissell traveled in relation to the changing elevation. The graphic coordinates his path with photographs shot along the way and an ongoing account of Bissell's rising heart rate and plummeting oxygenation level.*

On the aesthetics and ethics of information design, see Edward Tufte, *Envisioning Information* (Cheshire, Conn.: Graphics Press, 1990).

On designing accessible websites, see Jeffrey Zeldman with Ethan Marcotte, *Designing with Web Standards*, third edition (Berkeley, CA: New Riders, 2009) and Patrick Lynch and Sarah Horton, *Web Style Guide: Basic Design Principles for Creating Web Sites* (New Haven: Yale University Press, 2001). See also the site www.webstyleguide.com.

By creating cells that span multiple columns and rows, designers build layout structures that bear little relation to the logically ordered fields of a data chart. A master table typically establishes areas for navigation, content, and site identity, and each region contains a smaller table—or tables—inside itself. Grids propagate inside of grids.

Advocates of web standards reject such workarounds as spurious and unethical design tactics. Visually driven, illogical layout tables can cause problems for sight-impaired users, who implement various devices to translate digital pages into sound, cell by cell, row by row. Assistive screen readers "linearize" digital text into a stream of spoken words. Accessibility experts encourage web designers to "think in linear terms" wherever possible, and to make sure their tables make sense when read in a continuous sequence. Accessible websites also consider the needs of users working with older software or text-only browsers. Linear thinking helps not only sight-impaired audiences but also the users of mobile devices, where space is tight.

MICA.EDU Website, 2004. Designers: Carton Donofrio Partners. Publisher: Maryland Institute College of Art. *HTML tables, with their borders gently expressed, are an element of this neatly gridded webpage. Here, the table element is used not as a secret grid but as a structure for organizing content in columns and rows.*

HTML, the mark-up system that allowed the Internet to become a global mass medium, is the virtual counterpart to letterpress, which mechanized the production of the book and cleared the ground for a world culture of print. Like letterpress, HTML is a text-hungry medium that can be coaxed, with some resistance, to display images.

HTML coexists with other languages on the web, just as alternative technologies appeared alongside letterpress. Lithography, invented for the manufacture of images in the eighteenth century, soon incorporated words in addition to pictures, just as letterpress made space in its mechanical grid for woodcuts, engravings, and photographic halftone blocks. In the twentieth century, lithography replaced letterpress as the world's dominant printing method; used with digital or photographic typesetting, it conveys text and pictures with equal comfort.

Lithography is not governed by grids as relentlessly as letterpress; neither is Flash, the animation software that became a common web-design tool at the turn of the twentieth century. Flash was originally designed for the creation of vector-based cartoons. Although Flash's primary purpose was pictorial, designers were soon using it to construct the interfaces of entire websites. The Flash sites that became, in the late 1990s, icons of a new web aesthetic were more cinematic than typographic, often featuring a painterly mix of word and image. They were soon supplanted by template-driven sites built dynamically by content management systems. In such sites, elements are placed via CSS (Cascading Style Sheets); the resulting designs have a structured appearance that is predictable over time.

Hand-coding HTML *is as slow and deliberate as setting metal type. Empty table cells are used to define areas of open space, but* HTML *makes these collapse if the cells are truly empty, causing the grid to implode. The transparent images that often fill these spaces are virtual equivalents to the blank spacing material of metal type.*

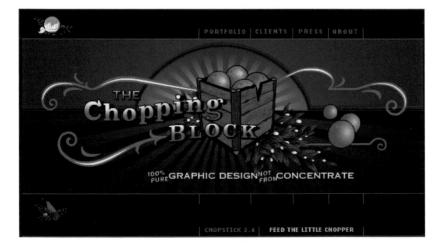

THE CHOPPING BLOCK
Website (detail), 2004.
Designers: Thomas Romer,
Jason Hillyer, Charles
Michelet, Robert Reed, and
Matthew Richmond/The
Chopping Block. *This website reprises the design of early twentieth-century fruit-crate labels, which were produced as lithographic prints that merge text and image. The webpage is animated, loading elements over time.*

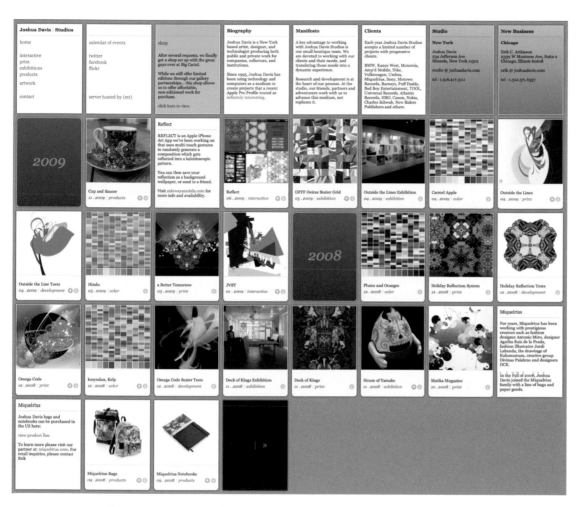

JOSHUADAVIS.COM Website, 2009. Designer: Joshua Davis. *In this template-driven site, elements are automatically arranged in a uniform grid.*

RETURN TO UNIVERSALS

William Gibson's 1984 novel *Neuromancer* envisions cyberspace as a vast ethereal grid. Gibson's data cowboy leaves behind the "meat" of his body and drifts off into a "transparent 3d chessboard extending to infinity." In Gibson's novel, this chessboard grid is projected on an internal surface of the mind, bound by no screen or window.

The grid as infinite space—defying edges and dominated by the mind rather than the body—is a powerful instrument within modernist theory, where it is a form both rational and sublime. In the early twentieth century, avant-garde designers exposed the grid in order to dramatize the mechanical conditions of print. After World War II, Swiss designers built a total design methodology around the grid, infusing it with ideological intentions. The grid was their key to a universal language. With the postmodern turn toward historical, vernacular, and popular sources in the 1970s and 1980s, many designers rejected the rationalist grid as a quaint artifact of Switzerland's own orderly society.

The rise of the Internet has rekindled interest in universal design thinking. The web was invented in the early 1990s (in Switzerland) to let scientists and researchers share documents created with different software applications. Its inventor, Tim Berners-Lee, never guessed that the web would become a design-driven medium connecting vast numbers of differently abled and divergently motivated people around the globe.

Universal design systems can no longer be dismissed as the irrelevant musings of a small, localized design community. A second modernism has emerged, reinvigorating the utopian search for universal forms that marked the birth of design as a discourse and a discipline nearly a century earlier. Against the opacity and singularity of unique visual expressions—grounded in regional preferences and private obsessions—ideas of commonality, transparency, and openness are being reborn as information seeks once again to shed its physical body.

On the invention of the web, see Tim Berners-Lee, *Weaving the Web* (New York: HarperCollins, 1999). For a contemporary account of universal design thinking, see William Lidwell, Kritina Holden, and Jill Butler, *Universal Principles of Design* (Gloucester, Mass.: Rockport Publishers, 2003). See also William Gibson, *Neuromancer* (New York: Ace Books, 1984).

To produce designs that are objectively informative is primarily a socio-cultural task. —JOSEF MÜLLER-BROCKMANN, 1961

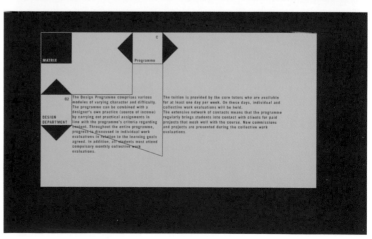

WWW.SANDBERG.NL
Website, 2003. Designer:
Luna Maurer. Publisher:
Sandberg Institute. *The grid is
a navigation device that warps
and changes as the user rolls
over it. The vertical axis
represents departments in the
school, and the horizontal axis
represents types of program
information. As the user passes
over the grid, cells fill with light
and appear to lift away from
the screen, indicating the
availability of information at
that intersection.*

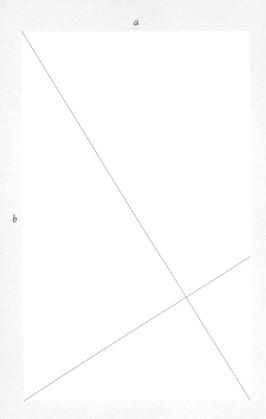

a

b

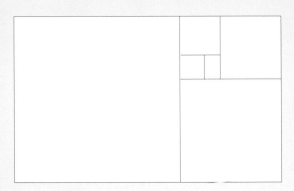

The golden section, which appears in nature as well as in art and design, has many surprising properties. For example, when you remove a square from a golden rectangle, the remainder is another golden rectangle, a process that can be infinitely repeated to create a spiral.

No book about typography would be complete without a discussion of the *golden section*, a ratio (relationship between two numbers) that has been used in Western art and architecture for more than two thousand years. The formula for the golden section is a : b = b : (a+b).

This means that the smaller of two elements (such as the shorter side of a rectangle) relates to the larger element in the same way that the larger element relates to the two parts combined. In other words, side *a* is to side *b* as side *b* is to the sum of both sides. Expressed numerically, the ratio for the golden section is 1 : 1.618.

Some graphic designers are fascinated with the golden section and use it to create various grids and page formats—indeed, entire books have been written on the subject. Other designers believe that the golden section is no more valid as a basis for deriving sizes and proportions than other methods, such as beginning from standard industrial paper sizes, or dividing surfaces into halves or squares, or simply picking whole-number page formats and making logical divisions within them.

A grid can be simple or complex, specific or generic, tightly defined or loosely interpreted. Typographic grids are all about control. They establish a system for arranging content within the space of page, screen, or built environment. Designed in response to the internal pressures of content (text, image, data) and the outer edge or frame (page, screen, window), an effective grid is not a rigid formula but a flexible and resilient structure, a skeleton that moves in concert with the muscular mass of content. Grids belong to the technological framework of typography, from the concrete modularity of letterpress to the ubiquitous rulers, guides, and coordinate systems of graphics applications. Although software generates illusions of smooth curves and continuous tones, every digital image or mark is constructed—ultimately—from a grid of neatly bounded blocks. The ubiquitous language of the gui (graphical user interface) creates a gridded space in which windows overlay windows. In addition to their place in the background of design production, grids have become explicit theoretical tools. Avant-garde designers in the 1910s and 1920s exposed the mechanical grid of letterpress, bringing it to the polemical surface of the page. In Switzerland after World War II, graphic designers built a total design methodology around the typographic grid, hoping to build from it a new and rational social order. The grid has evolved across centuries of typographic evolution. For graphic designers, grids are carefully honed intellectual devices, infused with ideology and ambition, and they are the inescapable mesh that filters, at some level of resolution, nearly every system of writing and reproduction. A grid can be simple or complex, specific or generic, tightly defined or loosely interpreted. Typographic grids are all about control. They establish a system for arranging content within the space of page, screen, or built environment. Designed in response to the internal pressures of content (text, image, data) and the outer edge or frame (page, screen, window), an effective grid is not a rigid formula but a flexible and resilient structure, a skeleton that moves in concert with the muscular mass of content. Grids belong to the technological framework of typography, from the concrete modularity of letterpress to the ubiquitous rulers, guides, and coordinate systems of graphics applications. Although software generates illusions of smooth curves and continuous tones, every digital image or mark is constructed—ultimately—from a grid of neatly bounded blocks. The ubiquitous language of the gui (graphical user interface) creates a gridded space in which windows overlay windows. In addition to their

Golden rectangle of text on
8.5 x 11-inch page (U.S. standard)

A grid can be simple or complex, specific or generic, tightly defined or loosely interpreted. Typographic grids are all about control. They establish a system for arranging content within the space of page, screen, or built environment. Designed in response to the internal pressures of content (text, image, data) and the outer edge or frame (page, screen, window), an effective grid is not a rigid formula but a flexible and resilient structure, a skeleton that moves in concert with the muscular mass of content. Grids belong to the technological framework of typography, from the concrete modularity of letterpress to the ubiquitous rulers, guides, and coordinate systems of graphics applications. Although software generates illusions of smooth curves and continuous tones, every digital image or mark is constructed—ultimately—from a grid of neatly bounded blocks. The ubiquitous language of the gui (graphical user interface) creates a gridded space in which windows overlay windows. In addition to their place in the background of design production, grids have become explicit theoretical tools. Avant-garde designers in the 1910s and 1920s exposed the mechanical grid of letterpress, bringing it to the polemical surface of the page. In Switzerland after World War II, graphic designers built a total design methodology around the typographic grid, hoping to build from it a new and rational social order. The grid has evolved across centuries of typographic evolution. For graphic designers, grids are carefully honed intellectual devices, infused with ideology and ambition, and they are the inescapable mesh that filters, at some level of resolution, nearly every system of writing and reproduction. A grid can be simple or complex, specific or generic, tightly defined or loosely interpreted. Typographic grids are all about control. They establish a system for arranging content within the space of page, screen, or built environment. Designed in response to the internal pressures of content (text, image, data) and the outer edge or frame (page, screen, window), an effective grid is not a rigid formula but a flexible and resilient structure, a skeleton that moves in concert with the muscular mass of content. Grids belong to the technological framework of typography, from the concrete modularity of letterpress to the ubiquitous rulers, guides, and coordinate systems of graphics applications. Although software generates illusions of smooth curves and continuous tones, every digital image or mark is constructed—ultimately—from a grid of neatly bounded blocks. The ubiquitous language of the gui (graphical user interface) creates a gridded space in which windows overlay windows. In addition to their

Golden rectangle of text on
A4 page (European standard, 210 x 297 mm)

Commercial printers generally prefer to work with pages trimmed to even measures rather than with obscure fractions. However, you can float golden rectangles within a page of any trim size.

For a more detailed account of design and the golden section, see Kimberly Elam, *Geometry of Design* (New York: Princeton Architectural Press, 2001). For an emphasis on applying the golden section to typography, see John Kane, *A Type Primer* (London: Laurence King, 2002).

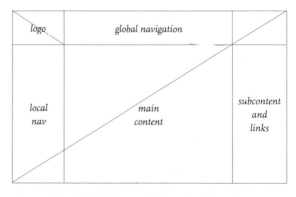

logo | global navigation
local nav | main content | subcontent and links

It may well be absurd to base a website on the golden section, but here, nonetheless, is a design for one. This wire frame diagram describes a webpage that is 500 x 809 pixels. The "golden screen" is then divided with squares and golden rectangles.

SINGLE-COLUMN GRID

A grid can be simple or complex, specific or generic, tightly defined or loosely interpreted. Typographic grids are all about control. They establish a system for arranging content within the space of page, screen, or built environment. Designed in response to the internal pressures of content (text, image, data) and the outer edge or frame (page, screen, window), an effective grid is not a rigid formula but a flexible and resilient structure, a skeleton that moves in concert with the muscular mass of content. Grids belong to the technological framework of typography, from the concrete modularity of letterpress to the ubiquitous rulers, guides, and coordinate systems of graphics applications. Although software generates illusions of smooth curves and continuous tones, every digital image or mark is constructed—ultimately—from a grid of neatly bounded blocks. The ubiquitous language of the gui (graphical user interface) creates a gridded space in which windows overlay windows. In addition to their place in the background of design production, grids have become explicit theoretical tools. Avant-garde designers in the 1910s and 1920s exposed the mechanical grid of letterpress, bringing it to the polemical surface of the page. In Switzerland after World War II, graphic designers built a total design methodology around the typographic grid, hoping to build from it a new and rational social order. The grid has evolved across centuries of typographic evolution. For graphic designers, grids are carefully honed intellectual devices, infused with ideology and ambition, and they are the inescapable mesh that filters, at some level of resolution, nearly every system of writing and reproduction. A grid can be simple or complex, specific or generic, tightly defined or loosely interpreted. Typographic grids are all about control. They establish a system for arranging content within the space of page, screen, or built environment. Designed in response to the internal pressures of content (text, image, data) and the outer edge or frame (page, screen, window), an effective grid is not a rigid formula but a flexible and resilient structure, a skeleton that moves in concert with the muscular mass of content. Grids belong to the technological framework of typography, from the concrete modularity of letterpress to the ubiquitous rulers, guides, and coordinate systems of graphics applications. Although software generates illusions of smooth curves and continuous tones, every digital image or mark is constructed—ultimately—from a grid of neatly bounded blocks. The ubiquitous language of the gui (graphical user interface) creates a gridded space in which windows overlay windows. In addition to their place in the background of design production, grids have become explicit theoretical tools. Avant-garde designers in the 1910s and 1920s exposed the mechanical grid of letterpress, bringing it to the polemical surface of the page. In Switzerland after World War II, graphic designers built a total design methodology around the typographic grid, hoping to build from it a new and rational social order. The grid has evolved across centuries of typographic evolution. For graphic designers, grids are carefully honed intellectual devices, infused with ideology and ambition, and they are the inescapable mesh that filters, at some level of resolution, nearly every system of writing and reproduction. A grid can be simple or complex, specific or generic, tightly defined or loosely interpreted. Typographic grids are all about control. They establish a system for arranging content within the space of page, screen, or built environment. Designed in response to the internal pressures of content (text, image, data) and the outer edge or frame (page, screen, window), an effective grid is not a rigid formula but a flexible and resilient structure, a skeleton that moves in concert with the muscular mass of content. Grids belong to the technological framework of typography, from the

This standard, 8.5 x 11-inch page has even margins all the way around. It is a highly economical, but not very interesting, design.

A grid can be simple or complex, specific or generic, tightly defined or loosely interpreted. Typographic grids are all about control. They establish a system for arranging content within the space of page, screen, or built environment. Designed in response to the internal pressures of content (text, image, data) and the outer edge or frame (page, screen, window), an effective grid is not a rigid formula but a flexible and resilient structure, a skeleton that moves in concert with the muscular mass of content. Grids belong to the technological framework of typography, from the concrete modularity of letterpress to the ubiquitous rulers, guides, and coordinate systems of graphics applications. Although software generates illusions of smooth curves and continuous tones, every digital image or mark is constructed—ultimately—from a grid of neatly bounded blocks. The ubiquitous language of the gui (graphical user interface) creates a gridded space in which windows overlay windows. In addition to their place in the background of design production, grids have become explicit theoretical tools. Avant-garde designers in the 1910s and 1920s exposed the mechanical grid of letterpress, bringing it to the polemical surface of the page. In Switzerland after World War II, graphic designers built a total design methodology around the typographic grid, hoping to build from it a new and rational social order. The grid has evolved across centuries of typographic evolution. For graphic designers, grids are carefully honed intellectual devices, infused with ideology and ambition, and they are the inescapable mesh that filters, at some level of resolution, nearly every system of writing and reproduction. A grid can be simple or complex, specific or generic, tightly defined or loosely interpreted. Typographic grids are all about control. They establish a system for arranging content within the space of page, screen, or built environment. Designed in response to the internal pressures of content (text, image, data) and the outer edge or frame (page, screen, window), an effective grid is not a rigid formula but a flexible and resilient structure, a skeleton that moves in concert with the muscular mass of content. Grids belong to the technological framework of typography, from the concrete modularity of letterpress to the ubiquitous rulers, guides, and coordinate systems of graphics applications. Although software generates illusions of smooth curves and continuous tones, every digital image or mark is constructed—ultimately—from a grid of neatly bounded blocks. The ubiquitous language of the gui (graphical user interface) creates a gridded space in which windows overlay windows. In addition to their place in the background of design production, grids have become explicit theoretical tools. Avant-garde designers in the 1910s and 1920s exposed the mechanical grid of letterpress, bringing it to

This page is an inch shorter than a standard U.S. letter. The text block is a square, leaving margins of varying dimension.

Every time you open a new document in a page layout program, you are prompted to create a grid. The simplest grid consists of a single column of text surounded by margins.

By asking for page dimensions and margin widths from the outset, layout programs encourage you to design your page from the *outside in.* (The text column is the space left over when the margins have been subtracted.)

Alternatively, you can design your page from the inside out, by setting your margins to zero and then positioning guidelines and text boxes on a blank page. This allows you to experiment with the margins and columns rather than making a commitment as soon as you open a new document. You can add guidelines to a master page after they meet your satisfaction.

GRID SYSTEMS

PAGE ONE

A grid can be simple or complex, specific or generic, tightly defined or loosely interpreted. Typographic grids are all about control. They establish a system for arranging content within the space of page, screen, or built environment. Designed in response to the internal pressures of content (text, image, data) and the outer edge or frame (page, screen, window), an effective grid is not a rigid formula but a flexible and resilient structure, a skeleton that moves in concert with the muscular mass of content. Grids belong to the technological framework of typography, from the concrete modularity of letterpress to the ubiquitous rulers, guides, and coordinate systems of graphics applications. Although software generates illusions of smooth curves and continuous tones, every digital image or mark is constructed—ultimately—from a grid of neatly bounded blocks. The ubiquitous language of the gui (graphical user interface) creates a gridded space in which windows overlay windows. In addition to their place in the background of design production, grids have become explicit theoretical tools. Avant-garde designers in the 1910s and 1920s exposed the mechanical grid of letterpress, bringing it to the polemical surface of the page. In Switzerland after World War II, graphic designers built a total design methodology around the typographic grid, hoping to build from it a new and rational social order. The grid has evolved across centuries of typographic evolution. For graphic designers, grids are carefully honed intellectual devices, infused with ideology and ambition, and they are the inescapable mesh that filters, at some level of resolution, nearly every system of writing and reproduction. A grid can be simple or complex, specific or generic, tightly defined or loosely interpreted. Typographic grids are all about control. They establish a system for arranging content within the space of page, screen, or built environment. Designed in response to the internal pressures of content (text, image, data) and the outer edge or frame (page, screen, window), an effective grid is not a rigid formula but a flexible and resilient structure, a skeleton that moves in concert with the muscular mass of content. Grids belong to the technological framework of typography, from the concrete modularity of letterpress to the ubiquitous rulers, guides, and coordinate systems of graphics applications. Although software generates illusions of smooth curves and continuous tones, every digital image or mark is constructed—ultimately—from a grid of neatly bounded blocks. The ubiquitous language of the gui (graphical user interface) creates a gridded space in which windows overlay windows. In addition to their place in the background of design production, grids have become explicit theoretical tools. Avant-garde designers in the 1910s and 1920s exposed the mechanical grid of letterpress, bringing it to

grid systems

page one

A grid can be simple or complex, specific or generic, tightly defined or loosely interpreted. Typographic grids are all about control. They establish a system for arranging content within the space of page, screen, or built environment. Designed in response to the internal pressures of content (text, image, data) and the outer edge or frame (page, screen, window), an effective grid is not a rigid formula but a flexible and resilient structure, a skeleton that moves in concert with the muscular mass of content. Grids belong to the technological framework of typography, from the concrete modularity of letterpress to the ubiquitous rulers, guides, and coordinate systems of graphics applications. Although software generates illusions of smooth curves and continuous tones, every digital image or mark is constructed—ultimately—from a grid of neatly bounded blocks. The ubiquitous language of the gui (graphical user interface) creates a gridded space in which windows overlay windows. In addition to their place in the background of design production, grids have become explicit theoretical tools. Avant-garde designers in the 1910s and 1920s exposed the mechanical grid of letterpress, bringing it to the polemical surface of the page. In Switzerland after World War II, graphic designers built a total design methodology around the typographic grid, hoping to build from it a new and rational social order. The grid has evolved across centuries of typographic evolution. For graphic designers, grids are carefully honed intellectual devices, infused with ideology and ambition, and they are the inescapable mesh that filters, at some level of resolution, nearly every system of writing and reproduction. A grid can be simple or complex, specific or generic, tightly defined or loosely interpreted. Typographic grids are all about control. They establish a system for arranging content within the space of page, screen, or built environment. Designed in response to the internal pressures of content (text, image, data) and the outer edge or frame (page, screen, window), an effective grid is not a rigid formula but a flexible and resilient structure, a skeleton that moves in concert with the muscular mass of content. Grids belong to the technological framework of typography, from the concrete modularity of letterpress to the ubiquitous rulers, guides, and coordinate systems of graphics applications. Although software generates illusions of smooth curves and continuous tones, every digital image or mark is constructed—ultimately—from a grid of neatly bounded blocks. The ubiquitous language of the gui (graphical user interface) creates a gridded space in which windows overlay windows. In addition to their place in the background of design production, grids have become explicit theoretical tools. Avant-garde designers in the 1910s and 1920s exposed the mechanical grid of letterpress, bringing it to

In this symmetrical double-page spread, the inside margins are wider than the outside margins, creating more open space at the spine of the book.

Books and magazines should be designed as *spreads* (facing pages). The two-page spread, rather than the individual page, is the main unit of design. Left and right margins become inside and outside margins. Page layout programs assume that the inside margins are the same on both the left- and right-hand pages, yielding a symmetrical, mirror-image spread. You are free, however, to set your own margins and create an asymmetrical spread.

In this asymmetrical layout, the left margin is always wider than the right margin, whether it appears along the inside or outside edge of the page.

MULTICOLUMN GRID

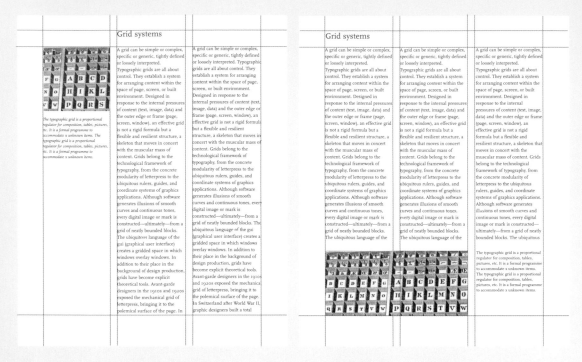

There are numerous ways to use a basic column grid. Here, one column has been reserved for images and captions, and the others for text.

In this variation, images and text share column space.

While single-column grids work well for simple documents, multicolumn grids provide flexible formats for publications that have a complex hierarchy or that integrate text and illustrations. The more columns you create, the more flexible your grid becomes.

You can use the grid to articulate the hierarchy of the publication by creating zones for different kinds of content. A text or image can occupy a single column or it can span several. Not all the space has to be filled.

Elements of varying width are staggered within the structure of the grid.

Grid systems

The typographic grid is a proportional regulator for composition, tables, pictures, etc. It is a formal programme to accommodate x unknown items.

The typographic grid is a proportional regulator for composition, tables, pictures, etc. It is a formal programme to accommodate x unknown items. The typographic grid is a proportional regulator for composition, tables, pictures, etc. It is a formal programme to accommodate x unknown items.

A grid can be simple or complex, specific or generic, tightly defined or loosely interpreted. Typographic grids are all about control. They establish a system for arranging content within the space of page, screen, or built environment. Designed in response to the internal pressures of content (text, image, data) and the outer edge or frame (page, screen, window), an effective grid is not a rigid formula but a flexible and resilient structure, a skeleton that moves in concert with the muscular mass of content. Grids belong to the technological framework of typography, from the concrete modularity of letterpress to the ubiquitous rulers, guides, and coordinate systems of graphics applications. Although software generates illusions of smooth curves and continuous tones, every digital image or mark is constructed—ultimately—from a grid of neatly bounded blocks. The ubiquitous language of the gui (graphical user interface) creates a gridded space in which windows overlay windows. In addition to their place in the background of design production, grids have become explicit theoretical tools. Avant-garde designers in the 1910s and 1920s exposed the mechanical grid of letterpress, bringing it to the polemical surface of the page. In Switzerland after World War II, graphic designers built a total design methodology around the typographic grid, hoping to build from a new and rational social order. The grid has evolved across centuries of typographic evolution. For graphic designers, grids are carefully honed intellectual devices, infused with ideology and ambition, and they are the inescapable mesh that filters, at some level of resolution, nearly every system of writing and reproduction. A grid can be simple or complex, specific or generic, tightly defined or loosely interpreted. Typographic grids are all about control. They establish a system for arranging content within the space of page, screen, or built environment. Designed in response to the internal pressures of content (text, image, data) and the outer edge or frame (page, screen, window), an effective grid is not a rigid formula but a flexible and resilient

The typographic grid is a proportional regulator for composition, tables, pictures, etc. It is a formal programme to accommodate x unknown items.

The typographic grid is a proportional regulator for composition, tables, pictures, etc. It is a formal programme to accommodate x unknown items.

The typographic grid is a proportional regulator for composition, tables, pictures, etc. It is a formal programme to accommodate x unknown items.

The typographic grid is a proportional regulator for composition, tables, pictures, etc. It is a formal programme to accommodate x unknown items.

A grid can be simple or complex, specific or generic, tightly defined or loosely interpreted. Typographic grids are all about control. They establish a system for arranging content within the space of page, screen, or built environment. Designed in response to the internal pressures of content (text, image, data) and the outer edge or frame (page, screen, window), an effective grid is not a rigid formula but a flexible and resilient structure, a skeleton that moves in concert with the muscular mass of content. Grids belong to the technological framework of typography, from the concrete modularity of letterpress to the ubiquitous rulers, guides, and coordinate systems of graphics applications. Although software generates illusions of smooth curves and continuous tones, every digital image or mark is constructed—ultimately—from a grid of neatly bounded blocks. The ubiquitous language of the gui (graphical user interface) creates a gridded space in which windows overlay windows. In addition to their place in the background of design production, grids have become explicit theoretical tools. Avant-garde designers in the 1910s and 1920s exposed the mechanical grid of letterpress, bringing it to the polemical surface of the page. In Switzerland after World War II, graphic designers built a total design methodology around the typographic grid, hoping to build from a new and rational social order. The grid has evolved across centuries of typographic evolution. For graphic designers, grids are carefully honed intellectual devices, infused with ideology and ambition, and they are the inescapable mesh that filters, at some level of resolution, nearly every system of writing and reproduction. A grid can be simple or complex, specific or generic, tightly defined or loosely interpreted. Typographic grids are all about control. They establish a system for arranging content within the space of page, screen, or built environment. Designed in response to the internal pressures of content (text, image, data) and the outer edge or frame (page, screen, window), an effective grid is not a rigid formula but a flexible and resilient

A horizontal band divides a text zone from an image zone. Elements gravitate toward this line, which provides an internal structure for the page.

HANG LINE In addition to creating vertical zones with the columns of the grid, you can also divide the page horizontally. For example, an area across the top can be reserved for images and captions, and body text can "hang" from a common line. In architecture, a horizontal reference point like this is known as a *datum*.

Columns of text hang from a datum, falling downward with an uneven rag across the bottom.

Ifang Leisalpa
(Schloss),
2090 Meter

und verdichtet, wie dies im Betonbau üblich ist. Da der Beton
bei diesem Vorgang die Vor- und Rücksprünge der Rückseite
der Steinplattenwand umfliesst, entstand eine vorzügliche
Verzahnung und Verbindung der beiden Materialien Kunststein
(Beton) und Naturstein.

Allerdings konnten die Wände nicht in ihrer ganzen Höhe
auf einmal hintergossen werden. Das musste in Höhenetappen
von 50 cm erfolgen. Erst wenn der Beton einer Lage eine bestimm
te Festigkeit erreicht und sich mit dem Mauerwerk verbunden
hatte, konnte die nächste Lage von 50 cm darüber betoniert
werden. Eine höhere Schüttmasse von flüssigem Beton hätte
die freistehenden Steinplattenwände seitlich weggedrückt.

Insgesamt wurden für die Wände der Therme 450 m³ oder
1300 Tonnen Valser Quarzitplatten zu 3100 m² Wandfläche in
20 Schichten pro m² verarbeitet. Die Länge aller verwendeten
Plattenstreifen zusammen ergibt ein Total von 62.000 Lauf-
metern, was der Strecke von Vals nach Haldenstein entspricht.
Peter Zumthor

Valser Quarzit	Boden	Fugen und Mörtelmasse	Grotten
Druckfestigkeit: etwa 217 N/mm² Rohdichte: 2.698 kg/m³ Wasseraufnahme-koeffizient: Masse –% 0,25 Gefräste Stein-platten: Stärken 6, 3, 4, 7 und 3,1cm Toleranz: 1 mm Breiten: 12–30 cm Längen: bis 3,20 m über 60.000 lfm Fugenbreite: etwa 2 mm	Breiten der Bahnen: 8–110 cm Längen: bis 3,20 m, je Platte zum Teil über 3 m² in einer Stärke von 2 cm Oberflächen: poliert, gefräst, gestockt, ge-schliffen in allen Möglichkeiten und einer Fugen-breite von 1 mm	EMACO R 304 BARRA 80 Firma MBT	Eckverbin-dungen, Schwel-len, Sturzplatten, Treppenunter-sichte und Tritte, Sitze als einzel-ne Werkstücke gefertigt	minimale Toleranzen (weit unter SIA-Norm) beim Schneiden und Vermauern der Steine, wie zum Beispiel auf 6 m Höhe weniger als 5 mm Toleranz	Trinkstein: polierte Quader aufeinander-geschichte Grösse etwa 0,5–1 m³ Quellgrotte: gebrochener Stein im Innern Schwitzstein: eingefärbter und polierter Beton Steininsel: grossformatige gespaltene Platten bis zu 3 m² je Platte

STEIN UND WASSER,
WINTER 2003|04 Booklet,
2003. Designer: Clemens
Schedler/Büro für konkrete
Gestaltung. Publisher: Hotel
Therme, Switzerland. *This
publication for a spa in
Switzerland uses a five-column
grid. The main text fills a four-
column block, and the smaller
texts occupy single columns.*

General Non-Fiction

Art

Photography

Collector's Editions

Film

Architecture

220 × 156 mm
8⅝ × 6⅛ inches
240 pp
c.80 b&w illus.

Paperback
0 7148 3164 6

£ **14.95**   UK
$ **24.95**   US
€ **24.95**   EUR
$ **39.95**   CAN
$ **49.95**   AUS

Béla Bartók

Kenneth Chalmers

- Sets Béla Bartók (1881–1945) and his work in the context of his homeland Hungary and h
  native city Budapest, where he lived for most of his adult life
- Covers the full range of his work from his early explorations of the folklore of Hungary to
  Third Piano Concerto composed on his deathbed in the United States
- Brings out the singular nature of his genius and the originality of his contribution to mus

Kenneth Chalmers is an author, translator and composer who has written on Bartók, Berg,
Stravinsky, Verdi and Weill, and collaborated on Decca's 20-volume Mozart Almanac

562

Design

Fashion &
Contemporary
Culture

Decorative Arts

**Music &
Performing Arts**
20th Century
Composers

Video

Index

6 mm
nches
40 pp
illus.

rback
203 0

UK
US
EUR
CAN
AUS

The Beatles

Allan Kozinn

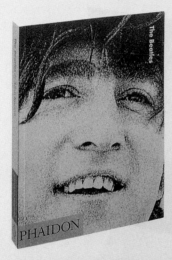

- Follows the extraordinary development of the four self-taught musicians from Liverpool from their beginnings until the break-up in 1970
- Examines why the innovative music of the Beatles – created, at least initially, as ephemera – has remained so durable
- Considers not only the commercially released disks but also studio outtakes, demos, unreleased recordings and broadcast performances
- Sets the group's evolution against the backdrop of the popular culture explosion of the 1960s

Allan Kozinn has written musical criticism for the *New York Times* since 1977 and won ASCAP awards for his work, including the book *Mischa Elman and the Romantic Style*

'A well-rounded, readable account. Makes a convincing case for putting the Beatles on the shelf between Bartók and Boulez.' *(The Sunday Times)*

563

PHAIDON: FALL 2003
Catalogue, 2003. Designer:
Hans Dieter Reichert.
Publisher: Phaidon.
Photograph: Dan Meyers. *This
catalogue for a book publisher
provides a rational and elegant
structure for displaying hundreds
of different books, each one
presented as a physical object
annotated with documentary
data. The margins act as a
navigational interface for the
catalogue. Divisions occur both
horizontally and vertically.*

Play serves learning though experimentation withou
risk. Learning occurs through quick, imprecise actions, conducted
within understood rules of a game, and free from threat or consum
mation. Play does not use up so much as build.

builds is common sense. Play's endlessly variable series of awkward, exaggerated motions seeks out the approximate arena for later development of tru competence.

There is much to be said for play in a mediur If a medium is defined by its affordances and constraints, then learning consists of exploring these properties. Experimentation is especially useful for becoming familiar with constraints: we learn from mistakes. We must accept that beginning work in a new medium will be full of setbacks. There will also be fortuitous discoveries, however particularly of affordances. Design is not only invention, but also sensitivity to a medium. Craft cannot be merely in service of technique, or of inappropriately conceive ends. The craftsman must begin to feel something about the artifacts, and only certain moves will fee right.

Of course when it comes to computation, we all must learn. In a sense, we're all children— the medium is *that* new. And of course, the most fluen experts here are often quite young. As all of us lear about this promising new domain, a chain of devel ments should be clear: play shapes learning; learni shapes the mind; mental structures shape software and software data structures afford work and play.

military-industrial world of computing, one important way to do so is to play.

Play takes many forms. For example, it can be individual or social. According to one classic taxonomy, individual play includes pursuit of sensations, exercise of motor apparatus and experimentation with higher mental powers. This mental play includes exercise of attention, emotion and will. Attention play includes tests of memory, imagination, focus and reason. On the other hand, social play includes fighting and rivalry, loving and courtship, imitation and status seeking. Imitative play includes movements, drama, behavioural constructions and emulation of inner states. [2]

Crafts and craft learning embrace quite a range of these playful forms. Arguably, no productive process combines so many so well. Sensation, skilled motion, attention, involvement, will — all must be balanced, and this is the basis for craft as recreation. Craft learning is a form of imitative social learning. Movements are physical skills taught directly, whether by demonstration or coaching. Drama is a lesser component here, although it may be understood in the willful suspension of disbelief that allows participation in an abstract medium. Constructions are the artifacts. They are the plastic play, the visual examples, the operational learning. Finally the inner state is the patience, reflectivity and intent that distinguish the master.

Play serves learning though experimentation without risk. Play often lacks any immediately obvious aim other than the pursuit of stimulation, but functions almost instinctively to serve the process of development. Learning occurs through quick, imprecise actions, conducted within understood rules of a game, and free from threat or consummation. Play does not use up so much as build. One thing it

Structure and Improvisation

The master at play improvises. Consider the jazz pianist. In *Ways of the Hand — The Organization of Improvised Conduct* (1978), the musician David Sudnow gives us a rare description of otherwise ta knowledge in action. Improvising on a piece takes much more talent than simply playing from a notation or learning by rote, Sudnow explains. Moreove improvising begins with a sense of structure, from which it builds a cognitive map. For example, the 'way in' to an arpeggio is mentally mapped. The structure of the keyboard presents a physical map a chord, which may be modified in countless ways physical moves. One could play the adjacent keys, example, or one could translate by any arbitrary int val. One could transpose or invert. One could chan the order in which the notes were played, or the

2 Karl Groos, *The Play of Man*. New York: Appleton and Co., 1901

the same pitches as the first, the doubled back and went fast again, but over different pitches... There were innumerable variations possible; looking at 'structure' in this way and corresponding to various continuity practices, ways of the hand were cultivated that were suited to the performance of such manoeuvres... Transposition of such a figure to a new segment and correct repetition with respect to pitch, without slowing it down or slowing down parts of it, involved coping with the topography of the terrain by the hand as a negotiative organ with various potentials and limitations. [3]

po, or the attack and decay. Of course one could stitute dominant, major and minor chords.

Sudnow argues that because these variations sequences of physical positions, they are learned active skills no longer necessary to be understood mental level. Each becomes a handful. That the d gets a hold of a variation on a chord is indicated by observed tendencies to start into particular uences with certain fingers on certain keys. The oeuvre is known by the hand, and the mind only s the way in. The ability to modify the run note by — which would require conscious attention — y comes later. Even without attentive intellectual dance, however, the natural tendency of the hand ot to repeat itself, even in a series of figural repeti-s. Thus once a sufficient repertoire of runs is ned, this tendency inherently ensures a richness e sound. The hand searches its territory for uences, which process replaces a faithfulness to score, and that makes jazz. For example:

The new run could be in various other ways only 'essentially related' to the preceding run. Say the first started slow and went up fast, then doubled back and went fast again, while the second started slowly and came back down through

Although jazz is the obvious case, it is hardly alone. Improvisation plays a role in many contemporary practices, and in many traditional crafts. Few of these worlds employ such a singular instrument as the piano; few are able to turn so much over to the hands, but all involve playful response to a structure. For example, of industrial design, Herbert Read insisted that "Art implies values more various than those determined by practical necessity." [4] As a modernist and industrialist, he felt admiration for fundamental structural laws, such as the golden section also admired by his contemporary Le Corbusier. He was convinced, however, that metrical irregularities based on a governing structure, rather than slavish adherence to the laws in their precision, was the basis for pleasurable expression. He cited Ruskin's line that "All beautiful lines are drawn under mathematical laws organically transgressed." [5] He held that this was the case even in the useful (industrial) arts.

Consider the case of processing a digital photograph. The makeup of the raster image file, the various tone scale and filtration operators, provides a very clear structure in which to work but demands no particular order of operation. The complex microstructure of the sampled pixels provides a sub-

The natural tendency of the hand is not to repeat itself, even in a series of figural repetitions. Thus once a sufficient repertoire of runs is learned, this tendency inherently ensures a richness to the sound. The hand searches its territory for sequences, which process replaces a faithfulness to the score, and that makes jazz.

IF/THEN PLAY: DESIGN IMPLICATIONS OF NEW MEDIA Book, 1999. Designers: Mevis and Van Deursen. Editor: Jan Abrams. Publisher: Netherlands Design Institute. Photograph: Dan Meyers. *In this book about new media, a two-column grid contains the main body of text. The pull quotes, running across two columns, are framed in thinly ruled boxes that suggest the overlapping "windows" on a computer screen. The top margin, which resembles the tool bar in a browser, provides an interface to the book.*

3 David Sudnow, *Ways of the Hand—The Organization of Improvised Conduct*, Cambridge, MA: Harvard University Press, 1978, p 7
4 Herbert Read, *Art and Industry—The Principles of Industrial Design* New York: Horizon Press, 1954 [1934]
5 *Ibid.*

wild wirkende, dem Lennéschen Ideal folgende, baumreiche Naturgarten weicht englischen Rasenflächen, die sich mit nur noch wenigen Baum- und Strauchgruppen und gepflegten Blumenbeeten abwechseln. Mit dieser Veränderung, so der dritte Direktor des Zoos, Heinrich Bodinus, soll es möglich werden, den belebenden und erwärmenden Strahlen der Sonne Zutritt zu verschaffen. Anders als zuvor finden sich in den Berliner Zeitungen nun immer häufiger positiv gefärbte Erlebnisberichte. Vorläufiger Höhepunkt und nicht zu unterschätzender rite de passage für die breite Anerkennung des Gartens war das DREI-KAISER-TREFFEN im Herbst 1872: Kaiser Wilhelm, Kaiser Alexander II. von Rußland und Kaiser Franz-Joseph von Österreich-Ungarn werden in einem zwanzig Wagen umfassenden Zug über das Zoogelände kutschiert. Obwohl der Zoo zu dieser Zeit noch außerhalb der Stadt gelegen ist, ist dessen neuartige Gestaltung schon ein Zeichen dafür, daß die preußische Hauptstadt um die Anbindung an die Kultur der großen europäischen Metropolen bemüht ist. Die Bevölkerungszahl Berlins steigt mit der industriellen Entwicklung jener Jahre erheblich, und dem Zoo kommt (neben den Stadtparks) zunehmend ein Erholungswert zu, der durch eine Reihe von technischen Neuerungen gesteigert werden kann: eine Dampfmaschine sorgt für Wasserzirkulation und verwandelt die früher im Sommer übelriechenden Gewässer des Gartens in belebte Weiher. Hinzu kommt die Erleichterung von An- und Abreise. Ab 1875 verbindet eine Pferdebahnlinie Berlin mit dem Zoo. Im Jahre 1884 folgt die Installation elektrischer Beleuchtung, die eine Ausdehnung der Öffnungszeiten bis in die Abendstunden zuläßt. Kinderspielhallen und -plätze werden eingerichtet. Wo sonst könnten sie sicher vor dem Getümmel der Weltstadt in frischer Luft ihre Glieder üben und ihre Lungen weiten? heißt es im Programmheft des Jahres 1899. ‖ Der Zoo entwickelt sich deutlich zu einem integralen Bestandteil der städtischen Kultur. Anders als in den Stadtparks — etwa dem Humboldthain — stellt hier der Eintrittspreis sicher, daß die das Vergnügen schmälernden Obdachlosen und Bettler vor den Toren bleiben. Zoofreunde werben um die Gunst von Kolonialoffizieren, die helfen sollen, die Tierbestände zu erhöhen und die in der Folge tatsächlich zunehmend als Donatoren fungieren. Forschungsreisen und Expeditionen in viele Regionen der Erde — häufig unter maßgeblicher Regie der Zoodirektoren — führen zur Entdeckung bislang unbekannter Tierarten. Die intensive Kooperation von Zoo und Naturkundemuseum setzt sich fort, so daß der Bestand des Museums 1894 auf etwa 2 Mio. Tiere, darunter etwa 150 000 Wirbeltiere, angewachsen ist. ‖ Der Berliner Zoo wird in den letzten Jahrzehnten des 19. Jahrhunderts zu einem repräsentativen Treffpunkt und zu einem Raum, in dem sich preußische Mentalität wenn auch nicht aufhebt, so doch relativiert. Fremdartige Tierwelt und eine Architektur des Orient, des Fernen Osten und der Savannen, verbindet sich, in einiger Entfernung vom hektischen und geschäftigen Leben der Stadt, zu einem den Stadtbewohnern bis dahin unbekannten Ambiente. Hier entwickelt sich Natur zum Unterhaltungsgegenstand. Die von Zirkussen, Menagerien und Märkten bekannten sensationellen und theatralischen Aspekte gehen mit dem zoologischen Erkenntnisinteresse eine eigenartige Symbiose ein. Getragen wird diese Entwicklung nicht zuletzt von ökonomischen Zwängen: immer wieder

kämpft die Zoogesellschaft um ihre Existenz. ‖ Der Zoo wird zu einem der Plätze der Stadt, wo sich Vorahnungen einer noch in Entwicklung begriffenen Weltstadt am ehesten materialisieren; kein Wunder, daß immer deutlicher auch Künstler und Gelehrte sich von diesem Raum angezogen fühlen. Neben einer Musiktribüne hilft ein erweiterter Restaurationsbetrieb den Aufenthalt in den meist nur unzureichend belüfteten Gebäuden aufzulockern. Ein Zeitgenosse beschreibt diese Bereicherung: Durch das neue Restaurationslokal ist die Zahl der großen Festsäle um ein Meisterwerk der Baukunst vermehrt worden. Wenn hier eine vortreffliche Militärkapelle aufführt, dann bildet, in Folge des erhöhten Eintrittspreises, die elegante Welt die Mehrzahl der Besucher. Draußen dehnt sich eine lange Reihe Equipagen bis in die Winkel des Thiergartens; drinnen sind alle Plätze im weiten Umkreise des muschelförmig gebauten Orchesters besetzt; beim Klange der Instrumente, beim Geplätscher der Fontänen sitzt man, sich erfrischend, rauchend, plaudernd und scherzend unter den schattigen Bäumen und blickt in das abwechselnde, stets rege Thierleben hinaus, wie es sich in den benachbarten Grotten, auf Aesten und Teichen kund giebt.³ ‖ Die Auswahl der Tiere und der Situationen, in denen sich ihre Präsentation bewegte, erfolgt sorgfältig und bedacht, die Kuratoren entscheiden sich für besonders exotisch wirkende, kuriose, lächerliche, niedliche Tiere.⁴ Dabei gilt es stets, die Konfrontation mit potentiell Abscheu oder starkes Befremden erregendem tierischen Verhalten zu verhindern. ‖ Die zunehmende Popularität des Zoos korreliert mit dem Verschwinden von Tieren aus dem Alltagsleben des städtischen Menschen. Das Tier ist entweder Haustier, also Mitbewohner der Wohnung, oder drastisch auf seine Rohstofffunktion reduziert und fristet in fabrikartigen Hallen abseits der Städte sein ökonomisch optimiertes Dasein. Mit den zoologischen Gärten beginnt ein Verdrängungsmechanismus, der sich später auch auf Naturparks und Reservate erstreckt: die Gefangenschaft erscheint angesichts der systematischen Zerstörung der Lebensräume als ein Schutz der Natur und dient dazu, das unterschwellig vorhandene schlechte Gewissen zu beruhigen.

NIEGER, TIERE, SENSATIONEN. BRAUNER (VERDI-ZWECK 1725B55)

(3) R. Springer: Berlin. Die deutsche Kaiserstadt. Reprint, Berlin 1877.
(4) Interessanterweise vollzieht sich in einigen nordamerikanischen Gärten heute eine dem entgegengesetzte Entwicklung: Sowohl in Washington — als auch in Montreal wurden gezielt ,unspektakuläre wirbellose Tiere eingeführt, die immerhin 98 Prozent des gesamten tierischen Lebens auf der Erde ausmachen. Diese Veränderung ist Teil einer Vielzahl von Eingriffen, in die traditionelle Gestaltung, um einem grundlegend veränderten Verständnis von Mensch und Tierwelt Rechnung zu tragen. Vgl. Alexander Wilson: The Culture of Nature. North American Landscape From Disney to the Exxon Valdez Cambridge 1992 / Seite 233 ff

90

architektur Franz Hessel erinnert sich in seinen Beobachtungen berlinischen Lebens an die merkwürdigen Behausungen der Tiere: Liebt das Zebra sein afrikanisches Gehöft, der Büffel sein Borkenpalais? Die Steine von Bärenzwinger, Vogelhaus und Löwenheim deutet Hessel als Baukastensteine, der Zoo wird in seiner Interpretation zur natürlichen Fortsetzung einer Kinderstube und einem Ort, wo die vorzeitlichen Tierkulte Gelegenheit haben, wiederaufzuleben. F. Lichterfeld bezieht sich in einem Artikel der ILLUSTRIRTEN ZEITUNG von 1873 auf die anfänglich vorhandene Verwunderung der Stadtbewohner ob der neuen, ungewohnten Bauwerke: ›Was sollen diese Thürme mit der flammenden Sonne und den phantastischen Drachen- und Elefantenbildern in einer christlichen Stadt wie Berlin?‹ Diese Frage wurde früher häufig aufgeworfen, zumal von Landleuten, welche ihr Weg nach der Stadt an dem fremden Heidentempel vorüberführte. Jetzt weiß jedermann in und um Berlin, daß der fremde Heidentempel das neue Elefantenhaus ist. […] Nicht diesen, sondern dem Publikum zulieb wurde der Neubau so reich ausgestattet, denn selbst dem Elefanten ist eine Portion Moorrüben oder ein Bund Heu lieber als der ganze architektonische und musivische Schmuck seines neuen Hauses, und nun gar erst dem Rhinoceros! ‖ Die stilistische Gestaltung der Bauten steht offensichtlich auch in Zusammenhang mit der Einbindung der zoologischen Gärten in kolonialistische Zusammenhänge. Die Repräsentation fremdkultureller Elemente erlaubt Rückschlüsse auf die Konturen eines rudimentär entwickelten Kosmopolitismus. Das Einbringen von Elementen aus anderen Kulturzusammenhängen markiert den Wandel vom systematischen zum geographisch orientierten Zoo. Wichtigen Einfluß auf die Idee, Tiere in einem baulich-stilistischen Rahmen zu zeigen, der gewisse Zusammenhänge zur Ethnographie der Heimatlandschaften aufweist, hatte der Zoologe Philipp Leopold Martin. In seinem 1878 in Leipzig erschienenen Kompendium DIE PRAXIS DER NATURGESCHICHTE — er maßte sich an, es als vollständiges Lehrbuch über das Sammeln lebender und todter Naturkörper zu bezeichnen — rationalisiert Martin dieses Vorgehen als ethnographisch-architektonische Belehrung: Was ist aber nun wohl natürlicher und zugleich lehrreicher, als die Natur in unseren Gärten nach Welttheilen, Zonen und lokalen Verhältnissen aufzustellen? […] Der Wisent verlangt Wald und der Buffalo die Prairie; und wenn wir dieses thun und in die Prairie noch ein Wigwam als Stall hinsetzen, so belehren wir damit zugleich das Publikum, denn es erhält Bilder, die es niemals vergißt. Die fremdkulturelle Architektur der Stilbauten — auch wichtiger Bestandteil der großen Weltausstellungen in dieser Phase — wird jeglicher zeitlicher Entwicklung enthoben. Zoodirektor Ludwig Heck schreibt rückblickend im Jahre 1929: Man denke nur, wenn wir

FORM + ZWECK 27
Journal, 1996. Designers: Cyan, Berlin. *In the pages of this experimental journal, compact columns of justified text are pushed to the outer margins. By marking paragraphs with symbols rather than indents and line breaks, the designers have maximized the density of the text field. Running heads, page numbers, and images are narrow channels cut into a solid wall of text. Footnotes are also treated as justified blocks, turned 90 degrees against the grain of the page.*

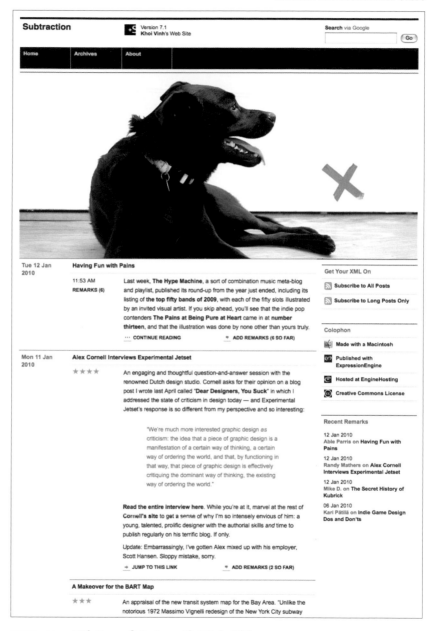

SUBTRACTION Website, 2008. Designer: Khoi Vinh. *While countless websites are divided into three or more columns, a fully functioning grid should allow some components to "break the grid" by crossing over multiple columns within a content area. The generous swaths of white space in Vinh's webpages free the eye from relentless clutter while emphasizing the underlying grid structure. Vinh sometimes uses a grid as a background image to check alignments as he works.*

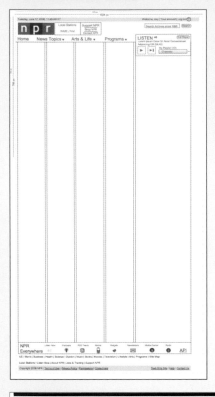

NPR.ORG Website, 2009–10. Designer: NPR staff (Darren Mauro, Jennifer Sharp, Callie Neylan, David Wright, Brian Ingles, K. Libner, Scott Stroud). *The web design process typically begins with designing a grid and wire frames that describe typical pages. The visual details, such as type choice, hierarchy, and styling of navigation elements, are added later. The site has eight page templates, each designed for a different editorial situation.*

POLITICS   BOOKS & ARTS   ECONOMY   ENERGY & ENVIRONMENT   HEALTH CARE   METRO POLICY   WORLD   LOGIN   SUBSCRIBE   Search TNR

THE NEW REPUBLIC

* Place of Grace: The Uncanny
Beauty of Peter Zumthor's
Out-of-the-Way Buildings

Unemployment Has Crept Over Ten Percent, and I Think That's a Good Thing. What?
Noam Scheiber

Did Rembrandt Reveal a Murder in One of His Paintings? An Intriguing Whodunnit Film. PLUS: 'The Maid.'
Stanley Kauffmann

The UN Report on Gaza Is Biased, Shoddy, and Unrealistic. But Israel Must Deal Honestly With Its Own Failures.
Moshe Halbertal

INTELLECTUAL RIGOR
HONEST REPORTING
INFLUENTIAL ANALYSIS
THE NEW REPUBLIC
Don't miss another issue of the magazine considered "required reading" by the world's top decision-makers.
Subscribe today and get two free issues, risk free.

Chait: Don't Blame Obama for the Bad Economic News. Blame Congress. »

From the TNR Archives: The Strange Genius of Oprah Winfrey »

Scheiber: Is David Brooks Punking Me? He's Got to Be Punking Me. »

Cohn: Is It Even Possible to Control the Cost of Heath Care? »

STAY IN TOUCH   GET THE MAGAZINE »   GET OUR E-NEWSLETTERS »   Enter Email Addre SUBSCRIBE   RSS »

SATURDAY NOVEMBER 7, 2009

WORLD
The UN Report on Gaza Is Biased, Shoddy, and Unrealistic. But Israel Must Deal Honestly With Its Own Failures.
Moshe Halbertal

FRIDAY NOVEMBER 6, 2009

POLITICS
Bush is a Genius! Health Reform is Dead! 'The Weekly Standard' and the Powerlessness of Wishful Thinking.
Jonathan Chait

HEALTH CARE
The House Has Seriously Weakened the Public Option—But It Still Works, and Is Still Worth Fighting For
Jacob S. Hacker and Diane Archer

ECONOMY
What Happens When Moderate Democrats Turn Into Pundits? Bad Things. Very Bad Things.
Noam Scheiber

WORLD
The Losers From This Week's Protests in Iran: Khamenei, Ahmadinejad, and Obama
Abbas Milani

WORLD
Is Barack Obama Causing a Real Estate Boom in the West Bank?
Sarah A. Topol

HEALTH CARE
Cohn: I'll Say This About the GOP Health Plan ... It's Even Worse Than I Imagined
Jonathan Cohn

POLITICS
How Obama Can Help Democrats Avoid a Repeat of the Virginia Debacle in 2010
John B. Judis

Multimedia   More Slideshows »

Slideshow: Where Have All the RINOs Gone?
Videos   Slideshows   Podcasts

TNR on Latin America

The Shah of Venezuela
The ideas that keep Hugo Chavez in power.

The Case of Honduras
A fragile democracy on the edge of a whirlwind.

Confessions of a 'Contra'
How the CIA masterminded the Nicaraguan insurgency.

The Death of Che Guevara
A firsthand account.

Boycotting Cuba
Whose interest does it serve?

THE **PLANK**
By the TNR STAFF and GUESTS
What Warren Buffett's Investment Says About the Global Economy
November 7, 2009 | 10:47 am - Simon Johnson
Phony Conservative Anti-Elitism, Revealed!
November 7, 2009 | 8:24 am - Isaac Chotiner
Today At TNR (November 7, 2009)
November 7, 2009 | 12:00 am - TNR Staff

THE **Treatment** By JONATHAN COHN
Your Must-Read Guide to Health Care Reform
The Drama Was in the History
November 8, 2009 | 12:16 am - Jonathan Cohn

THE **SPINE** By MARTY PERETZ
A Lesson From Fort Hood: Great Moments in "Psychologically Disturbed" Gunmen Committing Mass Murder
November 8, 2009 | 12:58 am - Barry Rubin

THE **(STA$H)** Inside the Battle to Fix Our Economy By NOAM SCHEIBER
WPA Revisited: Should Government Create Jobs Directly?
November 6, 2009 | 6:22 pm - Zubin Jelveh

THE **VINE** The Politics of a Greener Planet By BRADFORD PLUMER
Cap-And-Trade Politics: Carbon (Like Place) Matters!
November 6, 2009 | 4:25 pm - Mark Muro and Jonathan Rothwell

THE **AVENUE** Rethinking Metropolitan America
In Collaboration with the Brookings Metropolitan Policy Program
Cap-And-Trade Politics: Carbon (Like Place) Matters!
November 6, 2009 | 4:25 pm - Mark Muro and Jonathan Rothwell

William Galston

Simon Johnson

Ed Kilgore

Damon Linker

John McWhorter

THE NEW REPUBLIC Online magazine, 2009. *The home page of this online magazine uses a three-column grid to provide readers with direct links to a vast quantity of editorial content. Opinion sections each have their own logotypes, designed to reflect the literary tone of the overall brand.*

<small>DESIGNING PROGRAMS</small> Grid diagram, 1963 (redrawn).
Designer: Karl Gerstner. Publisher: Arthur Niggli, Zurich.
*This square grid consists of six vertical columns and six
horizontal modules, overlayed by grids of one, two, three, and
four units. Vertically, the grid is governed by a 10-pt measure,
which would determine the spacing of type from baseline to
baseline.*

Grid systems

A grid can be simple or complex, specific or generic, tightly defined or loosely interpreted. Typographic grids are all about control. They establish a system for arranging content within the space of page, screen, or built environment. Designed in response to the internal pressures of content (text, image, data) and the outer edge or frame (page, screen, window), an effective grid is not a rigid formula but a flexible and resilient structure, a skeleton that moves in concert with the muscular mass of content. Grids belong to the technological framework of typography, from the concrete modularity of letterpress to the ubiquitous rulers, guides, and coordinate systems of graphics applications. Although software generates illusions of smooth curves and continuous tones, every digital image or mark is constructed—ultimately—from a grid of neatly bounded blocks. The ubiquitous language of the gui (graphical user interface) creates a gridded space in which windows overlay windows. In addition to their place in the background of design production, grids have become explicit theoretical tools. Avant-garde designers in the 1910s and 1920s exposed the grid of letterpress, bringing it to the polemical surface of the page. In Switzerland after World War II, graphic designers built a total design methodology around the typographic grid, hoping to build from it a new and rational social order. The grid has evolved across centuries of typographic evolution. For graphic designers, grids are carefully honed intellectual devices, infused with ideology and ambition, and they are the inescapable mesh that filters, at some level of resolution, nearly every system of writing and

The typographic grid is a proportional regulator for composition, tables, pictures, etc. It is a formal programme to accommodate x unknown items. The typographic grid is a proportional regulator for composition, tables, pictures, etc. It is a formal programme to accommodate x unknown items. The typographic grid is a proportional regulator for composition, tables, pictures, etc. It is a formal programme to accommodate x unknown items.

This modular grid has four columns and four rows. An image or a text block can occupy one or more modules.

Grid systems

A grid can be simple or complex, specific or generic, tightly defined or loosely interpreted. Typographic grids are all about control. They establish a system for arranging content within the space of page, screen, or built environment. Designed in response to the internal pressures of content (text, image, data) and the outer edge or frame (page, screen, window), an effective grid is not a rigid formula but a flexible and resilient structure, a skeleton that moves in concert with the muscular mass of content. Grids belong to the technological framework of typography, from the concrete modularity of letterpress to the ubiquitous rulers, guides, and coordinate systems of graphics applications. Although software generates illusions of smooth curves and continuous tones, every digital image or mark is constructed—ultimately—from a grid of neatly bounded blocks. The ubiquitous language of the gui (graphical user interface) creates a gridded space in which windows overlay windows. In addition to their place in the background of design production, grids have

A grid can be simple or complex, specific or generic, tightly defined or loosely interpreted. Typographic grids are all about control. They establish a system for arranging content within the space of page, screen, or built environment. Designed in response to the internal pressures of content (text, image, data) and the outer edge or frame (page, screen, window), an effective grid is not a rigid formula but a flexible and resilient structure, a skeleton that moves in concert with the muscular mass of content. Grids belong to the technological framework of typography, from the concrete modularity of letterpress to the ubiquitous rulers, guides, and coordinate systems of graphics applications. Although software generates illusions of smooth curves and continuous tones, every digital image or mark is constructed—ultimately—from a grid of neatly bounded blocks. The ubiquitous language of the gui (graphical user interface) creates a gridded space in which windows overlay windows. In addition to their place in the background of design production, grids have become explicit

The typographic grid is a proportional regulator for composition, tables, pictures, etc. It is a formal programme to accommodate x unknown items. The typographic grid is a proportional regulator for composition, tables, pictures, etc. It is a formal programme to accommodate x unknown items. The typographic grid is a proportional regulator for composition, tables, pictures, etc. It is a formal programme to accommodate x unknown items.

Endless variations are possible.

A *modular grid* has consistent horizontal divisions from top to bottom in addition to vertical divisions from left to right. These modules govern the placement and cropping of pictures as well as text. In the 1950s and 1960s, Swiss graphic designers including Gerstner, Ruder, and Müller-Brockmann devised modular grid systems like the one shown here.

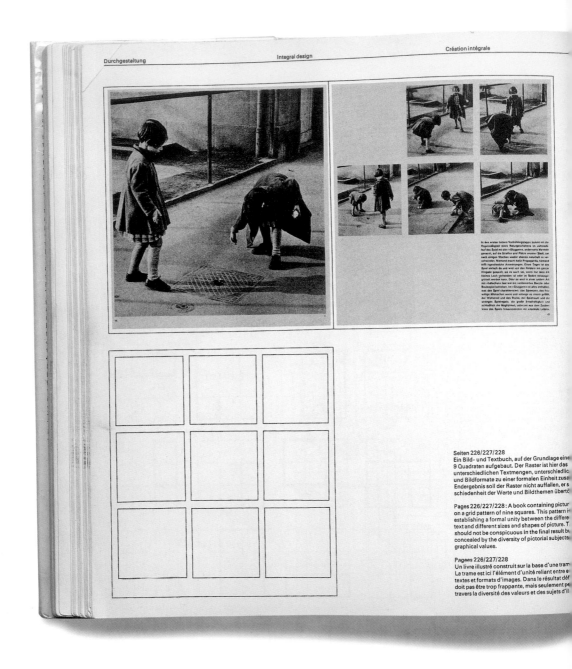

Durchgestaltung   Integral design   Création intégrale

Seiten 226/227/228
Ein Bild- und Textbuch, auf der Grundlage eine
9 Quadraten aufgebaut. Der Raster ist hier das
unterschiedlichen Textmengen, unterschiedlic
und Bildformate zu einer formalen Einheit zusa
Endergebnis soll der Raster nicht auffallen, er s
schiedenheit der Werte und Bildthemen übertö

Pages 226/227/228: A book containing pictur
on a grid pattern of nine squares. This pattern i
establishing a formal unity between the differe
text and different sizes and shapes of picture. T
should not be conspicuous in the final result bu
concealed by the diversity of pictorial subjects
graphical values.

Pagees 226/227/228
Un livre illustré construit sur la base d'une tram
La trame est ici l'élément d'unité reliant entre e
textes et formats d'images. Dans le résultat déf
doit pas être trop frappante, mais seulement pe
travers la diversité des valeurs et des sujets d'il

TYPOGRAPHY Book, 1967. Designer and
author: Emil Ruder. Publisher: Arthur Niggli,
Zurich. Photograph: Dan Meyers. *In this
classic design text, Emil Ruder demonstrates the
use of a modular grid.*

Modular grids are created by positioning horizontal guidelines in relation to a *baseline grid* that governs the whole document. Baseline grids serve to anchor all (or nearly all) layout elements to a common rhythm. Create a baseline grid by choosing the typesize and leading of your text, such as 10-pt Scala Pro with 12 pts leading (10/12). Avoid auto leading so that you can work with whole numbers that multiply and divide cleanly. Use this line space increment to set the baseline grid in your document preferences. Adjust the top or bottom page margin to absorb any space left over by the baseline grid.

Determine the number of horizontal page units in relation to the number of lines in your baseline grid. Count how many lines fit in a full column of text and then choose a number that divides evenly into the line count to create horizontal page divisions. A column with forty-two lines of text divides neatly into seven horizontal modules with six lines each. If your line count is not neatly divisible, adjust the top and/or bottom page margins to absorb the leftover lines.

To style headlines, captions, and other elements, choose line spacing that works with the baseline grid, such as 18/24 for headlines, 14/18 for subheads, and 8/12 for captions. Web designers can choose similar increments (`line height` in CSS) to create style sheets with neatly coordinated baselines.

Where possible, position all page elements in relation to the baseline grid. Don't force it, though. Sometimes a layout works better when you override the grid. View the baseline grid when you want to check the position of elements; turn it off when it's distracting.

BASELINE GRID *In InDesign, set the baseline grid in the Preferences>Grids and Guides window. Create horizontal divisions in Layout>Create Guides. Make the horizontal guides correspond to the baselines of the page's primary text by choosing a number of rows that divides evenly into the number of lines in a full column of text.*

NERD ALERT: Working in InDesign, you can make your text frames automatically align with the baseline grid. Go to Object>Text Frame Options>Baseline Options and choose Leading. If your leading (line spacing) is 12 pts, the first baseline will fall 12 pts from the top of the text frame.

BETTER TEXT FRAMES *The first line of the text starts 12 pts from the top of the text frame. In the default setting, the first line is positioned according to the cap height.*

MAIN HEADLINE
32/48 pt Scala Sans Pro Bold

SUBHEAD
18/24 Scala Sans Pro Italic

baseline grids

create a common rhythm

Captions and other details are styled to coordinate with the dominant baseline grid.

Modular grids are created by positioning horizontal guidelines in relation to a *baseline* grid that governs the whole document. Baseline grids serve to anchor all (or nearly all) elements to a common rhythm.

Create a baseline grid by choosing the typesize and leading of your text, such as 10-pt Scala Pro with 12 pts leading (10/12). Avoid auto leading so that you can work with whole numbers that multiply and divide cleanly. Use this line space increment to set the baseline grid in your document preferences. Adjust the top or bottom page margin to absorb any space left over by the baseline grid.

Determine the number of horizontal page units in relation to the numer of lines in the baseline grid. Count how many lines fit in a full column of text and then choose a number that divides easily into the line count to create horizontal page divisions. A column with forty-two lines of text divides neatly into seven horizontal modules with six lines each. If your line count is not neatly divisible, adjust the top and/or

bottom page margins to absorb leftover lines.

To style headlines, captions, and other elements, choose line spacing that works with the baseline grid, such as 18/24 for headlines, 14/18 for subheads, and 8/12 for captions. (Web designers can choose similar increments (line height) to create style sheets with coordinated baselines.)

Where possible, position all page elements in relation to the baseline grid. Don't force it, though. Sometimes a layout works better when you override the grid. View the baseline grid when you want to check the position of elements; turn it off when it's distracting.

InDesign, set the baseline grid in the Preferences>Grids and Guides window. Create horizontal divisions in Layout>Create Guides. Make the horizontal guides correspond to the baselines of the page's primary text by choosing a number of rows that divides evenly into the number of lines in a full column of text. Working in InDesign, you can make

CAPTION
9/12 Scala Sans Pro Italic

PRIMARY TEXT:
10/12 Scala Pro.
This measure determines the baseline grid.

DESIGN LIKE YOU GIVE A DAMN Book, 2006.
Designers: Paul Carlos, Urshula Barbour, Katharina Seifert, and Farha Khan/Pure + Applied. Authors: Architecture for Humanity, Kate Stohr, and Cameron Sinclair. *This book design uses a modular grid to bring order to complex content. Some pages are dense with body text, captions, and small images, while others feature full-bleed photography layered with short statements and hard-hitting statistics.*

"Architecture is a process of giving form and pattern to the social life of the community. Architecture is not an individual act performed by an artist-architect and charged with his emotions. Building is a collective action."

Hannes Meyer, director of Bauhaus, 1928 to 1930

Walter Gropius, slab apartment blocks on the Wannsee Shore, Berlin, 1931

built two prototypes based on his ideas for exhibition: The *immeubles villas* (1922) and the Maison Citrohan (1922), a play on the automobile name Citroën. Throughout the '20s Le Corbusier expounded on his ideas for a new industrialized architecture in a series of manifestos and urban plans.

Another early pioneer of prefabrication and component building systems was the German architect Walter Gropius. Gropius, who founded the Bauhaus and served as its director from 1919 to 1928, personified the architect as public servant and teacher. Throughout the '20s and '30s Gropius experimented with prefabricated wall panels and eventually whole structures. During his tenure and that of his successors, the Bauhaus became a nexus for socially conscious design.

Gropius, along with Marcel Breuer, is also credited with designing the first slab apartment block. This new building type, which would become the model for many future affordable-housing projects, was conceived to overcome the cramped, lightless tenement housing that had resulted from rampant land speculation at the turn of the century. The basic plan consisted of parallel rows of four- to 11-story apartment blocks. Each slab was only one apartment deep with windows front and back. The slabs were sited on a "superblock" at an angle to the street with communal green spaces between them to allow maximum sunlight into each apartment.[12]

Others would also experiment with standardized building components, modular systems, and prefabrication, including the French industrial designer Jean Prouvé and Frank Lloyd Wright, but perhaps none more passionately than the American inventor R. Buckminster Fuller.

Fuller arrived on what he termed "spaceship earth" in 1895. Like Gropius and Le Corbusier, he believed that mass-manufactured dwellings represented the future of housing. His most lasting contribution, however, was his fervent belief in the power of design to improve the human condition. In a sense Fuller, who was known for his eccentric use of language and his marathon lectures (the longest lasted 42 hours and only recently has been fully transcribed), was the first evangelist of humanitarian design.

In 1927, after the death of his elder daughter and the collapse of his first business, he found himself at the edge of Lake Michigan contemplating suicide. He was a failure, "a throw-away." What brought him from the brink, he later recounted, was the simple idea that his experience might ultimately be somehow useful to his fellow human beings. Rather than taking his own life, he decided to embark on a lifelong experiment, using himself as his own best research subject. He became "Guinea Pig B" (for Bucky), the world's first test pilot of a "design-science revolution," the sole purpose of which was to improve "human livingry," and he started with the house.

Conventional "handcrafted" homes had undergone "no structural advances in 5,000 years," Fuller argued. They were poorly lit, required much maintenance, and did not make efficient use of raw materials. Most conventional buildings depended on gravity for their strength. But what if a building could be suspended, as a sail from a mast, allowing for greater strength and the use of fewer materials?

Fuller's thinking led to the design of the Dymaxion House, a small-scale model of which was first exhibited at a Marshall Field's department store in Chicago in 1929. His radical scheme embraced the principle of tension and aimed to do "more with less." It was spherical, to make efficient use of materials, and clad in maintenance-free aluminum. It was naturally climate controlled and could be lit by a single light source through a system of mirrors and dimmers. All the mechanicals, wiring, and appliances were built into the walls and mast to allow for easy replacement. The house was also one of the first examples of self-sufficient (or "autonomous," as Fuller put it) green design. Wind turbines produced energy. The roof collected rainwater. Water-saving "fog guns" handled washing (including people), and Fuller's "package toilet" composted waste and recovered methane gas.[13]

While the Dymaxion House was unabashedly ahead of its time (it would be two decades before Fuller could find backing to build a full-scale prototype), the concept of building with tension rather than compression would become central to Fuller's work and would eventually lead to his most lasting contribution to the field of humanitarian design: the geodesic dome. Fuller's principle of tensegrity became a staple of tent design, and by extension, emergency shelter, that endures to this day.

Like the Dymaxion House, few of these early designs for "factory-built" housing achieved widespread commercial viability. For example, Le Corbusier's low-cost housing for workers in Pessac, near Bordeaux, France, went unoccupied for eight years after it was built. However, this concept of mass-produced housing would have a number of lasting implications for low-cost shelter. It prefigured a move away from the craft of building toward the technology of building. It took design out of the realm of the many and put it in the hands of an educated few. Perhaps more important, it negated the need for a dialogue between the architect and the occupant.

1929	1930	1931	1931	1931
Dymaxion House Chicago, Ill., USA R. Buckminster Fuller	**Housing Act of 1930** England	**Prefabricated houses built for the Hirsch Copper and Brass Works** Finow, Germany Walter Gropius	**Flood** China The Yellow River, the second largest river in China, floods. Death toll estimates range from 850,000 to four million. The flooding is followed by famine and outbreaks of disease.	**Modern Housing** Catherine Bauer
	1930–39 **Drought and Dust Storms** Midwestern and southern plains, USA	**1931** **Slab apartment blocks on the Wannsee shore** Berlin, Germany Walter Gropius		**1934** **National Housing Act of 1934** USA

The UNHCR's new Lightweight Emergency Tents is use in Minicathon, West Sumatra, following the Indian Ocean tsunami of 2004.

Lightweight Emergency Tent

Location_Various
Date_2002–present
Organization_Office of the United Nations High Commissioner for Refugees (UNHCR)
End client_Refugees, internally displaced populations
Design consultant_Ghassem Fardanesh
Manufacturer_H. Sheikh Noor-ud-Din & Sons (Pvt.) Limited, Lahore, Pakistan
Cost per unit_Approx. $100
Area_178 sq. ft./16.5 sq. m
Occupancy_4–5 people
Dimensions_18 x 9.8 x 6.9 ft./5.5 x 3 x 2.1 m
Weight_91 lb./41.5 kg

In war-torn countries and areas devastated by disaster, the presence of UNHCR tents is one of the first signs of aid.
Designers have tried to rethink this basic tent for decades. Everything from prefabricated structures to shipping containers to polyurethane yurts has been suggested or attempted. But as the agency politely points out in its guide to emergency materials, to date none of these systems has proven effective in refugee situations. Most fail simply because other emergency shelter arrangements will have been made before these systems even arrive. Some tent alternatives are perceived as "too permanent," making them difficult to site in host communities and creating less incentive for a refugee to return home. Others are difficult or costly to replicate.
But in recent years there has been a growing sense within the agency that the design of the standard family tent could and should be radically overhauled. In most emergencies the agency sends out plastic sheeting first. Depending on the size and complexity of the crisis, this sheeting may be the response of first and last resort. However, in cases where local materials are not available to build more permanent structures, where families cannot find shelter within the community or are displaced for longer periods of time, the UNHCR provides more durable alternatives—typically a ridge-pole or center-pole-double-fly tent made from canvas. Yet these canvas tents are not only heavy, cumbersome to carry, and costly to ship, but because canvas rots they deteriorate quickly and cannot be stockpiled for long periods. Wear and tear on the weakened material in the field significantly shortens the useful lifespan of the shelter.
In 2002 the UNHCR began testing a new design for the basic family tent it regularly dispatched to areas of crisis. The agency's

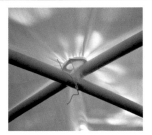

opposite
A GripClip, secured to a cross-piece of frame, shown from inside a shelter. The frame pieces are secured with plastic wrap.

above
GripClip's two plastic parts are designed to be twisted together with a piece of sheeting between them. The clip itself can be fastened to a frame structure with plastic ties, rope, or pipe clamps.

right
Robert Gillis inside a tent built with GripClips.
All photographs © www.spinettotc.com

GripClips

Location_Various
Date_1975–present
Designer_Robert Gillis
Manufacturer_Shelter Systems
Cost_$8–10 (set of 4)

It would be safe to say that few people know the ins and outs of tents better than Robert Gillis.

Not only did he design the first geodesic backpacking tent, based on Buckminster Fuller's ideas, for The North Face in the 1970s, but he also lived in a collection of tents (with his wife and three children) for more than 20 years—all of which he designed himself, including the tent that housed the family washing machine.
Although many of Gillis's tent innovations have stemmed from efforts to improve his own living conditions, from the beginning he saw the potential for translating his ideas to emergency shelter—in particular using the plastic sheeting that has become a standard

component of relief projects. However, working with plastic sheeting meant finding a way to "hold on to it." Gillis explains. "It was difficult to join the material without puncturing it. But puncturing it is a bad idea because it weakens it. The material deteriorates less if you don't injure it." The designer went through more than 10 different iterations before arriving at the GripClip, a small plastic fastener that clips onto any type of sheeting and ties it to a frame.
Reducing the shelter to its most fundamental element, the connection between the sheeting and the support, enabled Gillis to design a number of tents, from a basic shelter frame kit to more elaborate dome structures.
The clips also offered another advantage. They allowed for a range of shapes. Whereas most relief agencies distribute tunnel-shaped tents because the structure can be covered

with one large sheet of material, these tents are less stable in the wind than dome-shaped tents. Using GripClips, Gillis found he was able to layer sheeting in shingles to create a more stable structure that would also shed rain. "And I didn't have to sew it or heat-weld it or anything," he recalls. "Here was the perfect thing: It was totally wonderful."
More recently Gillis has focused on creating clips and fasteners to attach plastic sheeting to roofs, frameworks, piping, or plywood, allowing families to turn damaged structures into transitional homes while they rebuild.

Use a modular grid to arrange a text in as many ways as you can. By employing just one size of type and flush left alignment only, you will construct a typographic hierarchy exclusively by means of spatial arrangement. To make the project more complex, begin adding variables such as weight, size, and alignment.

Common typographic disorders

Various forms of dysfunction appear among populations exposed to typography for long periods of time. Listed here are a number of frequently observed afflictions.

typophilia
An excessive attachment to and fascination with the shape of letters, often to the exclusion of other interests and object choices. Typophiliacs usually die penniless and alone.

typophobia
The irrational dislike of letterforms, often marked by a preference for icons, dingbats, and—in fatal cases—bullets and daggers. The fears of the typophobe can often be quieted (but not cured) by steady doses of Helvetica and Times Roman.

typochondria
A persistent anxiety that one has selected the wrong typeface. This condition is often paired with okd (optical kerning disorder), the need to constantly adjust and readjust the spaces between letters.

Common typographic disorders

Various forms of dysfunction appear among populations exposed to typography for long periods of time. Listed here are a number of frequently observed afflictions.

typophilia

An excessive attachment to and fascination with the shape of letters, often to the exclusion of other interests and object choices. Typophiliacs usually die penniless and alone.

typophobia

The irrational dislike of letterforms, often marked by a preference for icons, dingbats, and—in fatal cases—bullets and daggers. The fears of the typophobe can often be quieted (but not cured) by steady doses of Helvetica and Times Roman.

typochondria

A persistent anxiety that one has selected the wrong typeface. This condition is often paired with OKD (optical kerning disordcr), the need to constantly adjust and readjust the spaces between letters.

Common typographic disorders

Various forms of dysfunction appear among populations exposed to typography for long periods of time. Listed here are a number of frequently observed afflictions.

typophilia
An excessive attachment to and fascination with the shape of letters, often to the exclusion of other interests and object choices. Typophiliacs usually die penniless and alone.

typophobia
The irrational dislike of letterforms, often marked by a preference for icons, dingbats, and—in fatal cases—bullets and daggers. The fears of the typophobe can often be quieted (but not cured) by steady doses of Helvetica and Times Roman.

typochondria
A persistent anxiety that one has selected the wrong typeface. This condition is often paired with OKD (optical kerning disorder), the need to constantly adjust and readjust the spaces between letters.

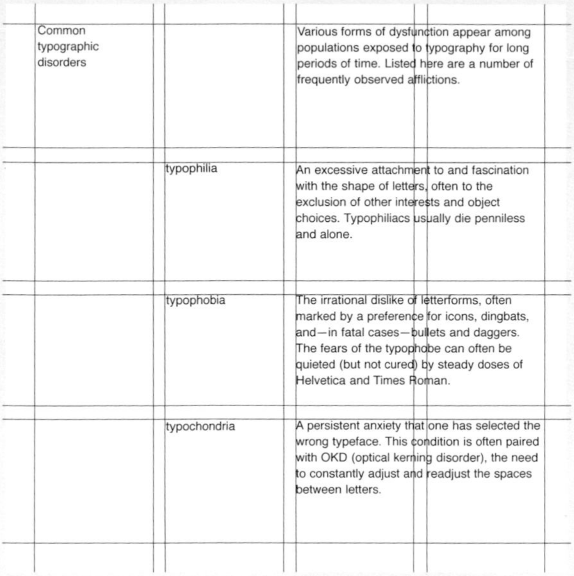

Quadrant 1 (top left)

Common typographic disorders		Various forms of dysfunction appear among populations exposed to typography for long periods of time. Listed here are a number of frequently observed afflictions.
	typophilia	An excessive attachment to and fascination with the shape of letters, often to the exclusion of other interests and object choices. Typophiliacs usually die penniless and alone.
	typophobia	The irrational dislike of letterforms, often marked by a preference for icons, dingbats, and—in fatal cases—bullets and daggers. The fears of the typophobe can often be quieted (but not cured) by steady doses of Helvetica and Times Roman.
	typochondria	A persistent anxiety that one has selected the wrong typeface. This condition is often paired with OKD (optical kerning disorder), the need to constantly adjust and readjust the spaces between letters.

Quadrant 2 (top right)

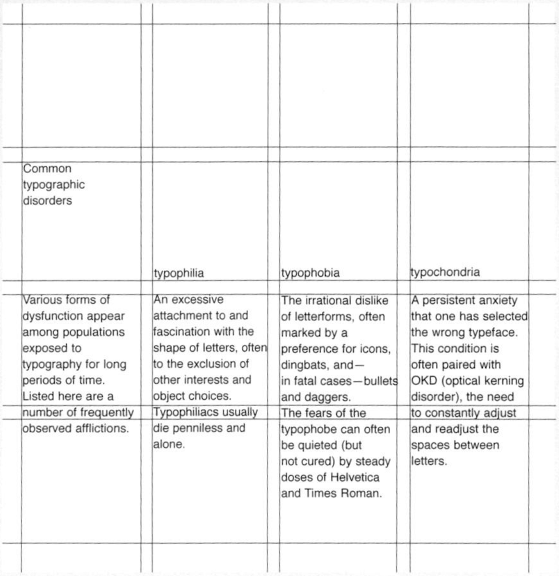 Common typographic disorders			
	typophilia	typophobia	typochondria
Various forms of dysfunction appear among populations exposed to typography for long periods of time. Listed here are a number of frequently observed afflictions.	An excessive attachment to and fascination with the shape of letters, often to the exclusion of other interests and object choices. Typophiliacs usually die penniless and alone.	The irrational dislike of letterforms, often marked by a preference for icons, dingbats, and—in fatal cases—bullets and daggers. The fears of the typophobe can often be quieted (but not cured) by steady doses of Helvetica and Times Roman.	A persistent anxiety that one has selected the wrong typeface. This condition is often paired with OKD (optical kerning disorder), the need to constantly adjust and readjust the spaces between letters.

Quadrant 3 (bottom left)

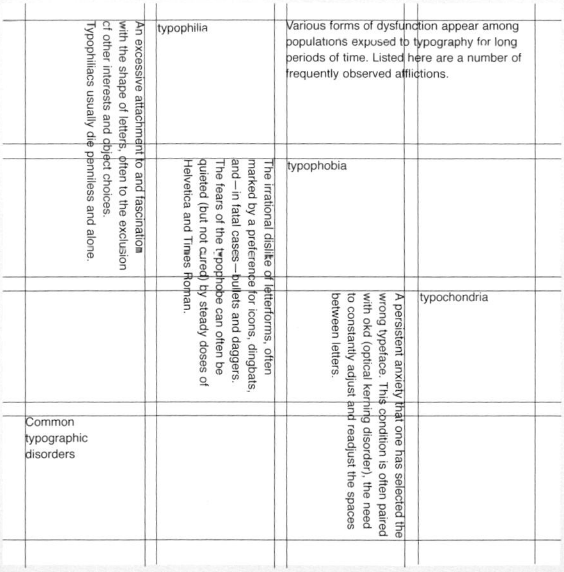 An excessive attachment to and fascination with the shape of letters, often to the exclusion of other interests and object choices. Typophiliacs usually die penniless and alone.	typophilia	Various forms of dysfunction appear among populations exposed to typography for long periods of time. Listed here are a number of frequently observed afflictions.	
		The irrational dislike of letterforms, often marked by a preference for icons, dingbats, and—in fatal cases—bullets and daggers. The fears of the typophobe can often be quieted (but not cured) by steady doses of Helvetica and Times Roman.	typophobia	
		A persistent anxiety that one has selected the wrong typeface. This condition is often paired with okd (optical kerning disorder), the need to constantly adjust and readjust the spaces between letters	typochondria
Common typographic disorders			

Quadrant 4 (bottom right)

	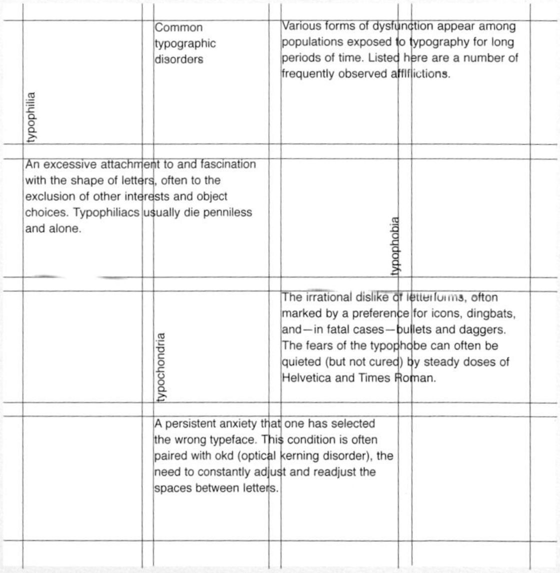 Common typographic disorders	Various forms of dysfunction appear among populations exposed to typography for long periods of time. Listed here are a number of frequently observed afflictions.
typophilia	An excessive attachment to and fascination with the shape of letters, often to the exclusion of other interests and object choices. Typophiliacs usually die penniless and alone.	
typophobia	The irrational dislike of letterforms, often marked by a preference for icons, dingbats, and—in fatal cases—bullets and daggers. The fears of the typophobe can often be quieted (but not cured) by steady doses of Helvetica and Times Roman.	
typochondria	A persistent anxiety that one has selected the wrong typeface. This condition is often paired with okd (optical kerning disorder), the need to constantly adjust and readjust the spaces between letters.	

The design of charts and graphs is a rich area of typographic practice. In a data table, the grid acquires semantic significance. Columns and rows contain different types of content that readers can scan and quickly compare. Designers (and software defaults) often over-emphasize the linear grid of a table rather than allowing the typography to command the page and stake out its own territory. As columns of text align visually, they create implied grid lines on the page or screen.

ACCOUNT	ACCOUNT NAME	TOTAL FOR ACCO
101001	Instructional Supplies	$3,65
101002	Office Supplies	$46
102004	Equipment - Non-Capital	$1,28
105009	Travel-Conference Fees	$56
110004	Miscellaneous Entertainment	$8
114006	Postage/Shipping-Local Courier	$21
151108	Temp Staff-Contractual	$7
151181	Honoraria-Critics/Vis Artist	$1,00
	DEPARTMENTAL EXPENDITURES	$7,35

TYPE CRIME: DATA PRISON *The rules and boxes used in data tables should illuminate the relationships among data, not trap each entry inside a heavily guarded cell.*

Train No.	3701	XM 3301	3801	A 67	3 3803	3 3201	A3 51	3 3703	3 3807	3 3203	A3 61	3 3809	A3 47	3 3901	3 3811	3 3903	3 3813	3205	3815	3817	3819	3207	3821	3823	3825	3209	3827	3829	3831
New York, N.Y.	A.M. 12.10	A.M 12.10	A.M. 1.30	A.M. 3.52	A.M. 4.50	A.M. 6.10	A.M. 6.25	A.M. 6.35	A.M. 6.50	A.M. 7.10	A.M. 7.30	A.M. 7.33	A.M. 7.45	A.M. 7.50	A.M. 8.05	A.M. 8.25	A.M. 8.40	A.M. 8.50	A.M. 9.10	A.M. 9.40	A.M. 10.10	A.M. 10.25	A.M. 10.40	A.M. 11.10	A.M 11.40	A.M 11.50	P.M. 12.10	P.M 12.40	P.M. 1.10
Newark, N.J. P	12.24	12.55	1.44	4.07	5.04	6.24	6.38	6.49	7.04	7.24	7.45	7.47	7.59	8.04	8.19	8.39	8.54	9.04	9.24	9.54	10.24	10.39	10.54	11.24	11.54	12.04	12.24	12.54	1.24
North Elizabeth									7.30			8.10																	
Elizabeth	12.31	1.03	1.51		5.11	6.31		6.56	7.11	7.32		7.54		8.13	8.26	8.46	9.01	9.11	9.31	10.01	10.31	10.46	11.01	11.31	12.01	12.11	12.31	1.01	1.31
Linden	12.36		1.56		5.16	6.36		7.01	7.15	7.37		7.59		8.18	8.31	8.51	9.06		9.36	10.06	10.36		11.06	11.36	12.06		12.36	1.06	1.36
North Rahway								7.03		7.39				8.20	8.33	8.54													
Rahway	12.40	1.11	2.00		5.20	6.40		7.06	7.20	7.42		8.03		8.24	8.36	8.57	9.10	9.18	9.40	10.10	10.40	10.53	11.10	11.40	12.10	12.18	12.40	1.10	1.40
Metro Park (Iselin)	12.44		2.04	4.26	5.24		6.56	7.10	7.25		8.04	8.07	8.15	8.40			9.14		9.44	10.14	10.44		11.14	11.44	12.14		12.44	1.14	1.44
Metuchen	12.48		2.08		5.28			7.14	7.29		8.11		8.44			9.18		9.48	10.18	10.48		11.18	11.48	12.18		12.48	1.18	1.48	
Edison	12.51		2.11					7.17	7.32		8.14		8.47		9.21				10.21		11.21		12.21		1.21				
New Brunswick	12.55		2.15		5.35		7.05	7.21	7.35		8.18	8.25	8.50		9.25		9.54	10.25	10.54		11.25	11.54	12.25		12.54	1.25	1.54		
Jersey Avenue	1.02		2.18					7.28		8.21			9.28				10.28		11.28		12.28		1.28						
Princeton Jct. S			2.31		5.50		7.19		7.50		8.34	8.41	9.05		9.41		10.09	10.41	11.09		11.41	12.09	12.41		1.09	1.41	2.09		
Trenton, N.J.			2.42	4.58	6.03		7.28		8.01		8.31	8.44	8.52	9.16		9.52		10.19	10.52	11.19		11.52	12.19	12.52		1.22	1.52	2.20	

	am ●																												
New York, NY	12.10	12.40	1.30	3.52	4.50	6.10	6.25	6.35	6.50	7.10	7.30	7.33	7.45	7.50	8.05	8.25	8.40	8.50	9.10	9.40	10.10	10.25	10.40	11.10	11.40				
Newark, NJ P	12.24	12.55	1.44	4.07	5.04	6.24	6.38	6.49	7.04	7.24	7.45	7.47	7.59	8.04	8.19	8.39	8.54	9.04	9.24	9.54	10.24	10.39	10.54	11.24	11.54				
North Elizabeth										7.30				8.10															
Elizabeth	12.31	1.03	1.51		5.11	6.31		6.56	7.11	7.32		7.54		8.13	8.26	8.46	9.01	9.11	9.31	10.01	10.31	10.46	11.01	11.31	12.01				
Linden	12.36		1.56		5.16	6.36		7.01	7.15	7.37		7.59		8.18	8.31	8.51	9.06		9.36	10.06	10.36		11.06	11.36	12.06				
North Rahway								7.03		7.39				8.20	8.33	8.54													
Rahway	12.40	1.11	2.00		5.20	6.40		7.06	7.20	7.42		8.03		8.24	8.36	8.57	9.10	9.18	9.40	10.10	10.40	10.53	11.10	11.40	12.10				
Metro Park (Iselin)	12.44		2.04	4.26	5.24		6.56	7.10	7.25		8.04	8.07	8.15	8.40			9.14		9.44	10.14	10.44		11.14	11.44	12.14				
Metuchen	12.48		2.08		5.28			7.14	7.29		8.11			8.44			9.18		9.48	10.18	10.48		11.18	11.48	12.18				
Edison	12.51		2.11					7.17	7.32		8.14			8.47			9.21			10.21			11.21		12.21				
New Brunswick	12.55		2.15		5.35		7.05	7.21	7.35		8.18	8.25	8.50				9.25		9.54	10.25	10.54		11.25	11.54	12.25				
Jersey Avenue	1.02		2.18					7.28		8.21							9.28			10.28			11.28		12.28				
Princeton Junction S			2.31		5.50		7.19		7.50		8.34	8.41		9.05		9.41			10.09	10.41	11.09		11.41	12.09	12.41				
Trenton, NJ			2.42	4.58	6.03		7.28		8.01		8.31	8.44	8.52	9.16		9.52			10.19	10.52	11.19		11.52	12.19	12.52				
TRAIN NUMBER	3701	3301	3801	67	3803	3201	51	3703	3807	3203	61	3809	47	3901	3811	3903	3813	3205	3815	3817	3819	3207	3821	3823	3825				
NOTES		XM		➤	3	3	➤3	3	3	3	➤3	3	➤3	3	3	3	3												

NEW JERSEY TRANSIT, NORTHEASTERN CORRIDOR TIMETABLE Original schedule with redesign by Edward Tufte. From Edward Tufte, *Envisioning Information* (Cheshire, Conn.: Graphics Press, 1990). *The original design (top) is organized with heavy horizontal and vertical divisions. Tufte calls this a "data prison." His redesign uses the alignment of the typographic elements themselves to express the table's underlying structure.*

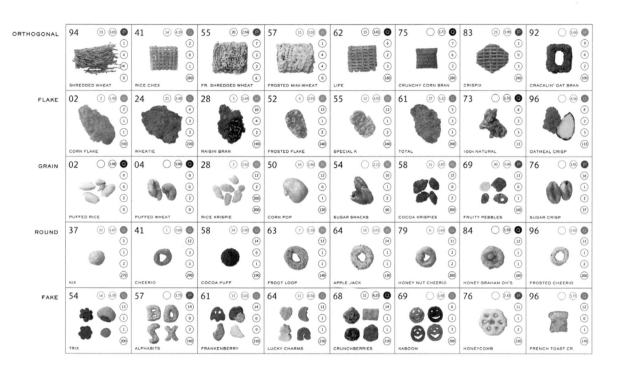

PERIODIC BREAKFAST TABLE Magazine page (detail), 1998. Designer: Catherine Weese. Photography: John Halpern. Publisher: Patsy Tarr, 2wice Magazine. *This chart organizes breakfast cereals by shape and annotates them according to a dozen characteristics, from fiber content to price per pound. Visual displays of data allow readers to quickly compare items. One might observe, for example, that in breakfast cereals, intensity of sugar is usually accompanied by intensity of color.*

Find a chart from an old science book or other source and redesign it. Shown at right is a nineteenth-century table documenting an experiment about ants. The old design emphasizes vertical divisions at the expense of horizontal ones, and it jumbles together text and numbers within the table cells.

The redesign below eliminates many of the ruled lines, replacing them, where needed, with a pale tone that unifies the long horizontal rows of data. The redesigned chart also replaces most of the numerals with dots, a technique that lets the eye visually compare the results without having to read each numeral separately.

CHLOROFORMED ANTS

	LEFT ALONE	TAKEN TO NEST	THROWN IN WATER	BOTH NEST AND WATER	LEFT ALONE	TAKEN TO NEST	THROWN IN WATER	BOTH NEST AND WATER
PT 10	••••						••••	
14			••••				••	••
15			•	•	••		••	
29			•••••				••••	
CT 02			•••••				••••	•
06			•••••				••••	
AL	04		20	01	02		20	03

INTOXICATED ANTS

	LEFT ALONE	TAKEN TO NEST	THROWN IN WATER	BOTH NEST AND WATER	LEFT ALONE	TAKEN TO NEST	THROWN IN WATER	BOTH NEST AND WATER
OV 20		•••	••		•		•••••	
22	••	••					••••••••	
EC 01		•••••••	••				••••••	•••
05		••••••••••••••	•••••				••••••••••••	•••
AN 15	••••				•		•••	
17		••••				••	••••••	•
AL	06	32	09		02	02	43	07

INTOXICATED FRIENDS Data table from Sir John Lubbock, *Ants, Bees, and Wasps* (New York: D. Appleton and Company, 1893). *The author of this experiment studied how ants responded upon meeting either "friends" (members of their own colony) or "strangers." In the first experiment, the friends and strangers were rendered unconscious with chloroform. In the second experiment, the ants were merely intoxicated. The chloroformed ants—whether friends or strangers—were usually taken for dead and pitched into a moat of water surrounding the colony. The intoxicated ants were treated with more discrimination. Many of the drunken friends were taken back to the nest for rehabilitation, whereas drunken strangers were generally tossed in the moat. Ants, one might conclude, should not rely on the kindness of strangers.*

118   BEHAVIOUR TO INTOXICATED FRIENDS.

Tabular View.—Experiments on Ants under Chloroform and Intoxicated.

	CHLOROFORMED ANTS					
	FRIENDS			STRANGERS		
	To Nest	To Water	Unremoved	To Nest	To Water	Unremoved
Sept. 10	...	...	4	...	4	...
14	...	4	...	2 and brought out again	2	...
15	1 and brought out again	1	...	...	2	2
29	...	5	...	...	4	...
Oct. 2	...	5	...	1 and brought out again	4	...
6	...	5	...	...	4	...
	1	20	4	3	20	2
	INTOXICATED ANTS.					
Nov. 20	3	2	...	...	5	1
22	2	...	2	...	8	...

In these cases some of the Ants had partly recovered ; in the following they were quite insensible.

	To Nest	To Water	Unremoved	To Nest	To Water	Unremoved
Dec. 1	7 none brought out again	2	...	3 all these brought out again	6	...
8	16 none brought out again	5	...	3 all these brought out again	15	...
Jan. 15	...	...	4	...	3	1
17	4 none brought out again	...	...	3 one brought out again	6	...
	27	7	4	2	30	1

{APPENDIX}

SPACES AND PUNCTUATION

Writers or clients often supply manuscripts that employ incorrect dashes or faulty word spacing. Consult a definitive work such as *The Chicago Manual of Style* for a complete guide to punctuation. The following rules are especially pertinent for designers.

WORD SPACES are created by the space bar. Use just one space between sentences or after a comma, colon, or semicolon. One of the first steps in typesetting a manuscript is to purge it of all double spaces. Thus the space bar should not be used to create indents or otherwise position text on a line. Use tabs instead. HTML refuses to recognize double spaces altogether.

EN SPACES are wider than word spaces. An en space can be used to render a more emphatic distance between elements on a line: for example, to separate a subhead from the text that immediately follows, or to separate elements gathered along a single line in a letterhead.

EM DASHES express strong grammatical breaks. An em dash is one em wide—the width of the point size of the typeface. In manuscripts, dashes are often represented with a double hyphen (--); these must be replaced.

EN DASHES serve primarily to connect numbers (1–10). An en is half the width of an em. Manuscripts rarely employ en dashes, so the designer needs to supply them.

HYPHENS connect linked words and phrases, and they break words at the ends of lines. Typesetting programs break words automatically. Disable auto hyphenation when working with ragged or centered text; use discretionary hyphens instead, and only when unavoidable.

DISCRETIONARY HYPHENS, which are inserted manually to break lines, only appear in the document if they are needed. (If a text is reflowed in subsequent editing, a discretionary hyphen will disappear.) Wayward hyphens often occur in the mid-dle of a line when the typesetter has inserted a "hard" hyphen instead of a discretionary one.

QUOTATION MARKS have distinct "open" and "closed" forms, unlike hatch marks, which are straight up and down. A single close quote also serves as an apostrophe ("It's Bob's font."). Prime or hatch marks should only be used to indicate inches and feet (5'2"). Used incorrectly, hatches are known as "dumb quotes." Although computer operating systems and typesetting programs often include automatic "smart quote" features, e-mailed, word-processed, and/or client-supplied text can be riddled with dumb quotes. Auto smart quote programs often render

apostrophes upside down ('tis instead of 'tis), so designers must be vigilant and learn the necessary keystrokes.

ELLIPSES consist of three periods, which can be rendered with no spaces between them, or with open tracking (letterspacing), or with word spaces. An ellipsis indicates an omitted section in a quoted text or...a temporal break. Most typefaces include an ellipsis character, which presents closely spaced points.

MAC OS KEYSTROKES *These keystrokes listed below are commonly used in word processing, page layout, and illustration software. Some fonts do not include a full range of special characters.*

DASHES		KEYSTROKES
—	em dash	shift-option-hyphen
–	en dash	option-hyphen
-	standard hyphen	(hyphen key)
-	discretionary hyphen	command-hyphen

PUNCTUATION		
'	single open quote	option-]
'	single close quote	shift-option-]
"	double open quote	option-[
"	double close quote	shift-option-[
...	ellipsis	option-;

OTHER MARKS		
( )	en space	option-space bar
†	dagger	option-t
‡	double dagger	shift-option-7
©	copyright symbol	option-g
®	resister symbol	option-r
€	Euro symbol	shift-option-2
fi	fi ligature	shift-option-5
fl	fl ligature	shift-option-6
é	*accent aigu*	option-e + e
è	*accent grave*	option-` + e
à	*accent grave*	option-` + a
ù	*accent grave*	option-` + u
ç	*cédille*	option-c
ü	*umlaut*	option-u + u
ö	*umlaut*	option-u + o

These interruptions—especially the snide remarks--are killing my buzz.

CRIME: *Two hyphens in place of an em dash*

Dashes express a break in the flow of a sentence. In a word-processed document, dashes can be indicated with two hyphens. Em dashes are required, however, in typesetting. No spaces are used around dashes.

El Lissitzky lived 1890–1941. Rodchenko lived longer (1891-1956).

CRIME: *Hyphen between numbers*

An en dash connects two numbers. It means "up to and including," not "between." No spaces are used around en dashes.

It's okay to be second-best, but never, ever second–best.

CRIME: *En dash in hyphenated word*

Do not use en dashes where the humble hyphen is required.

In the beginning was...the word....Typography came later.

An ellipsis character is used here in place of separate points.

The periods in an ellipsis can be separated with word spaces, or, as we prefer, they can be tracked open (letterspaced). Most typefaces include an ellipsis character, whose points are more tightly spaced. After a sentence, use a period plus an ellipsis (four dots).

She was 5'2" with eyes of blue. "I'm not dumb," she said. "I'm prime."

CRIME: *Prime marks (a.k.a. dumb quotes) used in place of quotation marks*

The purpose of prime marks, or hatch marks, is to indicate inches and feet. Their use to mark quotations is a common blight across the typographic landscape.

"I'm not smart," he replied. "I'm a quotation mark."

Unlike prime marks, quotation marks include an opening and closing character. Single close quotes also serve as apostrophes. Incorrectly used prime marks must be routed out and destroyed.

Don't put two spaces between sentences. They leave an ugly gap.

CRIME: *Two spaces between sentences*

Although writers persist in putting double spaces between sentences (a habit often learned in high school), all such spaces must be purged from a manuscript when it is set in type.

Since the onslaught of desktop publishing back in the dark days of the mid-1980s, graphic designers have taken on roles formerly occupied by distinct trades, such as typesetting and mechanical pasteup. Designers are often expected to be editors as well. Every project should have a true editor, a person with the training and disposition to judge the correctness, accuracy, and consistency of written content. Neither a project's author nor its designer should be its editor, who is rightly a neutral party between them. If a project team includes no properly trained editor, try to find one. If that fails, make sure that *someone* is responsible for this crucial role, for the failure to edit carefully is the source of costly and embarrassing errors.

Editing a text for publication has three basic phases. *Developmental editing* addresses broad issues of the content and the structure of a work; indeed, it can include judging a work's fitness for publication in the first place. *Copy editing* (also called line editing or manuscript editing) seeks to root out redundancies, inconsistencies, grammatical errors, and other flaws appearing across the body of the work. The copy editor—who must study every word and sentence—is not expected to question the overall meaning or structure of a work, nor to alter an author's style, but rather to refine and correct. *Proofreading*, which checks the correctness, consistency, and flow of designed, typset pages, is the final stage. Depending on the nature of the project and its team, each of these phases may go through several rounds.

ANATOMY OF AN ERROR After a document has been written, edited, designed, and proofread, a printer's proof is created by the printer from the digital files supplied by the designer. Many clients (or authors) fail to recognize errors (or make decisions) until the printer's proofs are issued. This luxury has its costs, and someone will have to pay.

PE'S (PRINTER'S ERRORS) These are errors that can be assigned to the printer, and they must be corrected at no expense to the designer or client. A printer's error is an obvious and blatant divergence from the digital files and other instructions provided by the designer and agreed to by the printer. Printer's errors are surprisingly rare in the digital age.

AA'S (AUTHOR'S ALTERATIONS) These are not so rare. Author's alterations are changes to the approved text or layout of the work. If the change originates with the designer, the designer is responsible. If it originates with the client or author, she or he is responsible. Keeping records of each phase of a project's development is helpful in assigning blame later. Designers can charge the client a fee for the AA on top of the printer's fee, as the designer must correct the file, print out new hard copy, get the client's approval (again), communicate with the printer (again), and so on. If agreed to in advance, designers can charge AA fees for *any* change to an approved document, even before the printer's proof is issued.

EA'S (EDITOR'S ALTERATIONS) Errors made by the editor are the responsibility of the editor's employer, typically the client or publisher of the work. Good editors help prevent everyone's errors from occurring in the first place.

For more detailed information about the editorial process, see *The Chicago Manual of Style, 15th Edition* (Chicago: University of Chicago Press, 2003).

Manuscript editing, also called copyediting or line editing, requires attention to every word in a manuscript, a thorough knowledge of the style to be followed, and the ability to make quick, logical, and defensible decisions. —*THE CHICAGO MANUAL OF STYLE*, 2003

Only an editor can see beyond a writer's navel.

No matter how brilliant your prose, an editor will discover errors in spelling, grammar, consistency, redundancy, and construction.

Writers should not over-format their texts.

The time you spend fiddling with formatting will be spent again by the editor and/or designer, removing extra keystrokes. Provide flush left copy, in one font, double-spaced.

Some lessons learned in high school are best forgotten.

One of them is dotting your i's with hearts and smiley faces. The other is leaving two spaces between sentences. In typesetting, one space only must be left between sentences.

The space bar is not a design tool.

Don't use the space bar to create indents (just key in a single tab), and don't use extra spaces to create centered effects or layouts (unless you really are E. E. Cummings).

Every change threatens to introduce new errors.

Each time a file is "corrected," new errors can appear, from problems with rags, justification, and page breaks to spelling mistakes, missing words, and botched or incomplete corrections.

Don't wait for the proofs to seriously examine the typeset text.

Changes made after a printer's proof has been made (blue line, press proof, or other) are expensive. They also will slow down your project, which, of course, is already late.

Famous last words: "We'll catch it in the blue lines."

delete
delete

transpose
transpose

stet ("let it stand")

add space
separate; add space

secondrate
add hyphen

left-over
remove hyphen

Dashing-no?
em dash (—)

1914-1918
en dash (–)

italic
italic

boldface
boldface

remove underline
remove underline

lowercase

case
uppercase

case
small caps

Writers, editors, and designers use special symbols to mark changes such as deleting, posing trans, or correcting words or phrases. *substituting* If you change your mind about a deletion, place dots beneath it. Remove a comma by circling it. Add a period with a circled dot. If two words run together, insert a straight line and a space mark.

To combine two paragraphs, connect them with a line and note the comment "run-in" in the margin. (Circling notes prevents the typesetter from confusing comments with content.)

Insert two short lines to hyphenate a word such as secondrate. When removing a hyphen, close up the leftover space. To replace a hyphen with an em dash-a symbol that expresses a grammatical break-write a tiny m above the hyphen. If a manuscript indicates dashes with double hyphens--like this-- the typesetter or designer is expected to convert them without being told. Use an en dash, not a hyphen, to connect two numbers, such as 1914-1918.

In addition to correcting grammar, spelling, punctuation, and clarity of prose, editors indicate typographic styles such as italic (with an underscore) and boldface (with a wavy line). Underlining, which is rarely used in formal typography, is removed like this. Draw A line Through A Capital Letter to change it to lowercase. underline a letter with three strokes to capitalize it. Use two underlines to indicate small capitals.

Double-space the manuscript and leave a generous margin to provide room for comments and corrections. Align the text flush left, ragged right, and disable automatic hyphenation.

Don't mark manuscripts or proofs with Post-It notes. They can fall off, block the text, and make the document hard to photocopy.

Editing an electronic file and allowing the author to see the changes is called *redlining* (also referred to as "editing online"). Basic housekeeping includes removing all double spaces and converting hatches (a.k.a. "dumb quotes") to quotation marks and apostrophes (a.k.a. "smart quotes"). The editor need not point out these changes to the author.

Changes to the structure and wording of the text must be communicated to the author. A visual convention is needed for showing ~~deleted~~ and added material. ~~Words to be removed~~ are typically struck out, and words added or substituted can be <u>underlined</u>, highlighted, or rendered in color. A line in the margin indicates that a change has been recommended. [Queries to the author are set off with brackets.][A]

Underlining,~~ ~~or striking out~~,~~ punctuation is visually confusing, so the editor often strikes out an entire word~~, or phrase,~~—or phrase—and types in the freshly punctuated passage as an addition. To hyphenate a word such as ~~secondrate~~ second-rate, strike it out and add the hyphenated form. When converting hyphens to en dashes (1914–18)—or changing double hyphens to em dashes—the editor simply keys them in. Typographic styles such as *italic*, **boldface**, and small capitals can also be changed directly.

Although redlining is wonderfully fluid and direct, it can be dangerous. The editor must scrupulously remove all traces of the editing process before releasing the file for design and typesetting. Potential disasters include words that are stucktogether, a missing , or a forgotten comment to the author [Are you out of your mother-loving mind?].

A. Queries to the author can also take the form of footnotes. Identify these notes with letters, so they are not confused with footnotes that belong to the text.

PROOFREADING

 PROOFREADING takes place *after* an edited manuscript has been designed and typeset. New errrors can appear at any time during the handling of a document, and old errors/previously unrecognized— can leap to the eye once the text has been set in type. The proofreader corrects gross errors in spelling, grammar, and fact, but avoid ∧ changes in style and content. Changes at this stage are not only expensive but they can affect the page design and introduce new problems.

  Proofreading is different task from editing, although the editor may play a role in it, along with or in addition to the author or client. Although the *designer or typesetter* 1 should not be given the role of proof reader, designers must nonetheless inspect their work carefully for errors before sending it back to the editor, author, or client.

 Mark all corrections in the margin of the proof, and indicate the position of changes within the text. Don't write between the lines. Many of the same interline symbols are used in proofreading and in copy editing, but proofreaders use an additional set of flags for marginal notes.

 Don't obliterate what is being crossed out and deleted so the typesetter can read it.

Mark all changes on one master proof. If several copies of the proof are circulated for approval, one person (usually the editor) is responsible for transferring corrections to a master copy.

Don't give the designer a proof with conflicting or indecisive comments.

TYPES OF *proofs* Depending on how a project is organized and produced, some or all of the following proofs may be involved.

  Galley proofs are typically supplied in a book-length project. They consist of text that has been typeset but not paginated and do not yet include illustrations.

  Page proofs are broken into pages and include illustrations, page numbers, running heads, and other details.

‖ ‖ *Revised proofs* include changes that have been recommended by the proofreader and input by the designer or typesetter.

  Printer's proofs are generated by the printer. At this phase, changes become increasingly costly, complex, and ill-advised. In theory, one is only looking for printers' errors—not errors in design or verbal style— at this stage. Printer's proofs might include blue lines (one color only) and/or color proofs.

---

1. The designer and typesetter may be the same person. In a design studio, as opposed to a publishing house, designers are generally responsible for typesetting.

EDITORIAL CHANGE	MARK IN TEXT	MARK IN MARGIN
delete	delete	
delete and close up	delete and close up	
let it stand (stet)	let it stand	stet
insert text or character	insert	text
run in paragraph	run in paragraph	run in
start new paragraph	start new paragraph	
insert punctuation	insert punctuation	
change punctuation	change punctuation	
insert hyphen	insert hyphen	
insert parentheses	insert parentheses	
insert en or em dash	insert en dash	N M
insert quotes	insert quotes	
capitalize	capitalize	cap
change to lowercase	LOWERCASE	lc
change to small caps	small caps	sc
change to bold	bold	bf
change to roman	roman	rom
wrong font	wrong font	wf

EDITORIAL CHANGE	MARK IN TEXT	MARK IN MARGIN
letterspace	letterspace	ls
close up	clo se up	
insert space	insert space	#
reduce space	reduce space	less #
transpose	pose trans	tr
flush right	flush right	fr
flush left	flush left	fl
indent 1 em	indent 1 em	
move to next line	move to next line	T.O.
superscript	superscript	
align vertically	align vertically	
align horizontally	align horizontally	
spell out abbreviation	spell out abbrev.	sp
use ligature	use ligature (flour)	
query that cannot be resolved by proofreader	query	?

Proofreader's marks derived from The Chicago Manual of Style *and David Jury,* About Face: Reviving the Rules of Typography *(East Sussex: Rotovision, 2001). Marking conventions do vary slightly from source to source.*

Think more, design less.

Many desperate acts of design (including gradients, drop shadows, and the gratuitous use of transparency) are perpetrated in the absence of a strong concept. A good idea provides a framework for design decisions, guiding the work.

Say more, write less.

Just as designers should avoid filling up space with arbitrary visual effects, writers should remember that no one loves their words as much as they do.

Spend more, buy less.

Cheap stuff is usually cheap because of how it's made, what it's made of, and who made it. Buy better quality goods, less often.

May your thoughts be deep and your wounds be shallow.

Always work with a sharp blade. Although graphic design is not a terribly dangerous occupation, many late-night accidents occur involving dull X-Acto blades. Protect your printouts from senseless bloodshed.

Density is the new white space.

In an era of exurban sprawl, closely knit neighborhoods have renewed appeal. So, too, on page and screen, where a rich texture of information can function better than sparseness and isolation.

Make the shoe fit, not the foot.

Rather than force content into rigid containers, create systems that are flexible and responsive to the material they are intended to accommodate.

Make it bigger. *(Courtesy of Paula Scher)*

Amateur typographers make their type too big. The 12-pt default—which looks okay on the screen—often looks horsey on the page. Experienced designers, however, make their type too tiny: shown here, 7.5-pt Scala Pro.

It is easier to talk than to listen.

Pay attention to your clients, your users, your readers, and your friends. Your design will get better as you listen to other people.

Design is an art of situations.

Designers respond to a need, a problem, a circumstance, that arises in the world. The best work is produced in relation to interesting situations—an open-minded client, a good cause, or great content.

No job is too small.

A graphic designer can set out to change the world one business card at a time— as long as it is the business card of a really interesting person.

An interface calls attention to itself at its point of failure.

Design helps the systems of daily life run smoothly, letting users and readers ignore how things are put together. Design should sometimes announce itself in order to shed light on the system, exposing its construction, identity, personality, and politics.

The idea is the machine that makes the art. *(Courtesy of Sol Lewitt)*

A powerful concept can drive decisions about color, layout, type choice, format, and so on, preventing senseless acts of whimsy. (On the other hand, senseless acts of whimsy sometimes lead to powerful concepts.)

The early bird gets to work before everyone else.

Your best time for thinking could be early in the morning, late at night, or even, in rare circumstances, during class or between nine and five. Whether your best time is in the shower, at the gym, or on the train, use it for your hardest thinking.

Build the discourse.

Design is social. It lives in society, it creates society, and it needs a society of its own— a community of designers committed to advancing and debating our shared hopes and desires. Read, write, and talk about design whenever you can.

Go forth and reproduce.

BIBLIOGRAPHY

LETTER

Bartram, Alan. *Five Hundred Years of Book Design.*
London: British Library, 2001.

Benjamin, Walter. *One Way Street and Other Writings.*
London: Verso, 1978.

Blackwell, Lewis. *Twentieth-Century Type.* New Haven: Yale
University Press, 2004.

Boyarski, Dan, Christine Neuwirth, Jodi Forlizzi, and Susan
Harkness Regli. "A Study of Fonts Designed for Screen Display."
CHI 98 (April 1998): 18–23.

Broos, Kees, and Paul Hefting. *Dutch Graphic Design: A Century.*
Cambridge: MIT Press, 1993.

Burke, Christopher. *Paul Renner: The Art of Typography.* New York:
Princeton Architectural Press, 1998.

Clouse, Doug and Angela Voulangas. *The Handy Book of Artistic
Printing.* New York: Princeton Architectural Press, 2009.

Christin, Anne-Marie. *A History of Writing, from Hieroglyph to
Multimedia.* Paris: Flammarion, 2002.

Crouwel, Wim. *New Alphabet: An Introduction for a Programmed
Typography.* Amsterdam: Wim Crouwel/Total Design, 1967.

———, Kees Broos, and David Quay. *Wim Crouwel: Alphabets.*
Amsterdam: BIS Publishers, 2003.

Cruz, Andy, Ken Barber, and Rich Roat. *House Industries.* Berlin:
Die Gestalten Verlag, 2004.

De Jong, Cees, Alston W. Purvis, and Jan Tholenaar, eds. *Type: A
Visual History of Typefaces, Volume I, 1628–1900.* Cologne:
Taschen, 2009.

Eason, Ron, and Sarah Rookledge. *Rookledge's International Directory
of Type Designers: A Biographical Handbook.* New York: Sarabande
Press, 1994.

Gray, Nicolete. *A History of Lettering.* Oxford: Phaidon Press, 1986.

Heller, Steven, and Philip B. Meggs, eds. *Texts on Type: Critical
Writings on Typography.* New York: Allworth Press, 2001.

Johnston, Edward. *Writing & Illuminating & Lettering.* London:
Sir Isaac Pitman & Sons, 1932.

Kelly, Rob Roy. *American Wood Type: 1828–1900.* New York: Da Capo
Press, 1969.

Kinross, Robin. *Unjustified Texts: Perspectives on Typography.* London:
Hyphen Press, 2002.

Lawson, Alexander. *Anatomy of a Typeface.* Boston: David R. Godine,
1990.

Lewis, John. *Anatomy of Printing: The Influences of Art and History on
its Design.* New York: Watson-Guptill Publications, 1970.

———. *Typography: Basic Principles, Influences and Trends Since the
Nineteenth Century.* New York: Reinhold Publishing, 1963.

McMurtrie, Douglas. *The Book: The Story of Printing and
Bookmaking.* New York: Dorset Press, 1943.

Morison, Stanley. *Letter Forms.* London: Nattali & Maurice, 1968.

Noordzij, Gerrit. *Letterletter: An Inconsistent Collection of Tentative
Theories That Do Not Claim Any Authority Other Than That of
Common Sense.* Vancouver: Hartley and Marks, 2000.

Pardoe, F. E. *John Baskerville of Birmingham: Letter-Founder and
Printer.* London: Frederick Muller Limited, 1975.

Perry, Michael. *Hand Job: A Catalog of Type.* New York: Princeton
Architectural Press, 2007.

Shelley, Mary. *Frankenstein.* New York: The Modern Library, 1999.
First published 1831.

Re, Margaret. *Typographically Speaking: The Art of Matthew Carter.*
New York: Princeton Architectural Press, 2002.

Triggs, Teal. *The Typographic Experiment: Radical Innovation in
Contemporary Type Design.* London: Thames & Hudson, 2003.

Updike, Daniel. *Printing Types: Their History, Forms, and Use,
Volumes I and II.* New York: Dover Publications, 1980.

VanderLans, Rudy, and Zuzana Licko. *Emigre: Graphic Design into the
Digital Realm.* New York: Van Nostrand Reinhold, 1993.

Vanderlans, Rudy. *Emigre No. 70: The Look Back Issue, Selections from
Emigre Magazine, 1984–2009.* Berkeley, CA: Gingko Press, 2009.

Willen, Bruce and Nolen Strals. *Lettering & Type: Creating Letters and
Designing Typefaces.* New York: Princeton Architectural Press,
2009.

TEXT

Armstrong, Helen. *Graphic Design Theory: Readings from the Field.*
New York: Princeton Architectural Press, 2009.

Barthes, Roland. *Image/Music/Text.* Trans. Stephen Heath. New York:
Hill and Wang, 1977.

———. *Mythologies.* Trans. Annette Lavers. New York: Hill and Wang,
1977.

Baudrillard, Jean. *For a Critique of the Political Economy of the Sign.*
St. Louis, MO: Telos Press, 1981.

Benjamin, Walter. *Reflections.* Ed. Peter Demetz. New York: Schocken
Books, 1978.

Bierut, Michael. *Forty Posters for the Yale School of Architecture.*
Cohoes, NY: Mohawk Fine Papers, 2007.

Bolter, Jay David. *Writing Space: Computers, Hypertext, and the
Remediation of Print.* Mahwah, NJ: Lawrence Erlbaum
Associates, 2001.

Derrida, Jacques. *Of Grammatology.* Trans. Gayatri Chakravorty
Spivak. Baltimore: Johns Hopkins University Press, 1976.

Diamond, Jared. *Guns, Germs, and Steel: The Fates of Human Societies.*
New York: W. W. Norton, 1997.

Kaplan, Nancy. "Blake's Problem and Ours: Some Reflections on
the Image and the Word." *Readerly/Writerly Texts,* 3.2 (Spring/
Summer 1996): 115–33.

Gould, John D. *et al.* "Reading from CRT Displays Can Be as Fast as
Reading from Paper." *Human Factors* 29, 5 (1987): 497–517.

Helfand, Jessica. *Screen: Essays on Graphic Design, New Media, and
Visual Culture.* New York: Princeton Architectural Press, 2001.

Lessig, Lawrence. *Free Culture: How Big Media Uses Technology and
the Law to Lock Down Culture and Control Creativity.* New York:
Penguin, 2004.

Laurel, Brenda. *Utopian Entrepreneur.* Cambridge: MIT Press, 2001.

Lunenfeld, Peter. *Snap to Grid: A User's Guide to Digital Arts, Media,
and Cultures.* Cambridge: MIT Press, 2001.

Manovich, Lev. *The Language of New Media.* Cambridge: MIT Press,
2002.

McCoy, Katherine and Michael McCoy. *Cranbrook Design: The New
Discourse.* New York: Rizzoli, 1990.

———. "American Graphic Design Expression." *Design Quarterly*
148 (1990): 4–22.

McLuhan, Marshall. *The Gutenberg Galaxy*. Toronto: University of Toronto Press, 1962.

Millman, Debbie. *The Essential Principles of Graphic Design*. Cincinnati: How, 2008.

Moulthrop, Stuart. "You Say You Want a Revolution? Hypertext and the Laws of Media" in *The New Media Reader*. Noah Wardrip-Fruin and Nick Monfort, eds. Cambridge: MIT Press, 2003. 691–703.

Nielsen, Jakob. *Designing Web Usability*. Indianapolis: New Riders, 2000.

Ong, Walter. *Orality and Literacy: The Technologizing of the Word*. New York: Methuen, 1982.

Raskin, Jef. *The Human Interface: New Directions for Designing Interactive Systems*. Reading, MA: Addison-Wesley, 2000.

Ronell, Avital. *The Telephone Book: Technology, Schizophrenia, Electric Speech*. Lincoln, NE: University of Nebraska Press, 1989.

GRID

Berners-Lee, Tim. *Weaving the Web: The Original Design and Ultimate Destiny of the World Wide Web*. New York: HarperCollins, 1999.

Bosshard, Hans Rudolf. *Der Typografische Raster/The Typographic Grid*. Sulgen, Switzerland: Verlag Niggli, 2000.

Cantz, Hatje. *Karl Gerstner: Review of 5 x 10 Years of Graphic Design etc.* Ostfildern-Ruit, Germany: Hatje Cantz Verlag, 2001.

Elam, Kimberly. *Geometry of Design*. New York: Princeton Architectural Press, 2001.

Gerstner, Karl. *Designing Programmes*. Sulgen, Switzerland: Arthur Niggli Ltd., 1964.

Gibson, William. *Neuromancer*. New York: Ace Books, 1984.

Higgins, Hannah P. *The Grid Book*. Cambridge: MIT Press, 2009.

Hochuli, Jost, and Robin Kinross. *Designing Books: Practice and Theory*. London: Hyphen Press, 1996.

Krauss, Rosalind. "Grids" in *The Originality of the Avant-Garde and Other Modernist Myths*. Cambridge: MIT Press, 1985. 9–22.

Küsters, Christian and Emily King. *Restart: New Systems in Graphic Design*. London: Thames and Hudson, 2002.

Lidwell, William, Kritina Holden, and Jill Butler. *Universal Principles of Design*. Gloucester, MA: Rockport Publishers, 2003.

Müller-Brockmann, Josef. *The Graphic Artist and his Design Problems*. Sulgen, Switzerland: Arthur Niggli Ltd., 1961.

———. *Grid Systems in Graphic Design*. Santa Monica: Ram Publications, 1996. First published in 1961.

———. *A History of Graphic Communication*. Sulgen, Switzerland: Arthur Niggli Ltd., 1971.

Nicolai, Carsten. *Grid Index*. Berlin: Die Gestalten, 2009.

Roberts, Lucienne, and Julia Shrift. *The Designer and the Grid*. East Sussex, UK: RotoVision, 2002.

Rothschild, Deborah, Ellen Lupton, and Darra Goldstein. *Graphic Design in the Mechanical Age: Selections from the Merrill C. Berman Collection*. New Haven: Yale University Press, 1998.

Ruder, Emil. *Typography*. Sulgen, Switzerland: Arthur Niggli Ltd., New York: Hastings House, 1981. First published in 1967.

Rüegg, Ruedi. *Basic Typography: Design with Letters*. New York: Van Nostrand Reinhold, 1989.

Samara, Timothy. *Making and Breaking the Grid: A Graphic Design Layout Workshop*. Gloucester, MA: Rockport Publishers, 2002.

Tufte, Edward R. *Envisioning Information*. Cheshire, CT: Graphics Press, 1990.

———. *The Cognitive Style of PowerPoint*. Cheshire, CT: Graphics Press, 2003.

Zeldman, Jeffrey with Ethan Marcotte. *Designing with Web Standards*, Third Edition. Berkeley, CA: New Riders, 2009.

MANUALS AND MONOGRAPHS

Baines, Phil, and Andrew Haslam. *Type and Typography*. New York: Watson-Guptill Publications, 2002.

Bringhurst, Robert. *The Elements of Typographic Style*. Vancouver: Hartley and Marks, 1992, 1997.

The Chicago Manual of Style, 15th Edition. Chicago: University of Chicago Press, 2003.

Dwiggins, W. A. *Layout in Advertising*. New York: Harper and Brothers Publishers, 1928.

Eckersley, Richard *et al. Glossary of Typesetting Terms*. Chicago: University of Chicago Press, 1994.

Felton, Paul. *Type Heresy: Breaking the Ten Commandments of Typography*. London: Merrell, 2006.

French, Nigel. *InDesign Type: Professional Typography with Adobe InDesign CS2*. Berkeley, CA: Peachpit Press, 2006.

Jardi, Enric. *Twenty-Two Tips on Typography (That Some Designers Will Never Reveal)*. Barcelona: Actar, 2007.

Jury, David. *About Face: Reviving the Rules of Typography*. East Sussex, UK: RotoVision, 2001.

Kane, John. *A Type Primer*. London: Laurence King, 2002.

Kunz, Willi. *Typography: Macro- and Micro-Aesthetics*. Sulgen, Switzerland: Verlag Arthur Niggli, 1998.

Lupton, Ellen and J. Abbott Miller. *Design Writing Research: Writing on Graphic Design*. London: Phaidon, 1999.

Lupton, Ellen and Jennifer Cole Phillips. *Graphic Design: The New Basics*. New York: Princeton Architectural Press, 2008.

Lynch, Patrick, and Sarah Horton. *Web Style Guide: Basic Design Principles for Creating Web Sites*. New Haven: Yale University Press, 2001.

Millman, Debbie. *The Essential Principles of Graphic Design*. Cincinnati: How, 2008.

Rosendorf, Theodore. *The Typographic Desk Reference*. New Castle: Oak Knoll, 2008.

Samara, Timothy. *Typography Workbook: A Real-World Guide to Using Type in Graphic Design*. Beverly, MA: Rockport, 2004.

Scher, Paula. *Make It Bigger*. New York: Princeton Architectural Press, 2002.

Spiekermann, Erik, and E. M. Ginger. *Stop Stealing Sheep and Find Out How Type Works*. Mountain View, CA: Adobe Press, 1993.

Strizver, Ilene. *Type Rules: The Designer's Guide to Professional Typography*. Cincinnati: North Light Books, 2001.

Strunk, William Jr. and E. B. White. *The Elements of Style*. Illustrated by Maira Kalman. New York: Penguin Press, 2005.

Tschichold, Jan. *The Form of the Book: Essays on the Morality of Good Design*. Point Roberts, WA: Hartley & Marks, 1991.

INDEX